COMMUNITY LIBRARY

S0-AWW-356

Remembering to Breathe

INSIDE DOG OBEDIENCE COMPETITION

Willard Bailey

Copyright © 2004 by Willard Bailey

All rights reserved. No part of this book shall be reproduced or transmitted in any form or by any means, electronic, mechanical, magnetic, photographic including photocopying, recording or by any information storage and retrieval system, without prior written permission of the publisher. No patent liability is assumed with respect to the use of the information contained herein. Although every precaution has been taken in the preparation of this book, the publisher and author assume no responsibility for errors or omissions. Neither is any liability assumed for damages resulting from the use of the information contained herein.

ISBN 0-7414-1860-6

Published by:
INFI∞ITY
PUBLISHING.COM
519 West Lancaster Avenue
Haverford, PA 19041-1413
Info@buybooksontheweb.com
www.buybooksontheweb.com
Toll-free (877) BUY BOOK
Local Phone (610) 520-2500
Fax (610) 519-0261

Printed in the United States of America

Printed on Recycled Paper

Published January 2004

IN MEMORIAM
Helen Myers Bailey (1907–1973),
who had time to listen at 3 A.M.

*"There is a fine line
between hobby and mental illness."*
—DAVE BARRY

■ PROLOGUE ■

cynophobia: irrational fear of dogs
—DORLAND'S MEDICAL DICTIONARY

In the bitter cold of a Cincinnati winter morning, a snowsuit stands on the sidewalk. There's a child inside but you can hardly tell. Except for the hole that reveals a tiny face, you see nothing but snowsuit.

"We're going to bundle you up good," Grandma had said before she sent Skippy out to play. "So you don't freeze out there."

Right now Skippy isn't playing. His body is rigid, frozen inside the snowsuit. Not from the two-degree cold. From fear. His face is contorted with terror. He's screaming bloody murder. His tricycle is on its side in the grass.

Nearby, a little dog looks puzzled. He's standing on the grass between the sidewalk and the curb. Wagging his tail tentatively. Wondering what gives with this tiny person. Why is he acting so strangely?

The problem is, in order to run to the driveway, then to the safety of the house, Skippy must pass the dog. So he'll stand there, petrified inside the snowsuit, screaming until Grandma comes out, shoos the little dog away and rescues him.

The year is 1935. Skippy is two years old. I am Skippy. So nicknamed by my mother, Helen, who thought her young son was so much like the comic strip character Skippy. Perpetually into mischief of some sort.

As a boy I was Skip to everyone. Later, as a striver, a career-builder, I shed the names Skip/Skippy, certain they did not convey the professionalism in which I sought to cloak myself.

Now, as the writer of this book, I am again Skip. For this book is about Honeybear and me. And I am her Skippy.

■ ■ ■

I can't pinpoint exactly when paralyzing fear began to give way to longing. But it had to do with neighbors' dogs I'd meet on the way home from grade school. Ginger in particular, a smelly, flea-ridden collie who became a surrogate pet; I wasn't allowed to have a dog of my own.

And it has continued in a marriage that shares a mutual love of animals and has survived 44 years, eight dogs and three cats.

■ CHAPTER 1 ■

The Beginning of a Love Affair

I, Skip, promise to
love and hug you
forever and ever
because you were
given to me
by
Barbara

PHOENIX, ARIZONA (FEBRUARY 10, 2001)

Fast-forward 66 years from the day Skippy stood in the bitter cold, frozen with fear.

I'm at Wendy's to celebrate the 11th anniversary of the day I first carried Honeybear into our house.

"Just a plain hamburger," I tell the kid at the counter. "Only a meat patty on a bun, nothing else."

"No toppings?" He eyes me suspiciously.

"No toppings!" I reply. "It's for my dog."

"You feed your dog Wendy's?"

"Only on special occasions."

"What kind of dog?"

"A golden retriever."

"Neat dogs," he says, smiling.

Understanding he's part of something special, he moves a few steps to his right where he can monitor the Mexican guy assembling the burgers.

The Mexican lunges for lettuce and the kid says, "No!" The guy lunges again for pickles, only to be stopped by a sharp, "No!" Finally the kid plants his feet firmly, puts his hands on his hips and says: "Nada! Nada! Nada!"

The Mexican gives up, wraps his sorry creation in foil and hands it over — peering around the corner to see what sort of demented gringo has ordered this atrocity.

Back outside, I let Honeybear smell the bag as I climb into the van. She is beside herself. Whimpering. Tail wagging. We battle for the driver's seat. I win … barely.

She's all nose as I unwrap the foil. Then, as much to prolong my pleasure as to help ensure she won't barf on the carpet later, I break the sandwich apart and feed it to her by hand.

Much too soon I have to say, "That's all." But she sticks her head all the way down into the bag, just to be sure. Finally, with a contented sigh, she sinks down between the bucket seats.

As I pull out of the parking lot, I get out my cell phone and call my wife, Barbara.

"OK," I begin, "we're just pulling out of Wendy's parking lot."

"Wendy's?"

"Yes, Honeybear just had a hamburger." Then I remind her of the occasion.

"Did she get all of it?"

"Yeah, I left everybody else home. It was just Honeybear and me. You know how she loves that."

"That's neat," Barbara says.

Honeybear rests her head on my knee all the way home.

■ ■ ■

The love affair began early in 1989.

On some street I can't recall, someone I hadn't seen before

and never saw again was walking two golden retrievers. I remember thinking, *What beautiful, happy dogs. They can't walk without wagging their tails.*

That starburst moment must have sent my antennae up. It seemed like thereafter I saw a happy, tail-wagging golden every few days. At some point my inner mandate became, *I've got to have one of those.*

I lobbied. I campaigned. "Here's what I want for Christmas," I told Barbara.

At first the answer was, "We already have two dogs and two cats." But over time the objections became less and less intense. And as Christmas approached, the signals became unmistakably positive.

At the time, Barbara was senior vice president, sales promotion and marketing, for Broadway Southwest, a chain of department stores based in Phoenix.

One evening before Christmas, Barbara was leaving for the Central Phoenix store to prepare for a special event being held the next day.

"Jan Nelson, one of our buyers, lives near the store," she told me. "She has two golden retrievers and she said she'll walk over with them tonight so you can see them. Want to go?"

"Oh no," I said as I dove for my coat.

I remember standing on the loading dock behind the store. Here came these two bundles of joy, eyes bright, tails wagging furiously. They greeted me like a best friend, nuzzling at my knees, competing for my attention. As I stroked those silky soft heads, it occurred to me that this was the first time I had petted a golden retriever. And I knew I was destined to pet a big soft head like that thousands of times.

■ ■ ■

On Christmas morning, my golden retriever arrived in the form of a plush, stuffed surrogate. The package contained a honey-colored toy dog with big dark eyes, a large black nose and huge floppy ears. Money was enclosed with a note: "From all of us." Which meant Barbara, her mother Gladys and step-father Bob.

The box also contained a three-inch-square folded card with a simple pledge:

> *I, Skip, promise to*
> *love and hug you*
> *forever and ever*
> *because you were*
> *given to me*
> *by*
> *Barbara*

That card, folded inside-out so I can always see the pledge, has been tacked to the bulletin board behind my desk for more than 11 years. The ink has faded. But the pledge is still clear.

I've tried with all my heart to keep that pledge. And it's been the most fulfilling thing I've ever done.

CHAPTER 2

Fluff Puff

The day after Christmas I called Jan Nelson. "Where did you get your dogs and how do I reach that person?" I asked.

The trail led to Debbie Wheat in Chandler, an eastern suburb of Phoenix. Yes, she told me, there was a litter I might find interesting. The puppies had been born three days before Christmas. They had been sired by Debbie's Guy (Birnamwood's Judge 'N Jury). Dawn Franklin had the mother, Gem (Wildfire-Starbuc's Gemini).

"Be sure to see both parents before you buy a puppy," we had been advised. Not that Barbara or I had a clue about what we were looking at or for. Worse, we didn't know we didn't know.

The first stop was Debbie's house to see the father of the litter. In the backyard I knelt to play with Guy. His head came up under my chin and almost knocked me out. But here was this big, friendly, playful, beautiful golden retriever and I could hardly contain myself.

The litter was at Dawn's house. We arranged to see the puppies when they were three weeks old. Dawn met us at the door with, "Hi! Come on back to the kitchen and wash your hands." From the sink we went into the living room where Dawn and her husband had built a large whelping box. Eight tiny balls of fluff — four males and four females — were asleep in the box.

I had first pick of the females. I held them and petted their tiny heads. I wanted them all. A few days later, my selection was narrowed when Gem rolled on top of one of the females and the puppy died.

I can't remember when or why I began to focus on the one Dawn's daughter Krista had named Fluff Puff. In fact, I'm not certain whether I picked the puppy or the puppy picked me.

■ ■ ■

The big day finally arrived. Saturday, February 10, 1990 dawned clear and chilly. I arrived at Dawn's house shortly after nine.

The puppies had just had a bath. There was little Fluff Puff, still damp, on the back porch. I worried she'd catch pneumonia. So I put her in a cardboard box on the front seat of my car and turned up the heater. She barked all the way home.

I can still point to the spot in our backyard where I put her down in the grass when we got home. She sat. I called. She sat. I coaxed. She sat. I worried. *Something's wrong with this dog*, I said to myself, *she won't move.*

Later, though, she would move. She would run and jump and retrieve and frisk and tail-wag through the most wonderful adventure of my life.

■ CHAPTER 3 ■

The Adventure Begins

"Whoever said you can't buy happiness
forgot about puppies."
—GENE HILL

Fluff Puff wasn't Fluff Puff for long. It took me just two days to come up with "Honeybear." She looked like a little bear. She was light-colored, the shade of honey. It fit.

Before long, Barbara shortened it to "HB." As in, "HB! Get your nose off the table!" Others thought "HB" was cute, and it stuck. Honeybear has always answered to both names.

I wanted to register her with the American Kennel Club (AKC) so I needed a "registered name." Dawn told me it was customary for the dog to carry the kennel name of the breeder. Her kennel name was Starbuc. And I had dreamed of owning a golden retriever, and now that dream had come true. So in the records of the AKC, Honeybear is known as Starbuc's Dream Come True.

■ ■ ■

"That's going to be a good-size dog," Barbara warned before HB had been in the house 24 hours. "You better get her into some kind of obedience training."

An accompanying package on Christmas morning had contained $250 for obedience lessons. Also included was the name and phone number of a guy who would come to our house and give lessons.

But when I called him, his hard-driving spiel assaulted my ears and my patience. "I'll think about it," I told him as I extricated myself from his blustering sales pitch.

Someone told me the Phoenix parks department held basic pet obedience classes. I called and got a schedule. A puppy kindergarten class would begin at Cactus Park, less than 10 minutes from our house, on Sunday evening, April 22. Honeybear would be four months old on that very date, would have had all her shots and would be ready to take on the world.

We arrived at the park shortly before 6 p.m., primed for our first class. April is one of the loveliest months of the year in Phoenix. The days are still pleasantly warm — the calm before the early, brutal and protracted summers — and it rarely rains. The evening was perfect, as the setting sun cast long, broad shadows.

Honeybear wore a brown buckle collar and was pulling me around on the requisite six-foot leash.

I was happy and only slightly apprehensive. As we joined the group that evening, I never dreamed the innocent little puppy kindergarten class would be the first of thousands of training sessions with Honeybear. Or that we would come to be joined at the soul.

Our instructors were Maureen Black and Lyndy McKay. Their business card read *Partners School for Dogs. "Watch the Loving Bond Grow."*

"Let's get started," Maureen said. "Bring your puppies over here." She indicated a shady spot of well-watered green grass.

We were told to sit in a circle — 12 eager owners with 12 fuzzy little hooligan angels.

Maureen first had us roll our puppies on their backs, heads in our laps, hind legs pumping. We were told to rub their tummies and chests while talking to them softly, soothingly. The idea was to get them to relax and enjoy being there.

For some it took several weeks to attain this relaxed state. One or two never did.

It took Honeybear only a couple of minutes. I didn't realize the significance at the time, but well before she was 16 weeks old Honeybear had begun to communicate clearly: "Skippy, I'll go anywhere with you. We can do anything you want. I just want to be with you."

Next, Maureen's partner Lyndy said, "Pass your puppy to the person on your right." It was a socialization exercise. I handed off Honeybear and received a squirming, gyrating, licking bearded collie. Around they went until Honeybear returned to me and promptly nailed me with a big wet smacker, right in the mouth.

The next thing I knew that first class was over, gone in a flash. As we made the seven-minute drive home, Honeybear was on the seat next to me, chin on my thigh, eyes turned upward adoringly. It was a scene that would be repeated thousands of times — returning from classes, practice sessions, shows, private lessons and matches.

Across six weeks, we got our puppies used to the leash, then used to walking calmly on the leash. All of that was done with treats used as lures. Thus began a habit that persists to this day. You will rarely find me anywhere at any time without treats in my shirt pocket. In fact, as I write this I have 17 Grreat Choice puppy/training biscuits in that pocket. Just in case.

The most memorable activity of that seven-week course was puppy recalls. They were introduced in the third week — the theory being that by the end of two classes the puppies would be more focused on their owners and less likely to run to the other puppies.

An instructor would hold your puppy. You would run away, calling the dog as you ran to create excitement. Then the instructor would release the puppy, and the idea was the puppy would run to its owner.

On our first recall, I placed Honeybear in Lyndy's hands, then sprinted about 50 feet, calling, "Honeybear come! Honeybear come!" I turned, fell to my knees and saw that Honeybear was thrashing to get loose. Lyndy released her. Honeybear came barreling toward me and launched herself into my arms. Not once during the remaining classes did she not leap into my arms when we did recalls.

Although I had no inkling at the time, those puppy recalls cast the die for the shape of things to come.

CHAPTER 4

"Harder, Willard!"

As we neared the end of our puppy kindergarten sessions, our instructors told us about the next level, beginners class, starting Thursday evening, June 7.

"Why not?" I said. Honeybear and I had done well in puppy kindergarten. And boy, had we had fun! It seemed logical to continue. A decision heartily endorsed by Barbara. HB was getting bigger and more challenging every day. Barbara was a bit overwhelmed by this rowdy, increasingly strong dog. Until then she had been a toy poodle person.

Off we went on Thursday evenings to beginners class, the same people but our number had shrunk to seven. For the next seven weeks there was a lot more emphasis on heeling, not just walking on leash. And we began to teach our dogs to sit and down and stay. For longer stretches of time and at greater distances.

Maureen suggested we practice sits and downs someplace where there were lots of distractions, like a PetsMart. There was one less than two miles from our house. I started taking Honeybear there several times a week.

At first, we practiced on a six-foot leash. Then, in small increments, I increased the distance to 20 feet on a green nylon longline. Once HB was solid on the sit and down at that distance,

I dispensed with the leash and we started over again … three feet, six feet, nine … out to 30 or 40 feet.

My time expectations increased incrementally as well. From 30 seconds on each exercise, we extended to 15 minutes on the sit and 30 on the down.

Putting a dog on a long sit or long down in the main aisle at PetsMart is an adventure. You are there for the distractions — people going by with carts, with dogs. The PA system blaring from time to time. A forklift in the next aisle stacking heavy cartons.

As a bonus, you get a dose of the innate knuckleheaded-ness of some people. Those who see your dog sitting or lying there and walk right up to pet her. Or worse, march their dogs right into your sitting dog's face, so that Fluffy — a 90-pound Rottweiler — can "meet" your dog.

Eventually Barbara made two tent-like signs, one to be put in front of and the other behind Honeybear. *Please don't pet me, I'm practicing obedience.* The signs diverted some, but not all, of the knuckleheads.

On the other hand, several PetsMart employees became Honeybear's friends. They'd wait until our training session was over, then come to pet her and give her treats. At times HB would be on the floor, on her back, having her tummy rubbed by two or three people. She came to regard PetsMart as one swell place.

An organization like PetsMart is subject to high employee turnover and many of those who fell in love with my gleeful golden early in our training eventually left. Two or three became long-termers and followed Honeybear's triumphs vicariously. I'd come into the store without HB and they'd say, "How's Honeybear? Has she had any big wins lately?"

Photo: Barbara Bailey

Honeybear at 15 weeks: Is that collar heavy enough?

Those friendly PetsMart employees were charter members of Honeybear's Fan Club, a group that is informal but very real and today is represented all over the western United States.

■ ■ ■

In retrospect, the 15-minute sit and 30-minute down were overkill. They represented a style of obedience training that was still in vogue when I entered the sport and has largely vanished.

When I began with Honeybear, obedience training was on the cusp, just a figurative moment before compulsion gave way to positive reinforcement.

In puppy kindergarten we employed methods that were gentle, using food to lure our puppies into the behaviors we wanted.

The tenor changed when we entered beginners class. Maureen Black became a harsh taskmistress. Coaxing gave way to sharp leash corrections.

"Yank that leash harder, Willard," Maureen would yell. "Honeybear doesn't even feel those little love pops you are giving her."

I spent those summer evenings jerking my puppy around by the neck. If she was standing and I wanted her to sit, I jerked on the leash. Once she was sitting and I wanted her to move, she got yanked again. If, when we were trying to heel, she got too far out front, she got snapped back. If she lagged, the jolt would go in the other direction.

As an instructor, Maureen was a product of her time. Jerking the dog around had been the training method of choice for more than three decades — longer than Maureen had been Maureen. After all, you had to show the dog who was boss.

The guru at the time was William Koehler. His book, *The Koehler Method of Dog Training*, was published in 1962. It set the standard for a generation … and then some. You still hear it referenced today. Now it is the Volkswagen bus of obedience training, "driven" by people who have yet to get the message that it's over.

The prevailing philosophy of the time — and still the gospel when I came upon the scene — was based upon Koehler's methods. But, in fairness to Koehler, often implemented in ways that badly misinterpreted his teachings.

Simply, the style of choice in 1990 was a master/slave approach. I want my dog to do something. He doesn't do it? Well then, he's being spiteful. Bad. He must be *corrected.*

Ah, now there's a word. *Correction* in dog obedience training more often than not is a euphemism for punishment. And in far too many cases for dog abuse.

"Corrections" went/go well beyond jerking the leash. The dog doesn't want to sit? He gets whopped on the butt. Doesn't sit the next time? Whop him harder.

Picks up his butt as you leave him on a sit-stay? Give him a good whack in the chest right before you leave. You say he continues to elevate his butt? Obviously you didn't whack him hard enough.

Your dog forges (gets out ahead of you) when you begin to heel? Carry a six-foot leash when you train and give the dog a couple of good lashes across the chest right before you step out. That'll make him think about staying back.

The Koehler method of training shows the dog where *not* to be. Don't be out there (wide). Don't be ahead of me. Don't be back there (lagging). He learns only by default where *to* be.

Koehler's method, correctly implemented, emphasizes this sequence of activities when the dog is corrected: For example, the dog forges. He experiences a sharp yank on the leash. If he immediately moves back into heel position, he is praised and the exercise ends.

That's the theory. But in most situations, such as our beginners class, the emphasis is on the *correction:* "Yank that leash,

Willard, get her back where she belongs. She's blowing you off." And the ensuing praise is all but forgotten.

At the point where Honeybear and I entered dog obedience, the emphasis was still on forcing the desired behavior by jerking the dog around until he learned by default to offer the behavior the trainer wanted. Or, in other situations, whopping or whacking. At the time, the concept of teaching the dog — *showing* him what was desired — was just peeking over the horizon.

A few forward thinkers were beginning to ask, "Wait a minute, does it really make sense to correct (punish) the dog before he understands what we want?" Soon, brilliant instructors such as AnneMarie Silverton would convince us that you shouldn't correct the dog at all during the learning phase. Corrections (and she didn't mean jerking his head off or knocking him across the ring), she told us, should come only after the dog had learned the behavior but chose not to comply.

In our beginners class we didn't "progress" far enough to employ whops on the butt, whacks on the chest or lashes with the leash. Those "corrections" were suggested by well-meaning people later in our career.

Nevertheless, my most vivid memories of our evenings in beginners class feature Honeybear being jerked around by the neck. Not forcefully enough to satisfy my instructor but certainly hard enough to upset Honeybear. Her body language made it clear she didn't like being jerked around.

■ CHAPTER 5 ■

Enter Billie Rosen

A few weeks into beginners class Maureen developed a conflict. Another instructor took her place. Billie Rosen was a tall woman with red hair and a loud voice. She brought along her three-year-old miniature schnauzer Kara as a "demo" dog.

It was immediately apparent that Billie was at ease in front of a group and used to taking charge.

More importantly, the teaching methods changed. To be sure, there were still leash corrections, but the emphasis was on helping the dog learn. Things became a lot more comfortable for me and for Honeybear.

One evening Billie said to the class, "There's a dog show in Prescott Valley this weekend. Part of it is obedience competition. If you've never been to a dog show, you might like to drive up and watch."

Translation: "I'm showing Kara in obedience this weekend. Why don't you guys come up and watch?"

Obedience competition? That was the first time I had heard the words. I was taking these classes to get control of a large, rowdy dog. I thought, *You mean people and their dogs actually compete in this stuff?*

So I went.

I parked, asked a few people and finally found the obedience rings. Only they weren't round, they were rectangles created with rebar and rope.

I hadn't known enough to bring a chair so I wandered around and watched what was going on.

Talk about heeling! Wow! Some of those dogs stayed right with their handlers all the way around the ring.

In one ring, a woman threw a dumbbell over a solid white jump. The dog soared over the jump, grabbed the dumbbell in his teeth, carried it back over the jump and sat in front of her. He gave it up willingly when she reached down to take it. Then he ran around behind her and sat at her left side.

In another ring, the handler rubbed a small dumbbell-like object briskly between his hands. Then the judge placed that object in the center of the ring among a bunch of similar dumb-bell-like objects. The dog ran to the objects, sniffed around for a while, snatched the object the handler had been rubbing and returned with it. This dog, too, sat in front of the handler and gave up the object politely when the man reached down to take it.

"What's this about?" I asked a bystander who seemed to understand what was going on.

"It's called the scent-discrimination exercise," the bystander told me. "The handler puts his scent on an *article* that no one else has recently touched. The judge then puts that article out there with eight others that have someone else's scent on them. The dog has been trained to find the article that was scented by his owner and bring it back."

"What if the dog gets the wrong one?" I asked.

"She flunks," my informant said. "It's referred to as an NQ, nonqualifying score. Lots of people NQ in this ring; the exercises are very difficult."

I saw other things that amazed me in what I learned was called the Utility ring. Dogs responded to hand signals at a distance of 40 feet. Others, sent away by their handlers, ran straight down the center of the ring, turned sharply and sat quickly on command at the other end. Then, at the handler's direction, returned via one of two jumps.

I was thrilled and impressed. *I can't believe they can teach those dogs to do such things,* I thought. *Honeybear and I could never learn to do that.* But a few minutes later I found myself thinking, *"Wow! Wouldn't it be something if I could teach Honeybear to do those things!"*

And that thought was as potent as the first hit of crack cocaine reaching the brain, releasing chemicals that demand *more!* — and will not be denied. I was hooked.

The next morning I called Billie. "Do you think I could teach Honeybear to do things like that?" I asked.

"Of course you can," she said. "Would you like to meet Kara and me sometimes in the afternoons and train with us?"

"Oh yes!" I said.

And so it began.

CHAPTER 6

Afternoons With Billie

Billie Rosen, I soon learned, is a fascinating, accomplished woman who is generous with her time and lavish with her encouragement.

The daughter of a San Francisco Bay area surgeon, Billie graduated from the University of California at Berkeley, then received a law degree from Hastings College of Law (the law school of the University of California, San Francisco).

She is an assistant attorney general for the State of Arizona. A strong-looking, big-boned woman with red hair and a loud take-charge voice, she must be formidable in the courtroom. It comes as no surprise that her caseload features actions against Hell's Angels, drug dealers, physicians accused of Medicare fraud, and chop shop operators. Billie is the lead prosecutor of drug dealers for the State of Arizona. From time to time, she finds herself under the protection of bodyguards.

In fact, on the evening of March 29, 2002, as this book was nearing completion, Billie escaped assassination when a bullet fired into her home wounded her brother Richard instead. Investigators believe a silencer may have been used to muffle the gunshots, which were fired through a screened back window.

Billie was home at the time of the shooting but her brother was seated at the computer where normally Billie would be found late in the evening. The heavily screened window may have obscured the view as to who was at the computer. Her brother was hit in the chest but survived.

The assassination attempt has been linked to one of her recent high-profile drug cases.

As this book goes to press, two suspects have been charged in the shooting and are awaiting trial. Billie has moved to a new home in an undisclosed location.

Undaunted, she continues vigorously to pursue her caseload.

■ ■ ■

Billie must have read the bumper sticker advocating random acts of kindness; her capacity for sharing exceeds even her capacity for throwing bad guys into the slammer.

We'd meet at Royal Palm Park in north central Phoenix at 4:30 each afternoon. Kara would greet us with that loud, prolonged schnauzer bark. She already had her first obedience title, Companion Dog, and I thought that was awesome.

I knew nothing about the world of American Kennel Club dog obedience competition. Billie seemed to know everything.

She told me about the competition levels. First you show in Novice A, a class exclusively for those showing their first competition dog. Once you get your Companion Dog (CD) title on that first dog, you may never start a dog in Novice A again. There is a Novice B class for those who have earlier put an obedience title on a dog.

In order to earn a CD, your dog must get three legs, Billie said. That requires a qualifying score from each of three different judges.

"Wait a minute," I said. "What does *qualifying score* mean?" I remembered the guy at the match talking about NQing, flunking.

Billie explained that you and your dog enter an obedience ring with a 200-point credit. As you proceed through the exercises, the judge deducts points for each error made by the handler or the dog. In order to qualify, you must finish with at least 170 of the 200 points. And you must score at least 50 percent of the available points on each exercise.

She also told me that ribbons are given to the four highest-scoring teams in each class — blue for first, red for second, yellow for third, white for fourth. *Wouldn't it be something*, I thought, *if someday Honeybear and I could bring home a ribbon?*

Once you have completed your CD, you are eligible to work toward your Companion Dog Excellent (CDX) title. The class is called Open A. At that level, the dogs have more fun, Billie said. "They get to run and jump and retrieve."

The next level is Utility Dog (UD). It's much more difficult. In fact, she told me, most dogs and handlers wash out before they reach that level. At the Utility level — which appeared stratospheric at the time — the dogs are tested on scent discrimination and hand signals, and they are required to work at a considerable distance from the handler. Aha! That's what I had been mesmerized by in Prescott Valley.

All that Billie told me became sugarplums that danced in my head. But at the time, I was more concerned about the butterflies in my stomach. They had to do with off-lead heeling.

■ ■ ■

Each afternoon we'd begin our session with a period of heeling. Billie also believed in ending our afternoon practice with additional heeling.

In the Novice A ring you begin with an on-leash heeling pattern. The scariest part, particularly for a green, anxiety-ridden Novice A person, comes a couple of exercises later when you are required to do the same pattern with your dog off leash.

Here's this animal that, at best, I'm not sure I can control, and now I'm supposed to do heeling (they call it *precision heeling* for God's sake) off leash with this wild thing. And this authority figure with a clipboard is going to score us on it.

Billie taught me pattern heeling, an effective way to transition from on-leash to off-leash heeling.

You do a short heeling pattern on leash. Maybe a forward, left turn, halt. Or a forward, about turn, halt. Or you can mix in a fast or a slow. If the dog does the pattern well on leash, you remove the leash and repeat the same pattern from the same starting point. If the dog makes a mistake, you put the leash back on, start over again and when you get to the spot where the mistake occurred, give a correction to remind the dog what you want. Then go back and try it again off leash.

Rome wasn't built in a day, and fine-heeling dogs aren't trained in a few sessions. Honeybear and I repeated pattern drills hundreds of times across many months.

It must have paid off. As I write this, Honeybear is 12 years old and tearing it up in the Veterans ring. Heeling-wise, today, with Honeybear at my side, I'll take my chances against any other dog/handler team on the planet.

After we practiced heeling, we'd do recalls and practice the stand for examination. I'd examine Kara and Billie would examine Honeybear. Of course that wasn't the greatest way to practice, both Honeybear and Kara quickly became comfortable with the not-at-all-strange pair of hands. If there was someone nearby in the park, Billie would say, "Would you like to help us train our dogs?" Presto! Another set of hands.

Near the end of each session, we'd practice the long sit and long down — little Kara and big Honeybear, so cute side by side.

■ ■ ■

Each session brought a new tidbit of information.

One afternoon Billie arrived with this announcement: "Willard, you'll be interested to know that six of the top ten obedience competition dogs in America right now are golden retrievers. The rankings are in the current issue of *Front & Finish*."

I had no clue. All I knew about golden retrievers was that they were pretty, had wonderful dispositions and wagged their tails a lot. Now suddenly I learned that I had lucked into an exceptional obedience breed. Wow!

"What's *Front & Finish*?" I asked, as an afterthought.

"It's a newspaper for dog trainers like us," she told me. "It comes out monthly and I read it cover to cover. You ought to subscribe."

I did. And later came to write a column for that publication for three years in the late '90s.

Another time Billie was talking about the top obedience competition dogs in America and she said something about The Gaines.

"The Gaines?" I said, "What's that?"

She told me it was a series of important regional tournaments each year, culminating in The Gaines Classic where the regional *winners* and many of those who had *placed* regionally squared off in one big showdown weekend. "To qualify, you need really high scores from your obedience trials," she said. "And you find yourself competing against the biggest-name, best dogs in the country."

All of which seemed light years beyond our reach. But I filed it away in my mind. And that night, as I was telling Honeybear good night, I whispered, "Wouldn't it be something if *we* could go to The Gaines?" She gave a big contented sigh, put her head on her paws and went to sleep.

■ ■ ■

From time to time I would use the words "Honeybear's world." Each time, Billie would respond, "Willard, *you* are Honeybear's world." Over time I came to realize how true that was. And that more and more Honeybear was *my* world.

■ ■ ■

Honeybear and I were Billie's project. With all her heart, she wanted us to do well.

When I look back on those afternoons with Billie, one mental picture transcends all others. It's a raw, blustery winter day here in the desert. There's a late afternoon downpour. Billie stands in the driving rain, no umbrella, calling heeling patterns for Honeybear and me. And that goes on for 20 minutes or so.

Tell that to the legion of bad guys she's sent to prison, and see if they believe it.

CHAPTER 7

Breaking The Ice

By the time Honeybear celebrated her first birthday, part of me was itching to see how well we could do. The other part was simply terrified.

At that point, with your first competition dog, you wake up at 3 a.m. and contemplate going into the ring in full view of a host of people you'd like to impress. With this wild thing you're sure you can't control. Under the eagle-eyed scrutiny of a sinister person who follows you around with a sharp pencil, quantifying just how much of a fool you're making of yourself.

Nevertheless, as 1991 got underway, I summoned the courage to enter the AKC-sanctioned match of the Sahuaro State Kennel Club. It was to be held on Sunday, January 13, at Paradise Valley Park, in northeast Phoenix.

We had participated in a few fun matches late in 1990, but a sanctioned match is much more stringent. At a fun match you may use food or toys to motivate your dog. You may physically correct your dog. In fact, you may train in the ring just about any way you wish. Training under ring conditions is the purpose of a fun match ... that and to generate revenue for the sponsoring group.

On the other hand, the AKC views sanctioned matches as "events at which dog clubs, judges, stewards, and exhibitors and their dogs gain experience needed for licensed events."

Food and toys are not allowed in the ring. The handler may correct the dog verbally but there's no laying on of hands. The judge may "at his/her sole discretion, allow the handler to repeat an exercise" — without a correction, you understand, thereby providing a golden opportunity for the dog to reinforce a mistake.

The longer I'm in obedience competition, the more ridiculous the sanctioned obedience match rules seem.

For instance, would someone please explain to me how carrying a toy under my arm during the heeling pattern diminishes the learning experience of the club putting on the match?

Or how it negatively impacts the match judge's opportunity to gain experience if I place a target in front of the pole before sending my dog on a go-out? Or if I march him out there and show him the pole after he has screwed up?

Beyond that, would someone clue me in, please, as to how I've chipped away at the fledgling steward's dry run if I spit food at my dog after he has given me a perfect front?

I was too green to question the match scheduled for January 13. All I knew was that it offered an opportunity under conditions close to "the real thing" to find out just how ready we were.

■ ■ ■

Billie had impressed upon me the importance of arriving at ringside at least an hour before any show. Honeybear, Barbara and I left home at eight o'clock for our 10 a.m. ring time.

As we entered the park that Sunday, it was deserted except for two cars and a couple of joggers. *Well, this can't be it,* I thought.

Then we saw a short bridge spanning a wash. We tried that road. It meandered west, then north. Soon we found ourselves passing a large dirt parking lot on our right and a golf course on our left. Just north of the parking lot, separated by a 30-foot-wide divider of grass with several Aleppo pine trees, was a 13-acre, fenced polo field. Another strip parking lot ran along the west side of the field, broken only by a slump-block "comfort station."

The west-side parking strip directly abutted the field. Several gates opened onto the grass.

Automobiles and vans had begun to gather in that strip lot. Several rings, fashioned of rebar and rope, were set up near the fence. We pulled in and parked.

The sun was brilliant, the sky was blue and the temperature had climbed to the 60s. It was the kind of day that motivates snowbirds from the midwest and Canada to pour hundreds of millions of dollars into the Arizona economy each winter.

There we were, ready for our first test — Barbara, Honeybear and I, two chairs, a water bowl and a leash. Thank God it was a cool day; we had not yet grasped the concept *bring your own shade*.

Little did I know on that first January morning that I would make that same 20-minute, nine-mile drive thousands of times. Or that the polo field at Paradise Valley Park would become Honeybear's favorite place on earth. And little could I foresee how deep my own emotional attachment to that grass field would become.

■ ■ ■

I had entered us in the Pre-Novice and Novice classes. Both feature the same exercises, but in Pre-Novice everything is done on leash.

Our Novice class was first. Our judge was a lady listed only as J. Savard. The judge's sheet from that frightening venture shows a score of 181. Of the 19 points we lost somewhere along the way, 18 were deducted on the two heeling exercises, on leash and off. She scored us for an occasional tight leash, lagging, sniffing, heeling wide, improper heel position, an extra command to heel, a no-sit, and lack of naturalness and smoothness. Well I guess! It's hard to be natural and smooth when you're holding your breath. I doubt I took two breaths during both heeling exercises combined.

Looking back, it's obvious we debuted with me stiff as a board and HB all over the ring.

Pre-Novice was somewhat better. We finished with a 191. Of the nine points we lost, eight were on the heeling exercises, both done on leash. After all, how far can the dog wander under those circumstances?

And on our first day in a real ring — two real rings — *we won both classes*!

Afterward, I saw several members of the Valle del Sol Golden Retriever Club (which I had joined) sitting outside the ring, some distance away. I managed to take Honeybear for a walk in that direction so I could gleefully announce, "We won both classes."

I was so proud I framed both score sheets, our ribbons and our armband, number eight. For days after the match, I referred to HB as "Number Eight." As in, "OK, Number Eight, here's your supper." Or, "Come on, Number Eight, let's go practice."

All of which is exactly as it should be. Obedience competition with your first dog is as fragile as a butterfly's wing. The dropout rate is staggering. An experience sparkling with excitement and delight right at the beginning can help cushion the disappointments that are certain to follow.

CHAPTER 8

The Wind Beneath Our Wings

On Monday morning, I couldn't wait to tell Dawn Franklin and Debbie Wheat about our "big wins" the morning before. During my conversation with Debbie, she told me about an instructor she thought would be good for us. Debbie had shown golden retrievers in obedience competition before I got Honeybear. She knew who was who around the obedience rings.

"What impresses me about Debby Boehm," she told me, "is the way her dogs watch her when they're in the ring." Indeed, I would quickly learn that focused dog attention was the cornerstone of Debby's teaching philosophy and the linchpin of excellence in obedience competition.

■ ■ ■

It all seemed simple enough, straightforward enough. "I think she lives over on your side of town," Debbie told me.

I found Debby's number. I called. An answering machine told me I had reached Precision Canine. It invited me to leave a message and promised a return call.

In retrospect, the day I left that message I should also have played the lottery. Had I done so, I would not only have become a pretty decent dog trainer, I might also have become rich. Debby returned the call. Yes, we could meet for a one-hour evaluation session. The charge would be $50. I didn't

know it at the time but the odds of Debby returning a phone call
— particularly from a stranger — were a bit more daunting
than the odds of winning the lottery.

Across the years, those of us who are close to Debby have
learned these two absolutes:

First, Debby is by far the best competition obedience instructor in Arizona. She's the person other instructors go to for lessons.

She has eyes in the back of her head; she sees everything. She
has a degree in psychology from Ohio State University with
emphasis on motivation and learning theory. And she is blessed
with the ability to apply what she knows (academically and from
training her own dogs) in a hands-on way to the poor soul and
the poor soul's dog who are struggling right there in front of her.

Second, Debby's Achilles heel is the telephone. She may or
may not return calls — a trait that has given her students fits for
as long as I have known her.

In later years, as I've gotten to know Debby better, I've pressed
her about her phone habits. "If you run a business and you adver-
tise your phone number, you should return calls," I've lectured.

To which she responds, "I use that as a screening device. If
they persist, if they call often enough, I know they're serious."

Yeah, right.

On the other hand, Debby's casual approach to the telephone
is the antithesis of her approach to classes or private lessons.
When you are with her for instruction, she is all yours. She gives
the same 100 percent focus she asks her students to develop in
themselves and their dogs.

■ ■ ■

At 1:30 p.m. on Monday, January 20, 1992, Honeybear and
I pulled up in front of Debby's house.

I was nervous. Stage fright. Debby had been built up in my
mind to be this super, all-knowing authority on training dogs

to compete in the obedience ring. And I was about to expose how inept we really were.

At the front door, the mat said:

Dog hiding in bushes.
Knows you're here.
Ring bell.
Act calm.

Somewhere in the house thousands of vicious-sounding dogs demanded my throat and a chunk of HB's flank.

I knocked. A slender thirty-something woman with long, blondish hair answered. Debby directed us around the side of the house. Through three gates. Past an outdoor stall with a single horse. The backyard was a bit more than half an acre of grass.

Debby emerged from the back of the house. A quick exchange of background information revealed we had a few things in common. Debby and I had lived in Columbus, Ohio, at the same time. I too had a degree from Ohio State University.

Now to the business of the visit: Honeybear and me.

Some 10 years later Debby and I sat down at my house to talk about those early days.

"I remember you being Honeybear's closest confidant," she told me. "Her secret was safe with you. You'd cover for her. That's a classic beginning dog trainer thing. Your reality was *the* reality. You thought Honeybear was doing great; therefore Honeybear *was* doing great, the greatest dog out there."

Our first session with Debby had come just eight days after winning two first-places in our first sanctioned match.

"You were feeling pretty tough about the whole thing — superconfident," she continued. "You felt you needed only a bit of polishing because your dog was dialed in; you had the whole thing licked."

Well, apparently I had managed to *look* confident.

That afternoon, as Debby began her evaluation, HB and I heeled. Honeybear lagged. "You gave me some excuse why that was," Debby recalled, "and why it was insignificant."

Near the end of the session, I assured Debby that HB was solid on the long sit. "Sit her right over here," Debby said, pointing to an area along the western perimeter fence. I called Honeybear into heel position right in front of the fence.

"Leave your dog," Debby said.

"Stay!" I barked and walked to a spot about 15 feet away.

After about 30 seconds, Debby sauntered in front of HB. "Honeybear," she said softly, sweetly. HB got up and ambled over to her, tail wagging, hind end undulating.

Debby looked at me. "Solid?" she said.

Looking back on that session, Debby recalled, "Honeybear was a nice little dog, trying to do what you wanted her to do. Not particularly motivated in a positive way. (Remember, she had been jerked around by the neck a lot during an impressionable formative period.) But certainly a willing little thing."

The day after our session Debby sent me a six-page summary of her impressions and recommendations. It began: "Willard Bailey and his 13-month-old female golden, Honeybear, present an appealing picture in the ring. They have the potential to put together some spectacular performances once they get locked in on each other."

Debby had zeroed in on the most important concept in dog obedience success — getting and keeping your dog's attention. She had quickly realized Honeybear and I had not been exposed to rigorous emphasis on dog attention. On focus. On "Watch!" As we heeled that afternoon in Debby's backyard, Honeybear had gawked, drifted, sniffed.

Shortly after that January afternoon in 1991, the words "Watch me" became the most used in my vocabulary.

A decade later, a believer, an evangelist, I often ask those less experienced in the sport, "What are the three most important elements in successful obedience competition training?"

Some may respond, "A leash, a collar and a dog."

But the correct answer is *attention, attention, attention*.

■ CHAPTER 9 ■

"Watch Me!"

"How can you expect your dog to know what you want her to do if she isn't paying attention to you?" Debby Boehm asked, as serious training began. "And the farther you go in obedience competition, the more lack of attention will kill you. Wait'll you get to Utility. There you'll have to leave your dog, go about 40 feet and hope she responds to your hand signals alone, no verbal commands. If she's not watching you, you're dead."

"Watch me" became our mantra, an incantation spoken in the hope of magically eliciting perfect attention from a dog who'd rather sniff.

"What's Honeybear's favorite toy?" Debby asked.

"She's a golden retriever," I replied. "On Christmas Eve, visions of tennis balls dance in her head."

Debby had me place Honeybear on a sit next to my left leg, in heel position. "Hold the tennis ball in your right hand," she instructed, "and bring it up by your left shoulder to mouth level."

I did and HB's eyes followed the ball.

"Tell her, 'Watch me,'" Debby said.

"Watch me," I said for the first of a zillion times. Honeybear's eyes locked on the ball.

"Praise her," Debby said. "Now say 'OK' and drop the ball."

I did and HB caught it cleanly.

"If she glances away, instantly say 'Aaaach!'" Debby continued. ('Aaaach!' is a harsh guttural noise that sounds like you're getting one up.) "Give her a quick, short jerk on the leash and remind her, 'Watch me!' When she glances back at your face, praise her right away."

We quickly extended the little watch from one second to five, to ten … all the way to a minute.

I bought an inexpensive full-length mirror at Target. At first I used it in the backyard, then took it with us to the park. It enabled me to observe Honeybear's attention without looking down at her. She'd sneak a glance at some distraction and I'd pop the leash instantly. She thought I'd developed eyes in the side of my head.

It's possible to include such teaching in daily activities. For instance, at meal time I'd hold her bowl of food up by my face and tell my excited, drooling little golden, "Honeybear, watch me!" Then, after a few seconds of perfect attention, "OK!" and put the bowl on the floor.

HB progressed rapidly. During the next lesson, Debby said, "This exercise isn't about watching the ball. We've used the ball to start her looking up. What we really want her to do is look at your face, right into your eyes. Eye contact is our goal."

At that point, instead of being the focal point, the ball became a distraction. I'd lower the ball. If HB's eyes followed it, I'd say, "Watch me!" followed by a quick pop of the leash if the verbal command didn't suffice. Again, we built the required attention time to a minute, still working in front of the mirror.

"Honeybear's doing great, Willard," Debby said the next time we met. "Now I want you to swing the ball — in front, at your side, anyplace it can catch HB's attention. If her eyes even flicker away from your face, correct her. When she resumes eye contact, praise."

It was about at that point that I first heard it. I was standing there swinging the ball — stiff as a board, waiting for HB to screw up — and Debby said, "Willard, *breathe.*"

It's a symptom common to rookie obedience competition handlers. Here you have this live four-legged teammate who at any second may bark, bolt, run in circles, jump on whoever is nearby, pee on the floor, or just break eye contact. You have this helpless, high-anxiety feeling. But maybe if you hold your breath you can fluke through whatever it is you are trying to do.

"Willard, remember to breathe!" became a staple of our instruction curriculum. In fact, only now, 12 years later, do I find myself remembering to breathe during heeling patterns. And even now it's a conscious effort.

Soon Honeybear was reasonably solid on watching me, with various distractions, as she sat at my side. In time she would become rock solid — much to the chagrin of a legion of show photographers. There isn't a show photographer alive who doesn't regard as a total artistic failure any presentation photo where the dog isn't looking directly at the camera.

And then they try to cope with Honeybear, the class winner or high-in-trial dog who, once she is seated on my left, refuses to look anywhere except into my face. The guy behind the camera throws toys, clucks and makes ridiculous animal noises, but HB continues to focus on my face.

Next Debby said, "It's one thing for the dog to watch you from a stationary position, quite another when the two of you are moving."

Back up to shoulder level went the ball. When I had HB's attention, I stepped forward slowly and encouraged her to move with me. A couple of steps, then release. I watched her intently, ready to correct when her attention flagged.

"This is strictly about attention," Debby cautioned.

"Corrections at this point are only for not watching, not for incorrect heel position."

She explained that many dogs tend to drop their heads momentarily when they start to heel forward. So it was with Honeybear. "Watch me," I'd say as we started to move. Then I'd quickly reward perfect head position after two or three steps.

Before long we were heeling short distances. Then we introduced turns and did short heeling patterns, some with reasonably good attention.

Finally we added the icing to the cake, the piece that has given Honeybear a paw up on every heeling pattern she's ever done.

"Visualize what happens when you go into the Novice ring," Debby said. She wanted me to picture everything that was going to happen, step by step.

You walk into the ring and set up where the steward indicates, your dog on your left, ready to go. The judge approaches you and says something like, "Good morning." (All too often in Novice A it's, "Good afternoon.")

Then the judge says, "This is the heel-on-leash exercise. Do you have any questions?"

The correct answer is, "No."

Next the judge asks, "Are you ready?" And that's when the opportunity presents itself. Your answer will be the last thing your dog hears before the judge says, "Forward."

"Imagine the judge has just asked, 'Are you ready?'" she told me. "Answer loudly, affirmatively, 'Ready!' then take off running to your right. At first this will surprise Honeybear and she will probably be left sitting there. And, in the process, as you dart to your right, she'll get a leash correction. As you run away, jolly her up: 'Where were you, HB? I fooled you.'"

Because the tone would be playful, Debby explained, Honeybear would not perceive the activity as a correction.

Rather, she would see the whole thing as a game where, unfortunately, she had been left behind. She'd quickly learn to respond to "Ready!" by looking up at me. And be locked in on me when the judge gave the next instruction, "Forward."

The next time we went out to train I practiced that little ploy a few times exactly as Debby had instructed. Then I added a twist of my own. I had learned that nothing in the world turned Honeybear on as much as food. So I reinforced the "Ready!" command with a treat instead of the "Gotcha!" technique of running away. I had experimented and had decided that Grreat Choice puppy/training biscuits met our needs perfectly. A handful of them fit into my top left shirt pocket and they were dry, so they didn't make a mess of my shirts.

My choice of treats ("cookies" as they are called by many in the dog obedience community) flew in the face of conventional wisdom. "Use soft food," everyone was advising, "so the dog doesn't have to stop and chew."

No problem with Honeybear. In later years Debby would tell bystanders, "Honeybear is the only dog I've ever known who can chew and maintain heel position at the same time."

So with HB in position to heel, I'd say, "Ready!" Her head would pop up and I'd drop a treat from my shoulder. If we did that once, we did it 5,000 times. The result? Not once in Honeybear's long career was she not ready — head up, eyes focused on me — when the judge said, "Forward."

■ CHAPTER 10 ■

Paradise Valley Park

Our affinity for Paradise Valley Park began inauspiciously, a result of beginner's anxiety. Because HB was the first dog I had trained, I was clueless. For a long time I was deathly afraid HB would decide to just take off and run away from me.

After our experience in the Sahuaro State Kennel Club match, held at Paradise Valley Park, it dawned on me that the polo field was grassy, immense and fenced in. Above all, fenced in. No way HB could run away. So why not train there? A few days later I gave it a try.

By the spring of 1991, more and more afternoons would find us pulling up outside the southwest gate of the polo field.

The location was close to ideal for training. The only drawback was "gopher" holes (actually the homes of ground squirrels). I knew where they were and we avoided them.

They weren't hard to find. In the late afternoon, as the sun began to dip toward the western horizon, the ground squirrels would come out of their holes and stand erect on their haunches, only to pop back into their holes if HB or I came near. To this day Honeybear feels a compulsion to put her nose down every "gopher" hole she encounters.

Although those holes presented a constant source of anxiety, it took many years for them to exact their toll.

■ ■ ■

As Debby began to get us straightened out, I began to take pride in our little watch-me victories. In fact, the watch-me exercises became the foundation for what we did during those afternoons at the park.

At first all of our heeling was done on leash. HB would glance away or drop her head to sniff and I'd pop the leash and say, "Watch me!" She'd look up. I'd say, "Good watch," and dispense a treat. I soon realized it made sense to carry the treats in the left breast pocket of my shirt. After all, if I wanted her to look up in that direction, that's where the food should come from.

Going from on-leash to off-leash was scary. The leash was psychologically a lot like the fence. No way HB could get far enough away to embarrass me when we were securely connected by the leash.

Debby eased the transition with a *light line* (some call it a *shark line*), a very thin plastic-coated, braided steel line with a wooden handle. It's an unobtrusive leash substitute.

We'd use it to con our dogs into thinking they were off leash when they weren't. We'd attach the regular leash and the light line to the collar and heel a few minutes with both in place. Then, with great ceremony and snapping of clasps, we'd remove the regular leash. Then we'd continue heeling, using only the light line — which the dog theoretically didn't know was there.

Nice try, but after more than a decade of training experience, I'm not buying the validity of that charade. If our dogs are smart enough to learn all the complex exercises we teach them, I'm convinced they are smart enough to see or feel the difference between being leash-free or being on a light line.

Nevertheless, all that on-leash and off-leash and off-leash-but-secretly-on-leash practice helped me build skill and confidence.

Much of what Honeybear and I worked on during those early days at the park was fear-driven. Make no mistake, the prospect of soon going into a real ring with a real judge and people watching — then having to surrender the leash — was downright frightening. But that anxiety led to practice habits that, I believe, overcame a lack of ability.

Decades earlier, at Ohio State University, I had been influenced by a public relations professor who told us, "A genius is someone who works like hell when no one is looking." Those words resonated in my mind as, out there alone on that polo field, HB and I struggled to find ourselves.

CHAPTER 11

Clueless

B y the time we walked into Debby's backyard for the first time, I had already entered our first real obedience trial. We didn't have a clue, but I didn't have a clue that we didn't have a clue. I was getting antsy. We had practiced, practiced, practiced. Never mind that in those days most of what we practiced was our mistakes. I thought it was high time to take the plunge.

Debby must have rolled her eyes at the prospect, though I don't recall that she tried to dissuade us. After all, the entry had been sent in. The deed was done.

Oh, how carefully I filled out that first entry. I sure didn't want anything to go wrong with this. If only I had been as meticulous about HB's attention.

Starbuc's Dream Come True, I printed. And in parentheses I put "Honeybear" so they'd know who that was. A female golden retriever, born December 22, 1989. Known to the American Kennel Club as SF759999. She would be entered in the Novice A class at the Phoenix Field and Obedience Club's trial on February 23, 1991. I checked it and rechecked it, then sent it off with a check for $14.

We ratcheted up the intensity and duration of our practice sessions. Lots of heeling, some with HB actually watching me.

We practiced the stand for examination, an easy exercise unless you and your dog are a green-as-grass Novice A team.

In the ring, I would be required to stand Honeybear, tell her to stay, then walk to a point six feet in front of her and face her while the judge moved in to "examine" her. In reality, the judge lightly touches the dog on the head, the back and rump before stepping back. Then the judge would say, "Return to your dog." I'd return to a position between HB's nose and right shoulder and wait for the judge to say, "Exercise finished," before releasing her.

During that exercise, HB would be required to freeze in place, not follow me, not shy away from the judge (or, heaven forbid, snap at the judge). She would not be allowed to dance around or shift her feet until I released her. Even shifting one paw could incur a penalty of half a point.

Now, in her 13th year and thoroughly seasoned, Honeybear could probably do that exercise 100 times in a row and get a perfect score. But back in 1991 the stand for examination was the stuff of acute anxiety.

We practiced the recall, the final individual exercise in the Novice ring. There was never any doubt that Honeybear would come on the recall exercise. (Whether she would come in real life when she had more interesting options was, at least in those early days, a matter of considerable doubt.) Her willingness to come on the recall had been established in puppy kindergarten when, joyously, she would come racing to me and launch herself into my arms.

But there were then, and continued to be throughout her career, other issues associated with the recall exercise. Issues that later would result in many points lost and many gray hairs gained.

The exercise goes like this: I would be required to take HB to the center of one end of the ring and tell her to sit in heel position ("Place" became my command to accomplish that). When the judge said, "Leave your dog," I would walk briskly to the opposite end of the ring, turn and face my dog. The recall is the first exercise in obedience competition where the dog is required to stay in position while the handler turns his back and goes to the other end of the ring.

The thing uppermost on any handler's mind — but particularly on the mind of the poor green, anxiety-ridden soul in Novice A — as he walks away on a recall exercise is, *What's going on back there? Is she still sitting? Is she up? Is she following me?* Sometimes, if there are people sitting at the end of the ring facing you and the dog, you can read their faces. Their expressions don't tell you exactly what has happened behind you, only that a disaster has occurred. Or that your fly is open.

Upon reaching the other end of the ring, I would turn, face HB and wait for the judge to say, "Call your dog." Whereupon I would shout "Come!" (Not, "Honeybear, come!" She'd break on her name, and that's points off.)

HB would be required to come briskly and sit perfectly straight directly in front of me. Then, upon the judge's command, swing into heel position (the finish).

The recall exercise is fraught with frustrating possibilities. It is common — routine in Novice — for the dog to front crooked or finish crooked. At that stage in their obedience careers, many dogs have yet to realize their heads and shoulders are connected to their rear ends. The head may be looking right up into your face but the rear end is 45 degrees off.

Worse, the dog might follow the handler across the ring. Or refuse to come at all. Or anticipate the handler's call and come too soon.

Or HB's favorite way of driving me toward an early grave: pick up her butt two or three inches as I walk to the opposite end of the ring, in anticipation of my command, "Come!" That's good for a three-point deduction, enough to ruin an otherwise excellent run.

Honeybear's career would be riddled with three-point deductions for elevating her butt when she was about to be called or sent somewhere.

But cruising toward my obedience competition debut with a dog whose fresh, bright face constantly radiated want-to, I was blissfully unaware of how exasperating dog obedience competition can be.

Just scared to death.

■ CHAPTER 12 ■

A Red Ribbon Day

By the time our Phoenix Field and Obedience Club (PFOC) judging program arrived in the mail, I was beginning to get a clue that I was clueless. Two private lessons and two class sessions with Debby had jarred me into realizing that maybe, just maybe, there was a world of stuff I didn't know about training a dog. Indeed, about training myself to train a dog. "Willard," Debby was fond of saying, "dog training is not about training dogs."

I held our first judging program as if it were the Dead Sea Scrolls — reverently, afraid it might crumble in my hands. There was HB's name! The little girl I had brought home in a cardboard box, and she had barked all the way home. Barbara pointed out that I had tears in my eyes.

Scanning the program, I saw that there would be 10 Novice A entries in Ring 2 at 8 a.m. under a judge named Gerald Daulton. Their armband numbers were 01 to 10 — and Honeybear was number one! We'd be first in the ring in our first trial. Oh, God.

Which is how I learned to send entries in later, hoping we'd find ourselves deeper in the judging order. The better to observe the heeling pattern, how the judge is running the ring and all the things a veteran handler would like to familiarize himself with before entering the ring.

But for right now, panic. Anxiety. Stage fright. And I was not alone. It comes with the territory. At our early matches and shows, when we were clustered with other Novice A people, Barbara would say, "There's enough nervous energy here to light the City of Phoenix."

Much later — when HB and I were competing against some of the best teams in the country at important national tournaments — Barbara looked around and asked, "If these people are having so much fun, why do they all look so stressed?"

Eventually I would learn that my instructor — my very own long-suffering Debby Boehm — who had all these books and tapes and philosophies about relaxation and focus and visualizing and getting into a zone — was one of the worst.

We learned not to talk to Debby before she took her dog into the ring. Not that that was a frequent problem. Her own competition anxieties were so deep-seated that she found more reasons than Iams has dog biscuits not to enter her dogs — or to pull them if, in a moment of reckless abandon, she had entered them.

■ ■ ■

As the days before the PFOC trial dwindled down to a precious few, my anxiety level rose exponentially.

"Well yeah, I love this and I want to do it. But oh God!"

The evening before the trial, Debby took three of us, her students, to the show site, Pierce Park, to practice. She whipped out some rebar and rope and in nothing flat had a ring set up. We did run-throughs with light corrections. The idea was to get dogs and handlers comfortable in the area where tomorrow they'd be in the ring.

Debby said, "Try to relax, Willard, and remember to breathe. The stress goes right down the leash and upsets your dog." And I tried to remember to inhale and exhale.

■ ■ ■

On the morning of the trial — in my anxious rookie mind our date with destiny — HB, Barbara and I arrived at Pierce Park at 6:30, as dawn was beginning to break. The site was peaceful and pretty. Five rings had been set up the afternoon before. Large rectangles of white ring gates were punctuated by red stanchions. The canopies over the judges', trial secretary's and trophy tables were red-and-white striped.

We found a spot that looked like it would be shady when the sun came up. Then we set up two folding chairs, a small portable pen and a water bowl. It was a far cry from the tent, 10-x-10-foot mat, crates, table, cooler, chairs, equipment bags and other assorted paraphernalia that today require an hour to set up.

I got Honeybear out of the car and immediately played ball with her. Debby continually emphasized that my training style was too formal, too regimented. Every exercise was done with a front and a finish. It was all life and death. Serious to a fault. "Play ball with her before you go into the ring and again when you come out," Debby told me. "Let her have fun. Break the stress."

I located Ring 2 and, again per Debby's instructions, walked HB around the perimeter, letting her sniff and, I hoped, get comfortable with the area.

And I beat a path back and forth to the Port-O-Let. "I hold the Arizona record for diarrhea before an obedience trial," I tell people today, "eight times before the PFOC trial in 1991."

All too soon I heard the weak strains of the Star-Spangled Banner being played on someone's cassette recorder at the trial secretary's table. It was eight o'clock and there was no longer anywhere to hide. Not even in the Port-O-Let.

The last thing Debby said to me as I put the leash on Honeybear and prepared to head toward Ring 2 and a fate worse than death was, "Willard, remember to breathe."

And then it all goes blank. Probably as a result of oxygen deprivation. I presume Judge Daulton told me the heeling pattern or had someone walk it. They do that if you're first in.

I know we went in there and did our thing because I have a little blue score card, framed and on the wall behind my desk, that says we weren't great but we weren't a disaster, either.

We lost four points on the heel-on-leash. HB undoubtedly dropped her head and drifted in and out of heel position. My footwork was probably comical.

Five points on the stand for examination??!! How on earth do you lose five points on the Novice stand for exam? What did she do, walk halfway across the ring? Was I out of position when I returned to her? We'll never know, but that's the one exercise in all of dog obedience competition where a perfect score should be a slam-dunk.

We lost another four points on the heel-free exercise. Proving we were no more sloppy off leash than on.

Two points on the recall. She'd always come like she was shot from a gun. But the front and finish … well, they were another matter. After working with this dog all her life, I'm now convinced she carries the sit-crooked gene.

Our score that frightening morning was 185. On my wall, next to my little blue scorecard, is a group photo of the four of us who placed. There we are, Honeybear and me with our red ribbon, so proud. We had finished second in our Novice A debut.

We drove home on cloud nine, HB's head on my lap.

■ CHAPTER 13 ■

Getting Our Feet Wet

We had survived our first encounter with a real AKC obedience competition ring. Our Companion Dog title was one-third in the bag. Now my advance planning looked pretty good — I had entered us in three more obedience trials the following weekend. The Valle del Sol Golden Retriever Club's spring specialty show would be held Friday at Paradise Valley Park. On Saturday we would be at Mesa Community College for the Superstition Kennel Club show. And Sunday would find us at Estrella Mountain Park, entered in the show of Sahuaro State Kennel Club.

We had sent Barbara's parents airplane tickets and invited them to spend ten days with us. During that time they could go to at least a couple of the shows. They adored Honeybear but had never seen her in competition. Barbara's mother, Gladys, and stepfather Bob Krieg arrived on Tuesday, February 26, in the afterglow of our triumph at PFOC.

■ ■ ■

Friday dawned (barely) in the throes of a downpour — a cold, driving rain that didn't let up all day. But nothing short of life-threatening lightning stops a dog show. There was no lightning, so off we went.

The day started off poorly right in the car. HB has always been terrified by the windshield wipers and rain on the car roof. As soon as we left home for the 20-minute ride, she began to tremble uncontrollably. Barbara covered HB's head with a towel, to no avail.

The weather was an even bigger problem when we arrived at the park. Gladys was a robust 81, game for anything. But Bob was frail at 90. Too frail to spend a cold day in a driving rain.

Neophytes in the dog show world, we had no tent and little of the outdoorsy gear veteran obedience competitors accumulate.

Barbara spent the day trying to keep her folks reasonably warm and dry, a thankless effort. First she tried umbrellas. They were of little use in the slanting downpour, even before one turned inside out. Late in the morning two kind souls offered space for the Kriegs in their tent. Eventually Bob wound up back in the car, engine running, heater on. Meanwhile, I was trying to focus on my dog, with wet glasses and water streaming into my eyes.

There were several specialty shows underway that soggy day on the 13-acre polo field.

Dog shows emphasize the conformation events. Those of us in obedience competition are "the other guys." At large all-breed dog shows, where there may be 18 or 20 conformation rings, we can be found off in the corner, doing our thing in two or three rings.

Which is just fine with us. There is no greater pleasure than to contort one's face into an expression of utter disdain, look a conformation handler and dog up and down, then say, "Our dogs can *do* something." Kiddingly of course … well, sort of.

The conformation handlers busy themselves with an exhausting routine of bathing, drying, scissoring, brushing, primping and generally fussing over their dogs right up until they enter the ring. And many carry a brush with them in the ring. Fluffy must look right … down to the last hair.

You can imagine the havoc a day-long downpour wreaks. We saw a woman not much more than five feet tall *carrying* her Great Dane to the ring, some 50 yards from her grooming tent.

The conformation ring for golden retrievers was a quagmire, made worse by the running of dogs and handlers. By late morning, handling became secondary to keeping one's footing.

Our obedience ring was much better because there was less traffic. But when it came time for us to enter the ring for the individual exercises the rain was beating and there was standing water in several spots.

We heeled better than we had at PFOC. And HB's stand for exam was perfect. Golden retrievers are water dogs and HB seemed to think the weather was swell.

Until the group exercises. The long sit and long down were done in a low spot with half an inch of standing water. Honeybear did fine during the long sit for one minute, stoic as the rain beat in her face. But somewhere around the second minute of the long down she got tired of lying in cold water and abruptly sat up. At which point "NQ" (nonqualifying score) became more than just a term I had heard.

So much for our second Novice leg. I learned later that we had been headed for first place when she blew it. Ah well, there was tomorrow.

They say dogs have a strong sense of place. If something positive happens they associate that experience with the place where it happened. Conversely, a bad experience is linked with the environment where it took place. Good vibes, bad vibes.

Handlers also have a strong sense of place. Honeybear and I were destined to spend thousands of afternoons on the polo field at Paradise Valley Park. And nearly a decade later I could still walk out there with HB, point to the spot and say, "Look, you big yellow rascal, that's where you broke the long down in Novice A when we were about to win the class."

But Honeybear would just wag her tail, as if to say, "Aw come on Skippy, throw the ball."

■ ■ ■

Saturday was a pristine Arizona morning. The storm had blown the smog out of the Valley, the sun was shining, the sky was blue. Forget Black Friday. On to Superstition Kennel Club. That show was held at Mesa Community College.

We arrived early and found we could park along the fence just outside the obedience rings. As we got out of the car, I heard *wop! wop! wop!* Followed by, "thirty love."

"Oh no!" I said to Barbara, "the obedience rings are right by the tennis courts." Golden retrievers are born with tennis balls in their mouths. If you have a golden who doesn't pounce on any tennis ball in sight, ready to play, have that dog checked.

"How am I going to heel HB with tennis balls bouncing a few yards away?" I said. "What will she do during the long sit and down?"

As it turned out, tennis balls weren't the problem. I was.

Our Novice A judge in Ring 2 that morning was a lady named Loma J. Hallissy. We were fifth in the ring. Plenty of time to study and practice the heeling pattern. Ample opportunity to run to the Port-O-Let a few times. When our turn came, I walked into the ring stiff as a board.

"Good morning," Mrs. Hallissy said.

"Good morning," I croaked. Breathe? You gotta be kidding.

Exactly at that point HB decided to sniff the grass. I gave her a sharp yank with the leash. Mrs. Hallissy looked startled, then stern. "One more like that and I'll have to excuse you," she said.

I stammered an apology. I was sure she thought I brutalized my dog in training. What a lousy beginning.

Our run in her ring wasn't all that bad for two beginners. HB even ignored the tennis courts during the group exercises.

Our score was 180. Of the 20 points we lost, 10 were for handler misbehavior. It was part of living and learning, but it was good for fourth place and our second CD leg.

Two down, one to go.

CHAPTER 14

The Worst Of Days, The Best Of Days

Across an obedience competition career, a few days, for better or for worse, are burned into your memory. But rarely do for-better and for-worse occur on the same day.

Sunday, March 3, 1991 was one of those days.

Everyone was there. We were on display. After a chilled-to-the-bone Friday when we wondered if Bob would come down with pneumonia or worse, the Kriegs had stayed home on Saturday. They had not seen us get our second leg.

But they came with us on Sunday, hoping to see their favorite golden retriever attain a Companion Dog title at the Sahuaro State Kennel Club show.

Debby was there, too. And of course I wanted to impress her.

Estrella Mountain Park is a huge county park that, in those days, was on the outer edge of civilization, the far western outskirts of the Valley. Unlike most Phoenix-area show sites, there are lots of trees and lots of shade. In many ways it's quite a pleasant place to be in a dog show.

So there were Barbara, Gladys, Bob, and Debby all lined up in the shade at ringside.

The judge was Sharon Ann Redmer, from Ann Arbor, Michigan. She was tall and friendly, a strong presence in the ring. Looking back, her style made the difference on a day when a neophyte handler and his fledgling golden added breadth and depth to the words "embarrassed themselves."

It was a tough ring, especially for newbies. The ground was dappled by sun and shade. I saw one Novice A dog break out of the heeling pattern to go lie down in a shady corner of the ring.

HB and I wobbled into Judge Redmer's ring full of hope.

"Forward," the judge said. And then the wheels came off. It was as if Honeybear had never been exposed to the concept of dog attention. Maybe it was the smells of the many critters that had scurried in the area. HB was in the same ring but definitely not in heel position.

"Halt," Mrs. Redmer said. And while we were standing there she said softly, "Breathe!" Then we were off again and the heeling was disgraceful.

Next, HB danced around on the stand for exam, heeled worse during the off-lead exercise and gave me a world-class lousy front and finish on the recall.

At the completion of the individual exercises, the judge said, "Just a second, let's see if you're still with us." She added up the points lost so far. We had lost 29. At that point our score stood at 171 — you need 170 to qualify.

Soon it was time for the group exercises, the long sit and long down. After the long sit, during which Honeybear went down, Judge Redmer said, "All right, now we've all proven we can hold our breath for one minute, let's see if we can do it for three."

HB also got up during the long down. Our final score was 111. A disastrous day.

In retrospect, that was *the* watershed day in our obedience career. I was embarrassed, humiliated, disheartened beyond words. But the balance was tipped by the pleasant, upbeat, encouraging, even witty, manner of Judge Redmer. Her friendly, supportive presence in the ring, on a day when a fragile new-comer could have been devastated right out of the sport, was a godsend.

I was able to go home, lick my wounds and come back stronger.

In the years that have followed, I have sat outside the Novice A ring on two occasions and heard judges make sarcastic, demeaning comments to fledgling competitors about their per-formances ... loudly enough to be heard by those at ringside. Thank God, on our darkest day as beginners in dog obedience, we didn't encounter one of those judges.

The next time I saw Sharon was two years later, again at Sahuaro State Kennel Club, this time indoors at the Phoenix Convention Center. What a difference two years can make. Honeybear and I were awaiting our high-in-trial photo when Judge Redmer walked by. We had not been in her ring that morning. We had shown in Open A, and won a runoff to cap-ture the blue ribbon and high in trial. But when Sharon com-pleted her judging and walked by I reintroduced us. Yes, she remembered when we had scarcely made it through the Novice A individual exercises, then flunked during the groups. And she took note of the high-in-trial blue and gold ribbon I was holding and warmly congratulated us.

Honeybear and I had come a long way since a sensitive judge did all she could to help a truly inept team feel better about themselves.

■ ■ ■

On the other hand, that disastrous March 3 was also the day we first saw Flash and Karen Price in action. They had been at Superstition Kennel Club the day before but I hadn't noticed them.

Photo: Barbara Bailey

July 1991: A big girl now.

Flash was known to the AKC as OTCH Sunfire Spontaneous Combustion, JH. Karen and Flash were from Chatsworth, California. Flash was a beautiful big male golden retriever. Oh, the heeling! They moved swiftly. Flash's head was up; he never took his eyes off Karen. He drove forward but was always in perfect heel position.

On the drop on recall, he came like a bullet, then dropped like he had been shot. He soared over the jumps. Flash was everything I wanted Honeybear to be. We were light years away but I could dream.

Later that afternoon I saw them again, standing so straight, so magnificent on a grassy knoll, a natural pedestal. It was their high-in-trial photo shoot.

You don't plan role models, they just *happen to you*. And that afternoon at Estrella Mountain Park, Karen and Flash not only rang our bell, they shattered it. Something inside me said, "That's it. That's the way I want Honeybear and me to look."

We saw a lot of them after that. I'd watch Flash: his drive, his explosiveness, how he strutted through the heeling pattern, his sheer joy during every ring appearance. Then I'd go out to train with Honeybear and I'd say, "Be like Flash!" Of course HB didn't know what that meant … but I did.

■ ■ ■

Honeybear and I weren't entered in the show the next day. But we went just to watch and play.

I made sure we were at the ring in time to see Karen and Flash in Open B. They did the heel-free and figure eight. It gave me goose bumps, brought tears to my eyes.

The drop on recall was next. Karen put Flash on a sit at her side … how straight, how attentive, how magnificent. The judge said, "Leave your dog." Karen walked briskly to the opposite end of the ring, turned and faced Flash. The judge gave a hand

signal for Karen to call her dog. A commercial airliner was passing overhead.

"Come," Karen said in a soft voice. Flash didn't budge. He
hadn't heard her. They flunked. Yesterday high in trial, today
zero. The imprint that left on my mind was deep and lasting.

There is a lot of noise around obedience rings, and jets are
the least of it. Breed ring people have generators blasting.
Squeaky-wheeled carts are being pulled by the rings. Other
dogs are barking. Commands are being given in adjacent rings.

It's been more than 12 years now and I have never had a
dog not hear me in the ring. My commands are loud. Urgent.
Some might say too strident, but I've never had a judge object.
And I have Karen and Flash to thank for that lesson.

CHAPTER 15

The Inner Game Of Training

"**B**ack to the drawing board," I said after HB and I had disgraced ourselves at Estrella Mountain Park. But I had only an amorphous idea of what I meant by that. It hadn't dawned on me — and it wouldn't for several years — how long and treacherous the journey would be and what it would take to get there. Or even where *there* was. Right now *there* was our third leg, our Companion Dog title. Which we'd probably get the next time we went into the ring. Oh the naiveté of the Novice A competitor!

The vague "drawing board" to which we would return was loosely envisioned as the park, lessons with Debby and classes at Precision Canine.

As an instructor, Debby sees everything, rationalizes nothing. And in the spring of 1991 she was beginning to see patterns of inhibitory behavior in my training approach. Most of them stemming from my anxiety. Deep down I was afraid I couldn't control my dog, or that I'd "break" her. After all, we had adopted Paradise Valley Park as our favorite place to train because the polo field was fenced and Honeybear couldn't run away, get hit by a car and die.

Anxiety manifested itself in other ways as well. There was a spasticity about my training. Everything was hurried. An explosive release terminated each exercise. If the dog gave me a perfect front or a perfect finish, I'd pop her a treat or release her so quickly she'd have no time to assimilate what she'd done right. No time to record what it should look like to her when she was, for example, perfectly straight in front of me.

My training was formal, formal, formal. Every exercise required a formal front and/or finish. It was all work for the dog. I had no idea how to incorporate play into the training. We'd train with rapid, spastic movements, done stiffly by me and wrapped in formality. Then, when we were finished, I'd throw up my arms in a grand gesture and say, "OK Honeybear, let's play ball!"

Without realizing it, I was teaching HB that training was stiff, boring, a chore. And the fun was to be found later, outside the training situation. It would follow that the dog's conditioned response would come to be, *Let's either get out of this or slog through it until we get to the fun part.*

What's more, the play itself took place through a fun *object*, a ball, thrown to a point some distance from me. In reality, Honeybear was playing with the ball. I was just the machine that made the ball fly away so she could chase it. Then she would bring it back so I could throw it again. The fun was in the chase and unless we tugged with the ball when she brought it back, she wasn't playing with me. There was no hands-on connecting, bonding element in that play.

Likewise, at the end of an exercise, petting, wrestling, tugging, roughhousing did not come naturally. Instead, I'd hand her a treat or spit it from my mouth. Notice that I said "at the end of an exercise." I was as likely to reward her at the end of an exercise for *being* as I was for doing something well.

The food itself surfaced as an issue early in our training. An issue destined to resurface in various ways, in various settings and with varying degrees of ugliness for as long as HB and I were significant figures (read *threats*) in obedience competition.

Part of the problem was that I was right on the cusp. I entered obedience competition when jerking the *bad, defiant* animal around, smacking him, using all types of force was still *the* way to train. The old-timers were wedded to that style of training. And for a brash newcomer to enter the sport and shamelessly begin to train with food in broad daylight — then begin to win for God's sake! — well, that was cheating of the most egregious, intolerable sort.

Debby Boehm herself had been kicked out of class for using food by one of the old-fossil instructors at PFOC. Which didn't mean Debby was supportive of my use of food. Rather, she was a proponent of the "appropriate" use of food. Our differences involved her take on my personal motivation for reliance on treats. It went right back to my deep-seated anxiety about my ability to motivate Honeybear.

"You don't feel that you're enough of a reward, Willard," she told me, and that became a constant refrain. In one dimension, she was right.

But there was another dimension, another valid point of view … mine.

When Honeybear did what I wanted her to, learned what I was trying to teach her, excelled in the execution of the exercises, she needed to be rewarded with impact. And Honeybear was the ultimate food-driven dog.

Deep in my stomach and deep in my psyche, I didn't think my hands were any match for one of the Grreat Choice training biscuits I had in my shirt pocket. And it didn't take my canine dispos-all long to reinforce what I felt.

Exercise well done? You bet. So I reach down to pet her as I congratulate her and she steps back and says, "Where's my treat?" There was reverse conditioning going on there.

Above all, the manifestation of anxiety that most influenced our early training was the fear that I'd "break" my dog. I had a comfort zone and I was reluctant to break out of that comfort zone. I feared I'd overload her to the point where she'd be unable to comprehend, or she'd fall apart and we'd have to start from the beginning. Or, the worst, she wouldn't love me anymore.

Once I found a method I was comfortable with and HB was comfortable with, I'd hold on to it stubbornly, even if giving it up was part of taking the next logical step. It was difficult for me to lay out a challenge for my dog — my buddy — and push her through to the next level. I felt more comfortable as an enabler.

Consequently I dealt with training problems by training, training and more training. Then, when we arrived at a show, I'd be petrified that she'd forget what to do. So I'd get her out and warm her up past warm. Then warm her up again. And again. Looking back, I suspect there were many times when HB was warmed up to the point of being warmed over and the word *fresh* had no appropriate place in describing the dog I eventually took into the ring.

So I'd enter the ring with a wound-down dog and myself in a state of anxiety-induced near-paralysis. During a halt, Sharon Ann Redmer had said, "Breathe!" Actually, in those days my halts weren't so much halts as they were mandated interruptions in our spastic heeling.

We'd stop. But instead of being planted, I'd be leaning forward, teetering there, holding my breath, ready to go. After all, the apocalypse would be upon us at any moment. And that pattern continued despite Debby's near-heroic efforts to break through. Years into the relationship I asked her, "Am I the most difficult student you've ever had?"

The pause lasted only a moment, then she replied, "Well, you'd certainly have to be in the top five."

Across nearly two decades of consulting with not-for-profit organizations in the field of fundraising, I encountered two varieties of neophytes. There were those who didn't know and realized they didn't know. They could be helped. Then there were those who didn't know and didn't know they didn't know … or would rather fail than admit it. They were impossible. And they drove me crazy.

Now, a decade later, I know I inflicted myself upon Debby as a student in the latter category. But perhaps it was less not knowing I didn't know than it was being afraid to know. What you don't know can't break your dog. Or so I thought.

So we remained at odds. A decade later Debby described the arm-wrestling that took place:

> "It might be over what we were seeing in training right now. Or it might be over training issues in general. It could be over what you needed to do about something or the need for you to address something you didn't think needed to be addressed.

> "The usual scenario would be we'd knock heads. I'd be trying to explain to the point that you could see where things were going or could understand the reality of what was happening. I'd keep saying the same thing, perhaps in different ways. And you'd keep saying, 'Yes, but …'

> "We'd part, disagreeing. You'd go your own way, training-wise, doing or not doing what I was talking about. But you'd kind of wander around, talking to a lot of people. Then, some time later, you'd come back to me and say exactly what it was I had said to you — as if it was your own idea."

Debby thinks it had to do with what she calls "the pet-person mentality." The vision you have is the reality. Maybe, but I think it also had to do with a maturation process, the development of a readiness to assimilate.

In the end, what worked for me was what I was comfortable with and what I sensed Honeybear was comfortable with. I was able to mold those comfort-zone methods into a training style that succeeded.

Best of all, head-knocking or not, the relationship with Debby survived, thrived and developed into a warm, lasting friendship.

■ CHAPTER 16 ■

Golden Afternoons

D ogs in vehicles have a way of reading every bump, every turn, every nuance of surface or change of direction. If the route is traveled frequently, they know where they are without lifting their heads.

Paradise Valley Park, just nine miles from home, quickly became a staple in our daily training routine. As soon as we'd turn into the park, Honeybear would pop up, tail hammering the back of the seat, and begin to whimper. I'd say, "Here we are, Honeybear, your very favorite place." And she'd nuzzle me in the face.

When she was young and in her prime, we'd finish the lesson, then play ball all around the 13-acre field. I'd throw the ball as far as I could. Honeybear would tear after it and bring it back. Or maybe she'd pause to stick her nose down a gopher hole. Or find a rabbit to chase.

Here in the west we raise *real* rabbits, jack rabbits. Big guys with long ears and powerful hind legs. Like the one HB flushed out one memorable afternoon to teach me about the power of motivation.

We were just beginning our late afternoon ballplaying when up jumped this jack rabbit, no more than ten feet in front of us. Before I could react, the chase was on.

I stood there yelling, "Honeybear, come! Honeybear, come!" What a joke.

At the far end of the field, nearly 1,000 feet away, the jack rabbit made a 180-degree turn and back they came, directly at me. HB was still close behind the streaking rabbit.

When he was almost at my feet, the jack rabbit finally saw me and turned sharply. Off he shot to the opposite end of the field with Honeybear right on his heels.

Suddenly the chase ended in an area close to the fence where there were a few trees. I figured the jack rabbit had found a hole in the fence.

I called, "Honeybear, come!" She trotted back, pooped but wagging her tail.

The next day, running a lap around the field, we reached the point where the chase had ended the evening before. There, on the ground, stiff as a board, without a tooth mark on him, was a large jack rabbit. I could only assume HB had run the poor rabbit to death.

She wasn't saying, only wagging her tail, impatient for me to throw the ball.

■ ■ ■

It didn't take Honeybear and me long to get to know the park rangers. The first two encounters were awkward.

Phoenix has a city ordinance regulating the control of dogs in public places. Boiled down, it says if Phydeaux is outside your yard, he must be on a leash.

I'd learned that during those afternoons with Billie Rosen. We'd be training Honeybear and Kara. Someone would bring a dog into the park and turn her loose. Before long, "Fluffy" would head our direction and Billie, in her no-nonsense voice, would call out, "There's a leash law in Phoenix." That usually led to the owner's indignant response, "Then how come *your* dog is off leash?" Then Billie, still in her best courtroom not-to-be-trifled-with tone, would explain that the Phoenix ordinance specifically exempts obedience competition dogs in training. That usually took care of the situation.

When Debby first learned we'd begun training at Paradise Valley Park, she warned me that she had had trouble with the rangers there. The point of contention being dogs off leash.

Sure enough, we had been practicing on the polo field only a few days when I saw the white City of Phoenix truck. The lettering on the side said Park Ranger. Into the parking lot it came, right up to the fence where we were practicing.

At that point there was only Honeybear and me with the two orange traffic cones we used to work on figure eights. That's all you need to practice for Novice. The ton of paraphernalia — the jumps, the ring, the scent articles, the chicken wire, the hernia-inducing training bag — all that comes later. I had nothing with me to show that I was training a dog for obedience competition, not just playing with my golden retriever off leash in a city park.

As soon as the ranger got out of the truck, came through the gate and started toward us, Honeybear started toward him. *Oh God!*

"Honeybear come!" I called. Lo and behold, she wheeled and came. "Honeybear down." She dropped. So far, so good; she looked like an obedience dog.

The ranger greeted me in a warm, friendly way, told me what a beautiful dog I had there, then began to tell me about the leash law.

"Oh but I'm training her for obedience competition," I interrupted and began to tell him about the ordinance's exemption of obedience competition dogs in training.

The ranger began to nod. He knew. Looking over my shoulder he checked out HB, who was still holding one of the most important down-stays of her embryonic obedience career. He allowed as how I was doing a pretty good job and again said what beautiful dog I had. Then he was gone.

And that's how I met Stan Bucher.

A few weeks later another white truck, with two rangers, pulled up. Only this time we had finished our lesson and were playing ball. I'd throw it as far as I could. Honeybear would fly after it, skid in a cloud of dust on the underwatered field, grab the ball and bring it back. *Oh, oh!* I thought, *this looks bad*.

Same drill. Out of the truck they came, through the gate and across the field. Down HB went.

When they got to the part about the leash law, I told them what I was doing. "Well, it sure looked to me like you were playing ball with your dog," said the senior man.

I was in the process of explaining the role of conditioning in training and the role of ballplaying in conditioning when HB joined us. Barking loudly. Tail wagging furiously.

I was certain she had just cost us a $50 ticket. But who can resist a gleeful golden? The dancing eyes. The whole back end undulating. Soon the rangers were crouched there in the middle of the polo field, rubbing the tummy of a large unleashed dog who only moments before had appeared to be playing ball in violation of Section 8-14 of the Phoenix City Code.

In due time the rangers left. Their parting shot was to caution me about allowing my dog to be off leash when we weren't actually training. "Someone else might not understand."

Good job, HB!

That incident warned me to be prepared. I visited the library and made a copy of the appropriate pages of the City Code. After Honeybear had finished her first three obedience titles, I copied the AKC certificates. I still carry that documentation in my training bag although I've never had occasion to show it.

Photo: Bill Kohler & Associates

Thanksgiving, 1991.

I never saw that team of rangers again, but Stan Bucher showed up from time to time. He'd get out of his truck, lean on the fence and watch us train. "You sure got that dog workin' good," he'd yell. If I took time out and walked over to the fence, he'd tell me about his own dogs.

One day he said, "It's too bad we won't have this park a lot longer."

I must have looked puzzled.

"They're going to put the expressway through here," he continued.

"I didn't know that," I said. "How can they take a nice park like this and bulldoze it for an expressway?"

"That's the government," he said.

I asked him when that was going to happen but he didn't know.

■ ■ ■

As you train and train and train, each session blends into the next. Without videotapes, it's hard to appreciate the progress you are making. But every so often you experience the joy of seeing it right there in front of you.

That happened a few months after I tried in vain to call Honeybear off the jack rabbit.

We were doing our late afternoon ballplaying and running. Suddenly HB peeled off to her right and went directly to the fence. From a distance of about 50 yards, I could see she was eating something, with explosive thrusts of her head. Eating anything off the ground is a cardinal sin in a place like Paradise Valley Park.

With all the power I could muster, I yelled, "Honeybear, COME!" She hesitated only a second, then wheeled and came full tilt. Right to front. "Good girl," I said and gave her a treat.

We continued on. When we arrived at the spot where she had been eating so frantically, I saw it … a large ham hock.

"Willard, you've got to get rid of the food. It's fine now but you can't use food in the ring at a trial, and if you don't train her to work for *you*, she'll quit on you in the ring."

It was a variation on Debby's theme: "Willard, you don't feel *you're* enough of a reward."

Training at the park, I'd try to be "good." We'd work without food. HB wanted to please, but her heeling was flat and spiritless. When I got discouraged, when I wanted to go home happy, I'd pull out the treats and Honeybear would "be like Flash."

Sometime later we made two pilgrimages to Chatsworth, California to take lessons from Karen Price. It was a hard 900-mile round trip.

Karen was wonderful. Many helpful training tips came out of those sessions. When she demonstrated her points using Flash, it was goose bump time.

But Karen, too, laid it on me. "Every few days, go out to the park with no food in your pockets," she told me. "Do your whole training routine with no food. Discipline yourself. You'll be surprised at how well you do."

It's hard to recall; I may have done that once after we returned to Phoenix. Or more likely I said to myself, *We didn't drive 900 miles to ignore what Karen told me. If I want Honeybear to be like Flash, I better do what she suggested. I'll train without food …* tomorrow.

■ ■ ■

As you begin to train your first obedience competition dog, the logistics are deceptively simple. You need only yourself, your dog and a leash and collar. And, if you train as I did, a pocket full of treats.

Such simplicity is short-lived. Particularly if you are 6'4", as I am, and have a long stride. It doesn't take long to figure out that heeling merrily about a 13-acre field is quite different than trying to respond to a judge's commands in a 40- by 50-foot

That was the day I knew the "Come!" command had sunk in. We were getting there.

■ ■ ■

"Come!" may have been looking good but heeling wasn't. Reality had intruded the day I first saw Karen Price and Flash. Flash pranced. HB paced. If Karen and Flash were an 11 on a scale of 10, we were a two. It was the obedience equivalent of "How ya gonna keep 'em down on the farm after they've seen Paree?" I had *seen* wonderful and I said, "Honeybear, this ain't it."

Honeybear's heeling was laggy. Her attention was sporadic. She just wasn't up there driving.

Except when I had one of those Grreat Choice training biscuits in my left hand. Then I had a supermotivated dog at my side — head up, eyes bright, full of herself. And if I lifted that treat to my shoulder, that raised her head even higher and I had ... why I almost had Flash.

In retrospect, I realize that for a long time — as long as the first eight years of her career — I had heeling-related motivation problems with Honeybear. The heeling experience imprint emanating from those pre-Billie beginners classes was one of being jerked around by the neck. "Harder, Willard," Maureen had yelled. "She doesn't even feel those love pops you're giving her."

She felt them, all right. She didn't like them. She remembered them. And they haunted us for a long time.

But food was Honeybear's hot button and I found myself going to it more and more to achieve the look and quality of performance that made *my* eyes bright, *my* tail wag.

And I sure heard about it, from everyone who had been around longer than I, who knew more than I, or professed to. In class, during lessons, at matches. Wherever the intelligentsia of obedience training paused to watch us, the refrain was:

ring. I began bemoaning the lack of a practice ring.

At the time, Barbara had just become one of the casualties of the bankruptcy of Carter Hawley Hale. CHH was the parent company of Broadway Southwest, the Phoenix-based department store chain where Barbara was senior vice president for sales promotion and marketing.

One Friday afternoon Barbara and several other vice presidents found themselves unemployed. For Barbara, it was the end of a 30-year career as a marketing superstar in the retailing industry.

She wasn't "between jobs," she was between careers. Unfortunately for her but fortunately for Honeybear and me, she had time to go with us frequently when we trained.

On May 17, 1991 Barbara asked, "What time do you plan to train today?"

"About two o'clock," I replied.

"I have some errands to run first," she said, "so I'll meet you at the park."

The park, at that time of the year, meant the picnic area. The city would padlock the polo field on May 1 and reopen it on September 1. It had something to do with rejuvenating the grass.

That afternoon, as Honeybear and I approached the picnic area, we saw it — our first practice ring.

Barbara had conferred with Debby to determine the correct dimensions. Then she had purchased rebar and rope. At intervals purple yarn was tied on the rope. If one placed the rope on the ground before hammering the rebar into place, the ring was laid out and the exact spots for the rebar were apparent. No measuring was necessary.

Barbara had arrived earlier that afternoon to set up the ring. "Happy birthday!" she said as HB and I got out of the car.

CHAPTER 17

Fourflushers In The Morning, Love In The Afternoon

"You don't realize it now, but you'll look back on your teenage years as the best days of your life."
MY MOTHER
(SHE WAS WRONG.)

It's been four months since I sent the proposal to Karen Walsh (not her real name) at a large Catholic hospital in southeastern Arizona, where she is chief fundraising officer.

We had met in her office at the hospital, then adjourned to a nearby restaurant for a *long* lunch. *Man, this woman talks*, I thought. *On and on and on.*

But sometime during the torrent of words, I had heard this: "I am definitely interested in annual giving, in building a donorbase. My predecessor was totally into special events — the golf tournament, the fashion show, the ball. I plan to turn this thing around."

Uh-huh.

Karen Walsh. Drop-dead blonde. Recently divorced from the football coach at a local high school. Her job was definitely not her top priority.

My assessment? She would be more comfortable behind the perfume counter at Macy's than in the role of chief fundraiser for one of the key healthcare institutions in a large metropolitan market. A Catholic institution at that. Wonder how she conned the Sisters?

But she occupied the position. And as the interminable lunch wound down she declared firmly, "Annual giving is my top priority. Send me a proposal ASAP."

Before launching my own fundraising consulting business several years earlier, I had spent nearly a quarter of a century on the other side of the desk. As a vice president in charge of fundraising and public relations for several large-market medical centers. My forte had been development of solid annual-giving programs. Now my efforts were directed at helping others achieve similar successes … or trying to.

A detailed proposal was FedEx'd to Karen within a week.

Ten days pass. Nothing. I call. Voice mail. I leave a message: "Hi, Karen. I'm calling to see what you thought about the annual giving proposal I sent you."

Two more days, no response. I call again. Voice mail again. I leave another cheerful message.

Two more days. Zilch. I call again. This time she screws up, picks up the phone. There's a momentary pause while she looks for someplace to hide. There isn't any, so she says, "Oh hi, Willard. I haven't had a chance to read it. I've been swamped. But I'll get to it tonight."

Yeah, right.

A month and several unreturned calls later she finally picks up the phone. "Oh, I *do* apologize. I've been inundated with the golf tournament. Call me after the middle of next month. I should have my head above water by then."

The seventeenth of the next month: "Oh, we have our ball coming up in a few weeks and … "

Now it's been four months since I FedEx'd the "top priority" proposal to Ms. Walsh. So I call. A few rings, then I hear it roll over, forwarding to another phone.

"Administrative office," a strange voice says.

"I was trying to reach Karen Walsh."

"I'm sorry, she's no longer with the hospital."

"Oh, my goodness!" I say in my best mock-surprised voice. "What happened?"

"Well, uh, things just didn't work out."

No shit.

■ ■ ■

And so it went across 17 years in the fundraising consulting business. Along the way I met more incompetent, dishonest fourflushers than one would imagine could populate a field known as charitable giving. Blink and they were gone. My motto became, "Sign 'em up right now, they're not going to be there very long."

A candidate for the position of chief fundraising officer (often called vice president for development) in a not-for-profit hospital would say (with validity), "You must realize it will take me at least three years to get the program up and running." On the other hand, industry-wide, the average tenure of persons in that position is between 23 and 24 months. Go figure.

My days were polluted with the likes and the antics of countless Karen Walsh types.

I might spend a morning trying to develop a charitable giving program with a glib fourflusher more focused on finding his next job. Or coming up with a plausible reason to leave work early that day. Or figuring out how to steal from his institution.

■ ■ ■

Through it all, Honeybear kept me sane. In the afternoon, HB and I would head for Paradise Valley Park, her chin on my leg. As we'd turn into the park, she'd sit bolt upright and begin her soft, anxious whimpering. As soon as we'd cross the little bridge and swing north toward the polo field, she'd stand on the seat, ears forward, tail whopping me in the face.

At that point, the day-in, day-out frustration that emanated from coping with the cast of misplaced characters in the fundraising industry would begin to dissolve. Relaxation and deep joy would take their place.

Teaching Honeybear, watching her learn and sharing her joy were what those afternoons were about. Imagine! An experience that fulfilling being repeated day after day, thousands of times.

■ ■ ■

My delight in watching Honeybear get better and better really took off the day I made a discovery I still can't quite explain. I rushed home that evening to tell Barbara. "You know what?" I said. "Today I realized HB has learned how to learn."

"What do you mean by that?" Barbara asked. I had to tell her I couldn't explain it.

When I was majoring in psychology at the University of Cincinnati, we used to talk about the *Eureka! phenomenon.* ("Eureka! I've found it.") The flash of insight that can be so important in the learning process or the inventing process.

Something like that happened to Honeybear. Not about a particular exercise or where heel position was or how to front. It was a flash of insight about the nature of the game, about how to adapt so as to make things go more smoothly.

Something like: *Oh, this is about how to do things I've never done before, things with my body, my mind. And the more I focus the faster I get rewarded and the more fun it is.*

Anyhow, at a definable point a light bulb went on in HB's head about the *process* of learning. Things proceeded more smoothly from that point. I wish I had had the foresight to write down the date and record where we were in our training when it happened.

One fact of significance can be recorded, though. By that time I had become committed to training with food — initially as a lure, then as a reward and reinforcer. And already the natives who were wedded to jerking their dogs around, or worse, were watching us and growing restless. Always the same little group of lowlifes expressing sullen, initially soto voce, disapproval. (Later soto voce would change to big-mouthed.) One wag at ringside called them "a coven" and it was so apt it caught on ... sotto voce of course.

■ ■ ■

Meanwhile, Honeybear and I were settling into a groove. The front end of thousands of afternoons at Paradise Valley Park. Thousands! How many afternoons are thousands of afternoons? Far too many to fathom now. Far too many to get my cerebral arms around and pull together into a ball that I can stand back and comprehend. I only know that strung together, single afternoon after single afternoon after single afternoon, they formed a life-defining adventure.

"What was the addiction?" some might ask. "What was the magic?

And the answer is ... Well, there is no simple answer.

I only know that those afternoons were about a man and dog getting more and more into each other's heads and hearts. Each getting more attuned to every behavioral nuance of the other. Both engaged in an experience that, snowball-like, gathered astounding emotional potency. We became joined at the soul.

Some call it *bonding*, a superficial word that doesn't begin to describe what's happening.

It has to do with softness.

The soft brown eyes that express eagerness to learn and joy in getting it right.

The silky head, the soft fur behind the ears — those places you stroke while you say, "Good girl, good job."

The soft body that occasionally you pick up and reposition to help her get it right.

And it has to do with motivation. Devoid of ulterior motives, hidden agendas, institutional politics.

Those afternoons were also about putting things together, tiny piece by tiny piece. Day after day. And then one day:

"She's heeling nicely now."

Or, "What a nice, fast drop!"

Or later, "Wow, Honeybear, that's 209 correct scent articles in a row."

Once in a while, during one of those halcyon afternoons, I'd flash back to the day I brought her home in a cardboard box and she barked all the way home, and neither of us even dreamed any of this stuff existed.

Or I'd recall that morning at the first obedience match I visited. *Oh, we could never do that.* But shortly, *Wouldn't it be something if I could teach Honeybear to do that?*

Then one afternoon you realize she *is* doing it. All the tiny pieces have come together … solidly enough that you now have a fighting chance against the "big dogs." And you stand there in the field while everything blurs because of the tears in your eyes.

Which is why Paradise Valley Park became our favorite place in all the world and those afternoons became the happiest times of our lives.

■ ■ ■

All was serene, except that from time to time someone would ask me, "Where do you train?" I'd answer, "Mostly at Paradise Valley Park."

They'd think a second, then ask, "Where is that?"

"Up there at 40th Street and Union Hills."

And once in a while someone would do the mental geography, then say, "That's where the expressway interchange is going, isn't it?"

I'd shrug my shoulders and say, "I certainly hope not, but I've heard rumors."

Such conversations would lead to disquieting afternoons at the park. I'd look around and think, *There's no way. They couldn't come in here, bulldoze this and pave it over. Could they?*

CHAPTER 18

Sit, Dammit!

As spring turned to the summer of 1991, Honeybear began to develop a disquieting pattern during the long sit/long down exercises. In the Novice class, handlers walk across the ring, turn and face their dogs. At most, 35 feet of separation. And the times are one minute for the sit, three for the down.

But at the soggy Valle del Sol show in March, Honeybear had sat up during the long down, blowing our try for a second CD leg. I attributed that transgression to the big puddle she was lying in.

Two days later she had broken both the long sit and down at Sahuaro State Kennel Club. Of course, we had stunk up the place on everything else as well. Just a world-class bad day. Or was it?

I thought HB was solid on the sits and downs, so I wasn't prepared for what was about to come down on my head. And as a Novice handler with no experience and less perspective, I was emotionally vulnerable.

As the summer wore on, the problem became more severe, more frustrating. I'd get to the other side of the ring, begin to turn and there would be my little golden, a few feet back, following me with a guilty look on her face.

Honeybear has always had this thing about being physically forced to sit. Tell her to sit and she sits. Try to maneuver her, hands-on, into a sit and she fights it. Further, once there has been a wrestling match over sitting, she never wants to sit in that spot again. All of which made correcting broken sits a nightmare.

Summer turned into fall. We were nowhere. I'd cross the ring. I'd turn. HB would be right behind me. My heart would sink. The more so because it was my first taste of how disheartening, how brutal obedience problems can be. And how they can get into the head of a neophyte.

It ate away at me. I'd wake up at 3 a.m., thinking, *This dog is impossible. I've tried everything. Nothing works. We might as well quit.*

The months of the fall shows, October and November, 1991, were two of the worst months of my life. We weren't just flunking in matches anymore. We had moved our act to the big time.

At many obedience trials, the sponsoring club gives you a small individual score card after your class is finished. The score is broken down by exercise. A perfect score — about as common as a no-hitter in baseball — is 200. In Novice, 60 of those points are awarded for the long sit and long down, done in a group. Flunk either the sit or the down and it's a long drive home.

The scores we would have earned that fall, had HB not broken the sit or the down or both, went like this:
- October 26, Superstition Kennel Club, 189
- October 27, Sahuaro State Kennel Club, 192.5
- October 28, Kachina Kennel Club, 191.5
- November 3, Phoenix Field and Obedience Club, 194
- November 9, Scottsdale Dog Fanciers, 193.5
- November 10, Prescott Arizona Kennel Club, 193

At that point we gave up for the season. "All those good scores!" I kept saying. "Right down the drain."

We pulled out of the final three Arizona shows, two at Tucson, one at Yuma. "You can't let her keep getting away with that stuff in the ring," Debby was telling me. "You've got to show Honeybear who's boss. She's blowing you off."

So here we were, mid-November, still pursuing the elusive third CD leg. It had been eight and one-half mentally excruciating months since we had gotten our second Novice leg at Superstition Kennel Club on March 2. Clearly it was time for a different approach.

Debby and I planned it carefully. Nothing that happened on that fateful evening was precipitous or done in the heat of anger.

Debby was holding evening classes at Washington Park in north central Phoenix, the site of a large, lighted city-owned tennis complex. Many courts, many bright lights at night. We held class in a large, grassy, adequately lighted area on the west side of the tennis courts.

HB and I joined Billie Rosen and eight or 10 other people for the group exercises. We lined up and heeled our dogs into place.

"Take your leashes and your imaginary armbands off and place them behind you," Debby instructed. "This will be the long sit for one minute. Sit your dogs."

HB was already seated in heel position, looking up at me, but I reinforced that with, "Sit!"

"Leave your dogs," Debby said.

I dropped my left palm in front of HB's face and said, "Stay!" Then I folded my arms across my chest and moved away. The handlers were a lateral straight line as we headed for a point about 35 feet in front of us.

Just as we were about to turn and face our dogs, I heard Debby's voice: "Here she comes, Willard."

I turned and there was that guilty face about five feet back. As she caught up, I grabbed her by the jowls, flipped her on her back, dropped to my knees, put my face in hers and began to bellow: "NO! NO! NO! NO! YOU CUT IT OUT! NO! NO! NO! NO!"

You could have heard me in Tucson, 125 miles away.

On and on I bellowed, shaking her occasionally. There was terror in Honeybear's eyes.

Finally Debby's voice cut through. "That's enough, Willard. Stop! That's enough."

We stood up. I took Honeybear by the collar and led her back to her spot in the line. I repositioned her and said, quietly, "Sit." Then I walked back and joined the other handlers, now waiting through the third minute of the one-minute sit. HB didn't budge. She was relieved to be back in the safety and comfort of the line of dogs.

Next she completed the long down without thinking of breaking. I had found the solution. And HB emerged as the most solid sits and downs dog I've ever known.

There was only one complaint. "If you're going to do that again, please tell me ahead of time," Billie said afterwards. "I want to get Kara out of there; you really upset her tonight."

But another classmate had a different view. "Willard, you really fixed a lot of dogs tonight. The rest of those dogs, sat there thinking, *Thank God that's not me.*"

■ CHAPTER 19 ■

Those California Dogs

After a few more classes and a couple of matches during which HB was rock-solid on her sits and downs, Debby and I decided it was time to resume our CD quest.

There would be no more local shows until the end of February 1992. But the Kennel Club of Palm Springs show, to be held the first weekend in January, had a classy ring to it. So we entered.

The show would be held at Indio, California, 245 miles across the desert from Phoenix. Indio is one of a string of small oasis cities — including Palm Springs, La Quinta, Indian Wells, Palm Desert, and Desert Hot Springs — best known for nationally televised golf events.

I had heard of Indio, but we had never been in that area. Honeybear had never even been in a hotel room because we had never shown so far from home that we had to arrive the afternoon before the show and stay overnight.

So where to stay? I looked in the American Automobile Association Tourbook for places that took dogs.

The Best Western Date Tree Hotel sounded good. Three diamonds. And the notes said, "Grounds landscaped with palms, fruit trees and cactus." *There should be someplace for HB to pee*, I thought. I made a reservation. We would arrive on Saturday, January 4, the day before the show.

We stepped up our training, haunted by the specter of "those California dogs." Debby had told us some of America's best trainers lived in California. Others had offered comments like, "You can't win over there, those dogs are just too tough."

But HB was working well, heeling better than she ever had. And no more broken sits or downs. *Forget the competition*, I kept telling myself, *to get a leg all you have to do is qualify*.

On Saturday morning Barbara and I loaded up and left for Indio shortly before noon. I had succumbed several months before and gotten a Chevy Suburban, the better to tote our growing volume of dog training stuff and show-related accouterments.

We reached the hotel at 4:30, but dark clouds were forming and it was already starting to get dark.

I began to worry. It was imperative that I work HB that evening. What if she forgot the exercises before we went into the ring tomorrow? We checked in and unloaded frantically, but it took us longer than I had hoped.

By the time we set out for the show grounds, it was nearly dusk. The show site was Empire Equestrian Park, only ten minutes from our hotel. But I had never been in the area and I got disoriented. Then I panicked. The worst-case scenario was happening. It would be too dark to work Honeybear. She'd flunk tomorrow.

Barbara recalls the next 20 minutes as sheer terror. I drove like a maniac, careening around corners, slamming the Suburban into reverse, wheeling around and tearing off in a new direction. Lost, confused, hysterical.

By the time I found the park, it was beginning to drizzle.

Stressed to the breaking point, I jumped out and began to run HB through the exercises. Each time she made a mistake, I reacted angrily, yelling at her and jerking the leash.

"I'll never go through a ride like that again," Barbara said when we got back to the hotel. "Next time I'm getting out."

I slumped in a chair as a new wave of anxiety rolled in. Had I ruined HB for tomorrow with my angry behavior?

On Sunday morning, we arrived at Empire Equestrian Park before 6 a.m.

The show grounds were 225 acres of white-fenced, verdant polo fields dotted with white gazebos and flower beds. Strategically placed wrought iron benches appeared to have been painted yesterday. White stables and equipment buildings were scattered about the green landscape. And all of it against the backdrop of the Santa Rosa Mountains.

This would be a great place to finish our Companion Dog title. And it was about time. It had been 10 months and four days since we had gotten our second CD leg. A painful eternity.

But the heavy black clouds that had been gathering the evening before still threatened. Rain was imminent. And the chill of the desert morning brought a penetrating dampness.

The obedience rings were well-separated from the breed rings, in a cozy little enclave. It was our first show set up by the Jack Bradshaw organization. I had never before seen rings constructed of white posts and white chain, and I was impressed.

The rings were located in a large grassy area that was immaculately groomed. The freshly painted wrought iron benches were scattered around the perimeter, as were tall, decorative wrought iron lamps with clusters of white globes high above the rings. At each end of the grass rectangle was a large white gazebo.

At first we set up on the perimeter sidewalk, a short distance from our ring. Then a light rain began and we moved inside one of the gazebos — our own luxury box for the morning.

Thirty-three teams were entered in Novice A that morning. The class was scheduled to begin at 8 a.m. under Judge Donna Ward. We were scheduled to be fifth in the ring.

Shortly before it was time for us to go into the ring, I took Honeybear for a brief walk, an extra precaution against an accident in the ring. I was unaware that two teams slated to show before us were absent and one had been moved back in the judging order due to a breed ring conflict. We were now scheduled to be second. As I returned from our walk, Barbara came running to meet me. "They called your number," she said. "You weren't there so they took the next dog."

Oh no! I thought, *all that preparation, and we drove all this distance and I've screwed up. We've missed our turn in the ring.* That was the day I learned always to ask whether all the handlers preceding us in the ring had checked in.

But not to worry. The judge said she'd work us in.

Pretty soon the steward called our number. The rain was still coming down steadily but lightly as we entered the ring and lined up for the first exercise, the heel on leash and figure eight. Barbara was at ringside, videotaping our run.

I had dressed to match HB. I wore tan Dockers and tan shoes so she would blend into my legs and feet, making errors of position less apparent to the judge.

On the videotape from that morning, HB's heeling is impressive. There is one crooked sit and a lag during the heel on leash. Her figure eight is beautiful, perfect. One point off on the exercise.

She moved two paws on the stand for exam. Another point off.

A crooked sit and a big-time bump during the heel off leash cost us another 1.5 points.

Finally, a crooked front on the recall resulted in the loss of another half point. But Honeybear's individual exercises that morning in Mrs. Ward's ring were among the best she had ever done.

Now the moment of truth was upon us — the group exercises, the long sit and down. As we lined up, a chocolate lab was on our right, a Dalmatian on our left.

On the judge's order, we left our dogs. It took the Dalmatian just 30 seconds to get up and amble across the ring. Honeybear watched with interest, perhaps with disdain for any dog who would break a stay.

Next the long down for three minutes — each seeming like an hour. Honeybear seemed relaxed. With 15 seconds left, a bird swooped low over the ring and caught HB's interest, taking her mind off any anxiety she might be feeling. I knew we were home free.

"Back to your dogs."

"Exercise finished."

We had done it! Armband in hand, I pumped my fist into the air as Barbara yelled, "All right, HB!"

The rain had been replaced by a biting wind when the Novice A qualifiers returned to the ring for the awards ceremony.

First, the formality of thanking the ring stewards. Then the judge told the little group of spectators at ringside, "In the Novice ring, a perfect score is 200 points. In order to qualify, a team must finish with at least 170 points and must get 50 percent of the points on each exercise. The teams you see in the ring have done that." (Applause)

She continued, "In first place this morning with a score of 197 (a loud "oooh" from the crowd), dog and handler 24." Predictably, first place went to a California dog — a flat-coated retriever from Chino.

The judge was speaking again. "In second place with a score of 196, dog and handler number nine." It was Honeybear and me. Again, Barbara yelled, "All right, HB!"

Of the 33 dogs entered in Novice A that morning, 27 had been from California. And we had not only finished second, we had missed first place by just one point.

There on a bleak morning in Indio, we had finally gotten our act together. Honeybear's career seemed poised to take off.

Many times during the trip home I stroked her soft head and said, "Good job, good girl."

And each time I could swear I heard HB mutter, "California dogs ... sheeit!"

Third CD leg: Skip, Honeybear, Judge Donna Ward

CHAPTER 20

Tiptoes On The Toilet Seat

Driving out of Indio that January afternoon, I was euphoric — now we could begin training for Open. As we drove back to Phoenix, I repeated over and over, "Now I get to teach her new things: the broad jump, the high jump, the drop on recall. It's time to teach my retriever to retrieve."

And time to acquire more stuff, mostly training equipment. If you attend classes or take private lessons, the equipment is available during the session. But if you are serious about doing well in the sport, you want to practice on your own. So we added high jump, bar jump and broad jump equipment to the stuff we lugged to the park each day. Equipment creep was well underway.

■ ■ ■

We resumed training each afternoon at Paradise Valley Park. I knew that when we moved into the Open ring the group exercises were going to get tougher. The long sit, now extended to three minutes, and the long down, now for five, would both be done with handlers out of sight.

But Honeybear was proving to be so solid on the sits and downs that I had little anxiety about the transition to out-of-sight sits and downs. The training dilemma was how to position myself out of sight — really out of sight — and still respond if HB broke the sit or the down. You either lose second-to-second track of what's going on or you compromise the dog's feeling that you are truly gone as you try to sneak a look.

I devised a solution using the facilities (pun definitely intended) close at hand, the park's "comfort station." It's a tan block building with baffled entrances on opposite sides and roof-level windows to permit ventilation.

I discovered I could put HB on a sit or a down in the shade, go into the women's john, stand on the tips of my toes on the toilet seat and observe her behavior through the heavily screened window. I could see her but she couldn't see me.

If she started to break the sit or the down, my booming, "No!" which resounded off the block walls of the interior, surely sounded like the voice of God to the poor dog.

One day I told a friend, Mark Shults, about my clever method of observing my dog. Mark is an accomplished cartoonist. A few days later I received Mark's rendition of the scene.

In the cartoon, I am standing on tiptoes on the toilet seat, looking out the high window. In my hand is one end of a long-line (which I no longer used) that goes through the window, extends down to the ground and disappears around the side of the building and back in the door. It's attached to the collar of a dog who is seated on the floor behind me, in front of the toilet, tail going furiously, looking up at my backside. Obviously wondering what her silly teammate is up to.

■ ■ ■

About that time, I began to hear more and more about The Gaines — the prestigious national tournaments where the best dogs in America duked it out across a two-day period.

Front and Finish ran articles about the events. Three regional tournaments culminated each November in a showdown called the Gaines Classic.

Tiptoes on the Toilet Seat: Mark Shults, 1992.

Those who told me about The Gaines spoke in near-reverential tones. I was advised that competing in The Gaines would be a must if Honeybear and I ever got good enough to qualify.

I filed it away in my mind. Maybe someday …

■ ■ ■

In the meantime, Honeybear was having the time of her life. Now she got to jump. She got to bound out and retrieve the dumbbell, and she got treats when she brought it back to front and presented it to me.

Well, she sort of came to front. HB has always had difficulty understanding that her back end is connected to her front end. She'd come in and plop down, front end at dead center, but the rear end would be angled just a little to my left — about half a point's worth.

Her rear end gave us other problems as well. She loved what we were doing. Too much so to wait on certain exercises. I'd throw the dumbbell. Before the judge said, "Send your dog," and before I could say, "Take it!" her butt would begin to elevate: an inch, two inches, three, sometimes halfway into a stand where it would hang.

Well into our Open career we showed under Judge Karen TenEyck. At that point HB was on a roll, performing beautifully, averaging 194 in the Open ring.

We came to the drop on recall. In that exercise you sit your dog in heel position, leave, walk to the opposite end of the ring, turn and face the dog. Upon a signal from the judge, you call the dog. At a second signal, using either a verbal command or a hand signal, you tell the dog to drop to the ground — ideally like she's been shot. Then you call your dog to front.

In Judge TenEyck's class, I walked to the opposite end of the ring, turned and there was Honeybear's rear end, up at least a foot. That was not an uncommon transgression during HB's butt-picking-up phase. From time to time I'd turn and there she'd be, standing up, still in place, looking guilty. Each caper like that cost us three points at a time when we were otherwise quite competitive.

On that morning in Las Vegas, as Mrs. TenEyck walked toward us at the conclusion of the exercise, she said, "What you need in order to fix that is a hammer and a tenpenny nail."

There were problems on the front end, too. Honeybear loved to chase the dumbbell, then she'd carry her head high as she brought it back. But she also liked to sit in front of me, open her mouth far enough to let the dumbbell roll back, then mouth it gleefully. That, too, cost us points.

Our training sessions across the first 10 months of 1992 featured the joy of learning new things and the exasperation of trying a variety of ways to straighten fronts, eliminate mouthing and keep HB's butt on the ground.

And both of us loved every minute of it.

■ ■ ■

Our Novice career was behind us and we weren't ready for Open. So HB and I seized as many opportunities as possible to enter a nonregular transitional class called Graduate Novice. In addition to the heeling exercises and stand for examination, the class required a drop on recall and the long sit and down with handlers out of sight. That was Honeybear's first opportunity to perform the out-of-sight group exercises under show conditions.

Without fail, I would return to the ring to find HB exactly where I had left her, solid as a rock.

■ ■ ■

Honeybear had been diagnosed with mild dysplasia of her left hip in February of 1991. At the time her veterinarian Dr. Chuck Toben X-rayed her, he had counseled, "Willard, I wouldn't ever jump her if I were you." I nodded but decided not to give up that easily.

I talked with several people I respected in the sport of dog obedience. Out of those conversations came these morsels for thought:

1. Dogs respond differently to dysplastic hips. Some who are severely dysplastic never show symptoms. Others who are even mildly dysplastic seem to have considerable pain.
2. Often arthritic conditions respond better with exercise than they do with sedentary behavior.
3. The dog or human who exercises is healthier — in terms of muscle tone and cardiovascular conditioning — than is a couch potato.

Honeybear was only 14 months old at the time of her hip X-ray and still jumping only 10 inches. I had been advised not to do any high jumping until she was 18 months old and her growth plates were closed.

Growth plates are zones of cartilage near the ends of the long bones where bone growth takes place in immature animals. As the bone grows, the cartilage calcifies and turns into bone. Prior to the time it calcifies, it is vulnerable to crushing injuries. Hence caution should be exercised in jumping young dogs.

HB was loving every minute of her 10-inch jumping, so I decided not to make a couch potato out of her. Rather, we'd keep going and I'd let her tell me if it hurt.

I did, however, train her gingerly. With knowledge of her dysplasia always in the forefront of my mind, when we began serious jumping training I did most of her jumping at 24 inches, raising the jumps to her AKC-mandated 28 inches* in two-inch increments across the final two weeks before a show.

---

*Calculated as follows: height at the withers, 22.75 inches, plus one quarter of that number, 5.7 inches, rounded to the nearest even number, 28 inches.

■ ■ ■

One offshoot of Honeybear's dysplasia diagnosis was psychologically devastating to me.

On May 16, the day before my birthday, I chaired a jumping seminar sponsored by the Phoenix Field and Obedience Club. The seminar was presented by Suzanne Clothier of Frenchtown, New Jersey. I had mentioned HB's hip dysplasia to Suzanne at dinner the evening before.

The seminar involved calling dogs over a series of five jumps in a chute. Jump heights and configurations varied, as did the distance between jumps.

At the seminar, Honeybear did her run through the chute with no problem. Suzanne then called us back in front of the audience for a demonstration of the rear end movement of a dog with abnormal hip structure. She had us walk, trot, and so on.

At the end of the seminar, she presented several awards. I have no idea what they were or what they were for — except for the final award. A large bag of dog kibble was presented to Honeybear, "the dog with the most heart."

By then I was feeling pretty bad.

That evening we had a party at our house. A come-meet-Suzanne-Clothier-up-close-and-personal affair for the people who had helped with the seminar. As parties often do, this one gravitated to the kitchen. Late evening found several of us on the kitchen floor around Suzanne and Honeybear. Suzanne examined HB like the veterinarian she was not, manipulating her hind legs and hip joints ... and decrying the verdict: Honeybear would not be able to compete in obedience competition beyond the Novice level. Her left hip would not permit it.

Time would prove that the whole episode was dramatically overplayed. In fact, HB would be nearly 10 years old before she gave the slightest indication of labored jumping.

All of which became apparent much too late to keep me from celebrating my 59th birthday in a funk.

■ ■ ■

The summer of 1992 was a blur of golden afternoons: Honeybear heeling, playing ball, jumping, playing ball, retrieving, playing ball, learning to come like a bullet, then drop on a signal, and playing ball.

By fall, the learning curve was headed through the roof. Debby agreed that HB was doing well. Not that Debby ever saw an exercise that was done as well as it should be.

"She's pacing, Willard, that's sloppy heeling."

"That mouthing's going to kill you, Willard."

"When she makes a mistake, don't just let her do the exercise over, FIX IT!"

But when all the teeth-grinding and hair-tearing and admonitions and epithets were over, we agreed it was time to bring HB out in Open. Time to pursue our Companion Dog Excellent title.

Honeybear was closing in on her third birthday.

■ CHAPTER 21 ■

Ptui!

If getting our Companion Dog title was an exasperating, gut-wrenching, nearly defeating experience, the path to our Companion Dog Excellent (CDX) title was a walk in the park. Honeybear and I — but most importantly HB — had learned to get out there and just do it. With tail-wagging, bright-eyed exuberance.

We finished our CDX in three straight shows. At the Palo Verde Golden Retriever Club's specialty show in Tucson, we did a 197.5 in Open A, our best score to date. The same weekend, at the Tucson Kennel Club show, we did a 194.5. Each leg was good for first place and a blue ribbon.

Two weeks later, at the Yuma Kennel Club — while pairs of Marine Harrier jets screamed over our heads at tree-top height — we scored a less-than-brilliant 190, finishing third. But it was enough for Honeybear to become a Companion Dog Excellent.

We finished under judge Ray Gates, a kindly older man from Santa Barbara who owned and loved golden retrievers. Across a decade of reencounters, he would become one of our favorite judges. Which is not to say we always scored well under him.

In the beginning I had a lot of anxiety about showing under Judge Gates. He liked to jolly you up and exchange pleasantries before he began to call the heeling pattern. Later I found out he did that largely with green-looking Novice handlers in an effort to put them at ease. And Lord knows if anyone ever walked into the ring looking like they needed to be put at ease, it was Willard Bailey early in his obedience career.

But Ray's relaxation strategy had an opposite effect on me. I would get Honeybear prepped to a T (I thought) right before we were ready to go into the ring. I wanted a dog who was right on the edge — close to being out of control, every hair bristling, rarin' to go. I was afraid she'd sit at my side and wilt while the pleasantries were exchanged.

In fact, after the second time we showed under him — indoors at the Phoenix Convention Center, under the banner of the Sahuaro State Kennel Club — I developed a little take-off, my exchange with Ray as we set up to begin the Open individual exercises:

Gates: "Good morning, young man."

Bailey: "Good morning."

Gates: "How are you this morning?"

Bailey (starting to fidget): "Fine, thank you."

Gates: "Are we having fun yet?"

Bailey (tersely): "Yes."

Gates: "Then why aren't you smiling?"

Bailey: "Because I'm getting ready to deck you, Ray, if you don't call the heeling pattern."

When we got our first CD leg, I began having a photo taken each time we got another leg. Those pictures, along with ribbons and in some cases score cards, have been matted and framed into large displays that dominate my office walls.

The photo taken the day we finished our CDX shows Honeybear, less than a month shy of her third birthday, sitting straight and eager between us. Her ears are at attention. Ray and I are kneeling. He holds our yellow third-place ribbon, a

Photo: Joan Ludwig

Third CDX leg: Judge Ray Gates, Honeybear, Skip.

green qualifying ribbon and a large green-and-white rosette and ribbon given by the Yuma Kennel Club to teams finishing a title at their show. I look proud as a peacock.

The next morning we unceremoniously flunked. Honeybear came exuberantly on the drop on recall exercise. At the judge's signal, I said "DOWN!" She dipped her left shoulder, acknowledging my command, then got a guilty look on her face and kept right on coming.

■ ■ ■

As we left the ring at the Tucson Kennel Club show, an older couple approached.

"We love the way you talk to your dog," the man said. "She seems to understand what you are saying."

"You bet she does," I replied. "It's an important part of what we do in the ring."

They had observed how I cued HB for the next exercise. "We're gonna do heelwork, Honeybear." Or, "This is the figure eight, HB." Or, "Broad jump, Honeybear, broad jump."

The constant flow of communication between exercises was part of the solid foundation Debby had given us. "Let her know what's coming next," she had emphasized.

I had accepted that advice with ease. As a young man, I had been impressed with the extensive vocabulary my mother's dogs had learned because she talked to them so much when they were together at home.

■ ■ ■

Having finished our CDX, I began to think seriously about The Gaines — the most prestigious dog obedience competition in America. I had torn the full page of qualifying and entry information out of *Front & Finish*. I knew that in order to enter the Open division at a regional I must submit three scores averaging 193 or better. And a quick calculation of the scores for the three legs that had taken us to our CDX — 197.5, 194.5 and 190 — revealed an average of 194, right on the nose. Voila! So I entered us in the Gaines Cycle 1993 Central Regional Dog Obedience Championship, to be held May 1 and 2 in San Antonio.

I was excited ... and terrified. To think that the little golden I had been given for Christmas three years earlier, that I had brought home barking in a cardboard box, would soon be at my side in the most prestigious dog obedience competition in America.

"I need for you to lean on us now," I told Debby. "I've got to get this dog ready for The Gaines." Lean on us she did. I would complain or start to argue. By that time we weren't comfortable unless we were arguing. Debby would stop me with a simple question: "Do you want Honeybear ready for The Gaines or don't you?"

And I would reply, "Of course I do, but ... ."

We spent the next five months polishing. I had become superorganized about our training, developing a lesson plan for each session on a 4x6 card. Focusing on our problems as I saw them each day (and with HB they've always been like shifting sands), I would write out what we were going to do and in what order. And now each card was headed *Honeybear's Gaines Lesson*, and the date.

We showed several times during that period, always in Open B. Our scores were consistently in the range of 194.5 to 196. In fact, a curious phenomenon began to develop. Time after time we would score exactly 196. On April 10, 1993, at Sahuaro State Kennel Club, we won a run-off for high in trial with — what else? — a 196+.

■ ■ ■

Those were heady times. We were going to The Gaines. Afternoons at the park were sublime.

And then a few weeks before we were to leave for San Antonio, Honeybear suddenly began retrieving the dumbbell, heading back with it, then dropping it 10 feet in front of me.

Panic. Here we were, bearing down on the biggest competition of our lives, and my dog was spitting out the dumbbell. Ptui! So I called Helen Phillips, an outstanding obedience competition trainer in Arvada, Colorado. Helen and I had become friends a year earlier when I was thinking about getting a second dog. I was weighing two attractive options: a golden or a border collie? A border collie or a golden?

A friend had said, "You should talk to Helen Phillips. She has both a golden and a border collie." She gave me Helen's phone number.

Thus began one of the most cherished and enduring friendships I've developed in the world of dog obedience. From Helen's lips and from her writings flows a seemingly inexhaustible stream of common sense and sound advice about dogs and training dogs.

Helen listened to my sad tale. Then she said, "When a dog does what you've described, it's because something awful has happened when she's come to her handler." Then she asked, "What are you doing when Honeybear gets back to you with the dumbbell?"

"Well," I began, "HB is a mouther. She comes in, sits in front of me, tilts her head back and rolls the dumbbell all the way back in her mouth. Then she begins to roll it around back there. She looks like a cow chewing its cud."

"Then what do you do?" Helen asked.

"In the past I've tried several things that didn't work," I replied. "Recently someone suggested I smack both ends of the dumbbell when she starts to mouth."

"And what kind of dumbbell are you using?"

"Hard plastic," I said. I had started using that kind because it didn't show teeth gouges, which tip off a judge that here's a mouthing dog.

"I would imagine the plastic is vibrating in her mouth and hurting her," Helen said. "Besides, smacking the ends of the dumbbell shouldn't be used as a correction for mouthing; it should be used as a correction for refusing to give up the dumbbell when you tell her to release it."

All of which made sense. Now how could I recover before the Gaines?

First of all, she suggested I work on the mouthing using a different tack. "Put the dumbbell in her mouth," she advised, "then go about your business — stroll around. While you stroll around, she must hold it. If she drops it, correct her. Ear-pinch her to pick it up again and keep it in her mouth. If she opens her mouth or rolls it around, gently put your thumb under her chin and your fingers over her nose. Don't squeeze. But close her mouth and say, 'Hold it.'"

At the same time, she told me, "You have to build up her positive feelings again about the retrieve. Have her come in carrying the dumbbell. As she gets to you, make an exchange, a treat for the dumbbell. You want her to start enjoying bringing it to you again."

I did all of that. Within a few days she was carrying the dumbbell all the way back — proudly, head held high, anticipating a treat, not painful vibrations.

Another crisis behind us.

By late April I was saying, "We're ready, but I'm scared." I could see us arriving in San Antonio, and there would be all those great dogs ... and Little Honeybear and Little Skip. And dear God, please, no ptui!

CHAPTER 22

The Gaines!

There was something mystical, almost unattainable about The Gaines. Obedience people would grab you by the arm when they told you about it.

Four national tournaments were staged each year: Eastern, Central and Western Regionals followed by The Classic, the culmination of the year's activities.

Each regional was a Saturday/Sunday event composed of the Red, White and Blue Shows. Entrants were required to compete in each of the three shows in the division for which they had qualified.

The divisions were Novice, Open and Super Dog. The latter was a grueling experience, requiring competition in both Open and Utility in each of the three shows — six rings in two days.

In order to qualify for a regional — in Open, for example — the dog must have earned a CDX but not have a third leg on the Utility Dog (UD) title prior to the date of the regional. And, of course, there were the three qualifying scores.

The top 10 teams in each division at a regional received cash awards and automatically became eligible to compete in The Classic in November.

■ ■ ■

My decision to enter HB in the regional at San Antonio was the beginning of what I would later refer to as Gaines Fever — a disease that explains why she was still in search of an Obedience Trial Championship at nearly 10 years of age.

A check of her career record shows her first qualifying score in Open came on our first try on November 13, 1992. Her first qualifying score in Utility, again on our first try, came on May 5, 1996. That's eight days shy of three and one-half years devoted to Open competition. During that period, Honeybear averaged 194.

I was so obsessed with qualifying for and going to The Gaines that I all but ignored Utility until HB was more than six years old. At that age most obedience competition dogs are retired.

■ ■ ■

We made a family affair out of our first Gaines. Gladys and Bob, Barbara's parents, flew in from Cincinnati. We rented a Pace Arrow, a large recreational vehicle. I had never even been inside an RV until we set sail for San Antonio, a round trip of nearly 2,000 miles.

Four adults — two of them *senior* senior citizens — and two dogs made things a bit cramped and testy at times. Worse, on that trip I learned about gray water and black water and how many valves and switches you have to tinker with on an RV.

We didn't arrive at the Alamo Kampgrounds of America until Thursday evening, so we postponed our first visit to the show site until the next morning.

On Friday morning we rented a car and drove to the Joe Freeman Coliseum. The large tan building loomed up out of the suburban San Antonio countryside. Its huge silver dome glistened in the morning sunshine. The facility must have been the talk of Texas when it was built in 1949.

We entered the coliseum on the ground floor and walked through a portal. I caught my breath. Far below us, six rings were laid out on the expansive coliseum floor. The famous blue mats were surrounded by gleaming white ring gates punctuated with red uprights. The red-white-and-blue theme was carried out in all aspects of the decor — banners, table cloths, signs.

For a moment I just stood there, drinking it all in, fighting back tears. At last, The Gaines!

While Barbara and her folks stayed on the plaza level, Honeybear and I walked down the steep steps to the floor of the coliseum, then around the deserted rings. "This is it, big girl," I told her. "This is what all those afternoons at the park have been about. Tomorrow and Sunday we'll find out how we can do against the Big Dogs."

And then it *was* tomorrow.

At five minutes to nine on Saturday morning, a color guard marched into the coliseum and presented the flag. "Ladies and gentlemen," the PA announcer said, "our national anthem."

We all stood and faced the flag. Honeybear was at my side in heel position. "Watch me," I whispered, and her eyes locked onto mine. At any dog show, the national anthem is a great time to practice patriotism and dog attention simultaneously.

Finally the Star-Spangled Banner was over. Then came the four most electrifying words in dog sports. The PA announcer said, "Let The Gaines begin!"

Suddenly the six rings sprang to life.

The Red Show was beginning in Rings One through Four.

In Ring One, 70 Novice teams would show under Judge John Blenkey.

In Ring Two, 43 Open teams — including us — would compete under the experienced eye of Nancy Pollock.

Joe Heidinger, holding forth in Ring Three, would judge the 37 aspirants in the Super Open class.

And Dee Dee Rose would have the same group in Ring Four for Super Utility.

The White Show was underway in Rings Five and Six.

The legendary Bernie Brown, at the time holder of the most OTCH points on one dog — 5,619 with OTCH Tanbark's Bristol Creme UDX, a golden retriever — was judging Novice in Ring Five.

And Judge Tom Masterson was in charge of the second Super Utility run in Ring Six.

Novice dogs would compete twice on Saturday, once on Sunday. Super Dog teams were required to compete in three rings both days — a test that was sure to bring the cream to the top … and cream the rest.

Those of us in Open would show once on Saturday, twice on Sunday.

■ ■ ■

Honeybear and I, team 334, would be 23rd in Nancy Pollock's ring. So I sat in the grandstand, watching the competition with Barbara, Gladys and Bob. And tried unsuccessfully to relax.

Freeman Coliseum was built in the typical arena configuration. A wide indoor concourse circled the perimeter. It was punctuated by bathrooms, concession stands and portals leading to the seats and to stairs that in turn led to the coliseum floor.

Dogs were crated in that hallway — indoors but outside the area where the action was. Out of sight of those seated inside the arena. A setup that made me very nervous. I kept jumping up from my seat to run out and make sure Honeybear was all right. Indeed, to make sure she was still there. Finally I gave up, brought her inside and let her lie at my feet.

Late in the morning our ring time drew near. I took HB outside for a walk, then warmed her up in the outer hallway.

As the dog right before us entered the ring, Barbara and her folks wished us good luck and we descended the steps to the coliseum floor.

"Good luck!" several people called out as we approached our ring.

"Be careful what you wish for," someone once said, "you might get it." So here we were, at our first Gaines, about to enter our first ring. And I was shaking in my boots. *Remember to breathe*, I kept telling myself. *Remember to breathe.*

Now we stood waiting, just outside Ring Two. I was wearing a large bib that said Cycle 334. Honeybear was at my side, looking up into my eyes. I was both scared and proud.

Then the steward beckoned us and I said, "Let's go show, Honeybear." Again I thought, *Remember to breathe!*

Next thing I knew, Nancy Pollock was saying, "Are you ready?"

"Ready!" I answered and Honeybear, whose eyes were already locked onto mine, ratcheted her head up another notch or two. At that point I'm certain I began holding my breath.

"Forward!" the judge said. Then came the sound I hold most dear from our Gaines experiences: pit-pat, pit-pat, pit-pat — HB's toenails on the blue mats that had been laid over the concrete. A most reassuring sound; she was right there all the way through the heeling pattern and the figure eight. By the time the judge said, "Exercise finished," I hadn't drawn more than two breaths.

The rest of our run seemed to go well, too. I had been afraid both of us would cave under the pressure. It hadn't happened.

As soon as the broad jump, the final exercise, was over, I said, "Good girl, Honeybear. Good girl!" Perhaps too enthusiastically.

HB looked at me, began to wag her whole back end, and before I could move to stop her she raced to Judge Pollock. Nancy is ... well, vertically challenged. So it was no problem for HB to put her front paws on the judge's shoulders and give her a big wet smacker right in the face.

I panicked. "Oh, I'm sorry," I said, and I hustled HB out of the ring. Clearly she had been out of control. And that's scorable — big-time scorable, particularly at a Gaines tournament where all the dogs are so good it becomes difficult to separate them for placement purposes. I figured that little caper had destroyed an otherwise excellent run.

At Gaines tournaments — unlike AKC obedience trials — scores were posted on a ringside pole immediately after you left the ring. Everyone present knew right away how that dog and handler had done. The scores were presented as the number of points deducted from a perfect score of 200.

Crestfallen, I led HB from the ring and turned to wait 30 seconds or so for the steward to post our score.

And there it was: minus three, the AKC equivalent of a 197, only half a point shy of the best score of our career to date. I was elated. Judge Pollock hadn't docked us for HB's little burst of jubilation. Years later, I asked her about it. She chuckled and said, "The first kiss is free."

HB and I rounded out that first magical Gaines morning with the group sits and downs. Honeybear was solid as a rock.

Our minus three in our only ring on Saturday put us in seventh place in the Open division. "Wow, Honeybear," I said, "we're seventh out of 43 dogs at our first Gaines. Good girl!"

Saturday had been our "easy" day. On Sunday morning we were required to do Open twice, in the White and Blue Shows.

We began our competition as the eighth team in Dee Dee Rose's ring.

We weren't quite as sharp in Judge Rose's ring as we had been in Judge Pollock's the day before. Later, when I got the little blue card that broke down our score, I learned that as we prepared for the final exercise, the broad jump, we were working on a minus 4.5.

We set up behind the broad jump, about eight feet back, HB at my side.

"Are you ready?" the judge asked. I nodded.

"Leave your dog," she said.

I walked to the side of the jump and placed my toes two feet from the jump. Honeybear sat ramrod straight, waiting for my command.

"Call your dog," Mrs. Rose said.

I looked at HB. "Jump!" I called.

Honeybear ran forward, leapt and cleared the 56 inches easily. But as she jumped she curved her trajectory to the right and landed with her right front foot less than a paw's width outside an imaginary line that extends straight forward from the right side of the jump.

Glancing at the judge, I saw a pained look cross her face. Honeybear's right paw had landed about an inch "out of bounds." In an ordinary AKC trial she might have gotten away with it. But this was The Gaines, and the judging, of necessity, was precise. With many of the top dogs in America competing, loose judging could result in a bunch of perfect scores.

Honeybear had missed ever so slightly, but she *had* missed. I saw it. Judge Rose saw it. And I saw that she saw it.

After she said, "Exercise finished," she walked over and said, "Oh, I'm so sorry, she missed by that much." And she held her thumb and index finger about an inch apart.

"I know," I said, "I was closer than you were. I saw it too."

We left the ring and waited for our score to be posted. We had lost 24.5 points, 20 of those (all the points available) on the broad jump. We finished the morning in Judge Joe Heidinger's ring, and we were flat. We lost six points, a very nice score at a Gaines. But nevertheless down among the also-rans for whom The Gaines would be "a wonderful experience."

■ ■ ■

Lunch was funereal. Until Judge Rose wandered by and spied us. She came over to tell me how much it had hurt her when that paw landed out of bounds. And how nicely Honeybear had been working up to that point.

She went on to tell me about her golden retrievers. Quite some dogs, it turns out. I later learned three of them are Obedience Trial Champions.

So much for our first Gaines. We wound up 20th out of 43 dogs — in the top half in spite of our little disaster. And I was hopelessly hooked.

■ CHAPTER 23 ■

The Coven

"Double, double toil and trouble;
Fire burn, and cauldron bubble."
MACBETH, WILLIAM SHAKESPEARE

Dee Dee Rose, Nancy Pollock, Debby Boehm, Billie Rosen —
those and many like them are the people who have
defined the best years of my life.

And then there is the other crowd, the few but odoriferous
bad apples in the obedience competition barrel.

Unfortunately, the world of dog sports attracts more than its
share of maladjusted people. Those who are lacking in self-
esteem, devoid of social skills, impotent in their dealings with
the world around them. Thwarted in their endeavors. Society's
misfits.

Some have turned to dog obedience as they grasp desperately for self-actualization. The dogs become crucial last-ditch
extensions of their frustrated owners. And by God those extensions had better show the world. Often, if they don't, if those
little esteem surrogates screw up, God help them when no one
is watching. Or never mind who *is* watching. God help them
anyhow. "Et tu, Fluffy!"

And God help anyone who, by attaining proficiency through methods other than that little clique's rough treatment of dogs, is perceived as showing them up.

■ ■ ■

Here in the Valley of the Sun, we have a few too many of those types. And they seem to gravitate to each other, to cluster. Likes attract. At shows or matches, you'll see six or eight of them piled into and around one tent (with dogs), cackling in unison at any misfortune experienced by a competitor they perceive as threatening.

Once, someone who had had her fill of the antics of our local band of misfits observed, "They're like a coven of witches, aren't they?" It stuck. Henceforth, they've been known as The Coven.

Across the years I've watched The Coven target handler/dog teams whose success has assailed the group's already fragile egos.

Erik Hoyer is a gentleman and a gentle man. Retired now, he was a captain in the Phoenix Fire Department. As a member of a response team sent to Oklahoma City by the Phoenix Fire Department, he spent 16 hours in the rubble inside the Murrah Federal Building, searching for survivors or bodies.

Erik is also an accomplished trainer of obedience competition dogs and tracking dogs. He is an obedience judge and a tracking judge. His late bouvier des Flandres, Max, was the most-titled bouvier in the history of the breed. And the only bouvier ever to attain the title of Obedience Trial Champion (OTCH) — until Erik also completed an OTCH on Max's daughter, Bronte, in 2001. Now there are two.

Through it all, Erik has suffered the slings and arrows of The Coven. He has his own Erik-like way of dealing with their abuse. "I kill them with kindness," he says.

Then there is the journeyman trainer/handler, septuagenarian Orrin Stine and his Belgian sheepdog Nero. The Coven nearly drove Orrin out of the sport with aggressive attacks aimed at "Orrin and his vicious dog." The fact is Nero has never attacked a dog or a person. But perception is everything, and Nero is a big black dog with big white teeth. The downfall of this man and his dog at the hands of The Coven has been galvanized by Nero's penchant for sniffing other dogs — particularly little ones — and Orrin's unwillingness and/or inability to control his dog.

The Coven watched Honeybear and me wobble into the sport, clueless, then take food training farther than anyone in Arizona had ever dared. There was a strong correlation between our success and the overt hostility of The Coven. We'd do well, they'd scowl … or worse.

One day when HB and I had been particularly successful in the ring, I was talking to Marilyn Abbett, a snowbird from Connecticut who winters in Scottsdale. Marilyn has been quite successful in her own right. She has recently completed a Utility Dog Excellent title on her first obedience competition dog, a joyous, wired-out-of-her-gourd Italian greyhound, aptly named "Ziti Zoom Zoom." After HB and I had accepted our blue ribbon for first in our class, Marilyn came over to offer warm congratulations. Then, pointing to a tent bursting with Covenites, she said, "Willard, how come they get so mad when you win?" I shrugged and laughed.

It was killing them, that's why.

One weekend Honeybear and I were entered in an obedience trial in Prescott, Arizona, about a hundred miles from home. We arrived on Friday afternoon and stayed in a Motel 6. That evening clouds covered the moon and the motel grounds were poorly lighted. I was walking HB behind the motel in near-darkness when, suddenly, a voice from the shadows said, "You know, Willard, there are people who don't like it that you train with food."

I recognized the voice. It was the one whose physical attributes most typified Coven members — her butt and her mouth were far bigger than her I.Q. Let's call her the Queen of Darkness.

"There's a name for people like that," I replied.

"What is it?" the Queen of Darkness asked.

"OTCH fodder," I responded.

Time passed. One Sunday I entered Honeybear in a match in Flagstaff, a mountain town about 120 miles north of Phoenix.

HB, Barbara and I were in our tent, awaiting our turn in the ring. Suddenly, from behind the tent, I heard that voice again, the Queen of Darkness. Her dog, a German shepherd, had just lagged and slogged through the Novice exercises. The Queen of Darkness was telling a friend, another member of The Coven, "I'm not surprised. He didn't even want to get out of the van when we got here today."

"Yep!" I said to Barbara, "that's a Coven-trained dog."

■ ■ ■

The unfortunate corollary to all of this is that for many years, since well before I came into the sport, The Coven has had a stranglehold on the so-called "leadership" of Phoenix Field and Obedience Club, the only obedience club in the Central Arizona area.

Time and again good people — folks capable of contributing leadership and talent to the club — join, get the picture and are never seen again. As a result, the old guard prevails and the organization remains stagnated in a time warp 25 years out of date.

For example, Billie Rosen joined the club and soon became community service chair. For the next couple of years PFOC volunteers were everywhere — dog shows, pet fairs, shopping centers — putting on demonstrations and disseminating information about responsible dog ownership and how to have fun with your dog.

Then, near the dawn of agility's popularity in the United States, Billie started a fledgling agility program for PFOC. Coven members and hangers-on were sharply critical of the program and abusively critical of Billie. Eventually Billie resigned and started her own independent agility club, Jumping Chollas.

Now, a decade later, Jumping Chollas, with 190 members, is the most successful agility club in Arizona. Meanwhile, the agility program run by PFOC's Coven-dominated board has shriveled up and died.

The PFOC obedience training program is a cash cow for the club with upwards of 1,500 enrollees each year. Unsuspecting members of the public, seeking training for themselves and their dogs, see the name Phoenix Field and Obedience Club and think, *These people are the experts.* And they eagerly sign up for class. But astute observers conclude the majority of the "instructors" are barely qualified to be students in the classes they are trying to teach. And the drop-out rate is staggering.

■ CHAPTER 24 ■

Honeybear's Fan Club

I had tasted The Gaines. We had come within a paw's width of placing in our first encounter with the Big Dogs. What everyone had told me was true, just being there was the thrill of a lifetime. That happy, tail-wagging, strutting big girl at my side. The reassuring pit-pat, pit-pat of those toenails on the mats. Priceless. And what I wanted was more.

Utility? It could wait. It would take a long time to get her ready to show at Gaines level in Utility. And the Western Regional was scheduled for Las Vegas in February of 1994. We had to be there.

The last six months of 1993 were a blur of happy training and successful shows.

Honeybear knew the Open exercises. I joked that she could go into the ring by herself and do quite well. So we polished and proofed.

Sometimes we'd head for Terminal Two at Phoenix Sky Harbor International Airport. For reasons that still remain a mystery to me, dogs in training were allowed in Terminal Two but not One, Three or Four.

Once, I marched HB right into the baggage claim area the morning before Thanksgiving — one of the busiest travel days of the year. A great time and place to practice heeling and dog attention. Lots of people milling around (many of them fasci-nated by what we were doing), two luggage carousels going, and "Honeybear, watch me!"

Or we'd practice at Town & Country Shopping Center in north central Phoenix. It's an open-air center with several inte-rior walkways well away from the parking lot and moving automobiles. Again, excellent distractions.

And, of course, there was our old standby, PetsMart. Although by that time HB was a bit too comfy there.

Much of our work during afternoons at the park focused on chronic, nagging problems. Her crooked fronts, her proclivity for gleefully mouthing the dumbbell. And the one that hurt most — the over-eager elevation of her butt as I'd turn my back and walk to the other end of the ring for the drop on recall exer-cise. That frequently cost us three points, blowing an otherwise sensational run.

Add it up. To a score of 195, add three points for picking up her butt, a half point for a crooked front and half a point for cud-chewing. Absent those transgressions, you have a 199 out of a possible 200, enough to win Open B about 95 percent of the time.

On balance, though, the words that best describe HB's ring performance during the last six months of 1993 were *solid* and *consistent*. My big girl had matured into a seasoned competi-tor. And I wasn't doing too badly myself; I no longer led the state in diarrhea before a show.

Between June 1993 and the end of the year, we missed being in the ribbons (first through fourth places) only once. We scored a bunch of 196s, a 197, a 195, and a 194.5. Not spectac-ular, but steady.

■ ■ ■

I began to realize that Honeybear — a happy, happy dog in the ring — was becoming a crowd favorite. Her performances contrasted sharply with those of dogs who had been harshly trained. They were working out of fear and it showed in the ring.

A surprising number of people I could not recall seeing before began to approach me, call me by name and give me the big hello. I'd respond with a hearty hello, but my eyes must have betrayed me because they'd say something like, "You don't remember me but I remember Honeybear." They were members of a group that began way back when we used to practice sits and downs at PetsMart — Honeybear's Fan Club.

It's still going on today. Except for an occasional appearance in the Veterans ring, Honeybear has been retired since October of 1999.

Several weeks ago I took HB to the Kachina Kennel Club shows at Estrella Mountain Park. At shows and matches, I place the dogs in EEZI-CRATES. They are lightweight but durable. They telescope flat and I can carry three in one hand. They are made of tough, tan industrial strength vinyl-coated polyester. Walking by the tent you can discern that there's an animal in there, but nothing more.

That afternoon at Kachina two men came strolling along. When they reached our tent, they stopped. "Is Honeybear in there?" one of them asked.

"Yes," I replied, "but how did you know?"

"Oh, I know Honeybear from back at Mildred's," he said. He was referring to a place where we used to practice once in a while many years ago.

I let Honeybear out. While the men petted her, she danced around and wagged her tail. A good time was had by all, then the men went on their way. I have no idea who they were.

Honeybear's Fan Club included those who were waiting timidly outside the ring as we finished our run. Often with a tiny child, two years or less. Hesitantly the parent would ask,

"Would it be all right if my little girl pets your dog?" What a
pleasure it was to have a dog who was so well socialized, so
nice with kids that I could relax and say, "Oh, she'd love it."

As the whole family kneeled down to pet HB, the next
words I'd hear would be, "She's so soft!"

Invariably the real test would come when my great big
golden (relatively speaking) would give the tiny child a big wet
smacker right in the puss. That would either send the child into
joyous, dancing-around laughter or cause the little face to cloud
up and the tears to come. Oh well, you never know.

Another type of ringside groupie is the one who says, "Wow,
that was great! I wish you'd come to my house and train my
dog."

To those people I love to respond, "Yeah, my dogs are just
great in the ring." Then I lean closer and in a conspiratorial
near-whisper I say, "But they're a disaster at the front door."

Which is true. My dogs are a wagging, barking, jumping,
irresistible force when visitors come.

■ CHAPTER 25 ■

Strange Things Are Happening

We sailed through the end of 1993 in grand style. But there must have been black magic working as the new year began; everything fell apart.

I entered us in an obedience trial at the Kennel Club of Palm Springs the first weekend in January. It was during a period when they had moved their shows to the convention center in downtown Palm Springs. The setting was cramped, a far cry from the Empire Equestrian Center in Indio, but doable. Obedience was outdoors.

Honeybear did well. But I flunked us. On the first group exercise — the three-minute long sit with handlers out of sight — the judge said, "Sit your dogs." All the handlers told the dogs, "Sit." Except me. I said, "Honeybear, down!"

Then the judge said, "Leave your dogs," and we started across the ring. About three steps out, it hit me. Then I hit me; I slapped my forehead with the palm of my hand and said, "Oh no!"

Behind me was a row of dogs sitting obediently side by side — except for the golden retriever who had been told to lie down. In front of me, the Santa Rosa Mountains were beautiful in the morning sun. That's what I saw as I continued across the ring, realizing that our run and our trip were now reduced to a big zero.

That disastrous moment imprinted itself so indelibly on my psyche that now, driving across I-10, every time we approach the Palm Springs area and I see those mountains, the first thing that comes to mind is the picture I saw before me that morning as I slapped my forehead in frustration and disgust.

That faux pas may have set the tone for the strange happenings that were to follow.

■ ■ ■

We went back to Southern California two weeks later. The show was hosted by the Shoreline Dog Fanciers of Orange County. It was held on Sunday, February 15 at the Orange County Fairgrounds in Costa Mesa, just up the road from trendy Newport Beach.

We arrived at noon on Saturday. That afternoon we took HB down to the beach. It was the first time she had seen the ocean. After a few minutes of deciding it wasn't going to get her, she loved it. I didn't want her coat to be a mess the next morning and I sure didn't want to give her a bath in the motel room, so I let her puddle around in the surf a little bit and that was it.

All fairgrounds dog show environments are alike. The buildings are big barns. Inside, a cacophony of noise bounces off walls and ceiling — hundreds of dogs barking, PA system babble, carts with squeaky wheels, the chatter of excited exhibitors.

At Shoreline, the rings were rubber mats over concrete. The ring barriers were ropes stretched between stanchions — not the most effective crowd control. They weren't even double-roped to keep the spectators a reasonable distance from what were supposed to be focused performances in the rings. What's more, indoor rings weren't HB's thing; nearly all her training and showing had taken place outdoors on grass.

Sure, The Gaines had been indoors, but inside a fairgrounds building was a far cry from the exhibitor-friendly Gaines environment.

Still, Honeybear had been around. She was seasoned. None of the environmental conditions should have mattered. But something did.

Under Judge Fred Effinger, HB turned in her worst heeling performance since that Novice A disaster under Sharon Ann Redmer. She was about a foot behind me through most of the heeling pattern.

In the middle of the pattern the judge called a halt. HB caught up and sat. And sat. And sat. Judge Effinger was behind us and I couldn't see what was going on. Was he waiting for HB's butt to go all the way down? I looked over my left shoulder cautiously. HB was planted firmly, looking up at me, saying, "So what's next?"

Finally Mr. Effinger said, "Forward," and we slogged through the rest of the exercise. She dropped two feet behind on the fast.

The rest of our run that Sunday was equally uninspired. Our score was 189.5. It had been a long time since we had disgraced ourselves like that.

And the long pause in the middle of the heeling pattern? When we came out of the ring, Barbara told me that several kids had been sitting on the floor under the rope, legs protruding into the ring. The judge had gone over and told them to move, in mid-pattern.

I didn't realize it at the time, but something had clicked off in HB's little head that morning. Something having to do with upbeat heeling. It was several years before Honeybear again began to heel as I knew she could.

■ ■ ■

Our distraction was mild compared to the one suffered by a West Highland white terrier.

During the Novice A long sit, a large fire extinguisher fell off the wall and crashed about ten feet behind the line of six or seven dogs. To everyone's surprise, all the dogs except the Westie held their positions. The Westie panicked and fled across the ring to "Mom."

The nonbreaking dogs then finished the group exercises, doing the long down. But Judge Effinger told the lady with the Westie, "Take your dog outside. Walk him, play with him, get him calmed down. Then I'll let him repeat the group exercises by himself."

About 15 minutes later the woman and dog reappeared. They entered the ring and she put the little guy on a sit. As she left him and started across the ring, the dog looked behind him, at the spot where the fire extinguisher had crashed, then bolted to the lady's side again.

So they took another break while the lady tried to calm her terrified dog. They tried again in about 30 minutes and the dog successfully completed both the sit and down, followed by a rousing ovation.

Finally, the day's proceedings were extended through several run-offs.

By the time we got out of the show it was nearly 4:30. "Let's stay overnight and drive back in the morning," I suggested. Barbara agreed.

We were staying at a Holiday Inn Express in downtown Costa Mesa.

At dawn the next morning I was awakened by the bed shaking. I thought it was Honeybear leaning against my side of the bed, scratching. But a moment later Barbara said, "It's an earthquake."

It sure was. The date was January 16, 1994. We were experiencing the devastating Northridge earthquake.

I looked out the door and saw water sloshing out of the swimming pool. On the radio we heard news about large upheavals, sinkholes, damaged bridges and obstructions that had closed freeways in that part of Southern California. We were fortunate; our route home was not affected by the earthquake.

Back home several people ventured this theory:

"Dogs have a sixth sense. Maybe Honeybear sensed that the earthquake was coming and that affected her performance."

Yeah, well, if that was the case, she must also have sensed that the apocalypse itself was coming somewhere down the road; her Shoreline behavior was destined to last a long time.

Even when we were getting good scores on our heeling exercises, I felt I didn't have enough dog at my side. She wasn't what I refer to as "up and driving." Her heeling was lackluster. I wanted to say, "Come on, Honeybear. Let's go!" The other Open exercises weren't bad, but the heeling had no zing.

A few days after our Shoreline collapse, I called Karen Price in Chatsworth. She said she'd like to look at the videotape. I FedEx'd it to her. She called back to ask whether I was certain HB wasn't sick. "That just wasn't Honeybear I saw on the tape," she said. Then she suggested I have HB's thyroid checked.

It was borderline and Dr. Toben put her on a low dose (0.1 mg.) of Soloxine. But time would reveal that her thyroid had nothing to do with her lackluster heeling. It might have been a comfortable rationalization, but it was without substance.

The 1994 Gaines Western Regional was scheduled for February 26 and 27. I had been counting the weeks. Now this. I pulled our entry. The Gaines was all about excellence, and that starts with pristine heeling. The kind HB was capable of but presently chose not to offer. "I'm not going to The Gaines and embarrass us," I said.

Debby said Honeybear looked bored. And that time I agreed with her.

■ CHAPTER 26 ■

Enter Dick And Kay

I had heard about Dick and Kay Guetzloff of Palatine, Illinois. Largely from the wrong sources. Members of The Coven and hanger-on wannabes who, from long before my time, had held the PFOC "leadership" in a chokehold. They were the people who couldn't and who resented those who could, did and did well.

What was their beef with the Guetzloffs? Several times, from the lips of The Coven, I heard, "All they do is come in here from Chicago and win everything." I was unable to grasp what was wrong with that, but being new to the sport I kept my mouth shut.

Of course Dick and Kay weren't exactly their own best public relations ambassadors.

When Dick would place other than first, he would often wad up his ribbons and stuff them in his pocket before he left the ring. Contrast that with the less fortunate exhibitor who cherishes a rare fourth-place finish, carries the ribbon proudly from the ring, then spends the rest of the day making sure it doesn't get wrinkled. Or the handler who has taught her dog to carry the ribbon from the ring proudly in his mouth.

But what mental set can be expected after 40 years as one of the winningest handlers in the sport? How many thousands —

tens of thousands — of ribbons and useless knickknacks have Dick and Kay accumulated? What can they do with them all?

One of the anecdotes repeatedly mentioned by the whining Coven members concerned the time Dick won a big prize at the PFOC trial, one of the countless times he had the highest scoring dog in the trial. The trophy was a clock. Dick, the story goes, gave it away "before he ever left the showgrounds." The PFOC "leadership" — The Coven — resented that.

■ ■ ■

Our first meeting with Dick and Kay had come just as Honeybear was beginning her Novice A quest for a CD. There had been a feature in *Front & Finish* about a man from Palatine, Illinois who had recently retired from a career as a long-haul truck driver. He had been showing dogs in obedience competition with unusual success for more than 30 years. Mostly golden retrievers.

Now, having recently retired, he was planning to campaign a border collie, Heelalong Chimney Sweep, and see how far they could go. He had shrugged off the travel grind he was undertaking. "Heck," he said, "I've been making long drives all my life."

Several of his other comments along with the fact that he was steeped in experience with goldens stimulated my interest.

The morning HB and I were seeking our second CD leg at Superstition Kennel Club I looked up and there was a tall man in a black Greg Norman-style hat walking a border collie. Why that was the man I had been reading about a few days earlier.

At the time, one of Honeybear's most frustrating habits was her compulsion to sniff. Anywhere, anytime, but mostly at all the wrong times. Maybe the famous Mr. Guetzloff had the solution.

It took me a few minutes to approach the somewhat austere-looking man. Later I would learn that one of Dick's regrets, as he and Sweep went where no dog and handler had gone before, was that people held him in such awe they were afraid to approach him at shows.

That morning in March of 1991 I encountered a warm, friendly man who was happy to talk about my problem. He told me that sometimes spaying helped alleviate the sniffing problem in females. Of course Honeybear had been spayed as soon as we learned she was dysplastic. So much for that remedy.

Later Debby would utter the pearl of wisdom that put me on track to wipe out the problem once and for all: "Willard, it's physically impossible for the dog to sniff if she's watching you."

Barbara had brought coffee and a box of doughnuts to the Superstition show. As Dick and I talked, his wife Kay joined us and Barbara offered them coffee and doughnuts. Now, a decade later, Barbara laughs as she recalls, "Dick took one doughnut, Kay took two."

The next day, when HB and I had that horrible performance in the ring of Sharon Ann Redmer, I hoped Dick and Kay had been occupied with their own dogs and hadn't seen us.

Early in 1993 rumors began to circulate that Dick and Kay were planning to sell their residence in Palatine and move to Prescott, Arizona. They were looking for a milder climate than the Chicago area offered. Prescott, at 5,200 feet and 100 miles from Phoenix, seemed to meet their needs.

Those rumors set off a new wave of jealous backbiting and retelling all the old stories about Dick's attitude and Kay's personality. One Coven member/PFOC "leader" got to the real heart of it when she said, "You mean they're going to be here all the time? My God, the rest of us might as well quit."

Sure enough, a few months later it became common knowledge that the Guetzloffs had established temporary residence in Prescott while they built a new house and training area a few miles out of town.

■ ■ ■

The year after Dick and Kay moved to Prescott, they agreed to be obedience co-chairs at the Prescott Arizona Kennel Club's (PAKC) show. One of the changes they instituted was cash prizes in obedience competition. That, combined with a few other progressive changes, sent the PAKC old guard into apoplexy. "But we've never done it that way," they said.

The whole thing ended in a fusillade of bickering, accusations, charges and countercharges. The Guetzloffs did not renew their PAKC membership the following year.

Much of the heartburn emanated from Kay's abrasive manner. The raps against Kay were she won too much, had a big mouth, was tactless and loudly opinionated — and often popped off with garbled facts.

None of which took away from her mastery of dog obedience competition. Not only was she a formidable opponent in the ring, she was also an outstanding teacher.

"The Guetzloffs aren't going to teach you anything that will enable you to beat them in the ring," some people said. The operative word there is *enable*. During the five years Dick and Kay lived in Arizona, I took lessons from each from time to time. Beyond that, I found Dick to be a kindly, generous coach at ringside. My experiences satisfied me that both were not only willing but anxious to share all they knew. The problem was that those of us who sat at their feet were mere mortals and nothing they could teach us could elevate us to a level where we could threaten their dominance of the Open B and Utility B rings.

Kay took fierce pride in the success of her students. In particular, there was a group of five or six in the Flagstaff area who, at best, bumbled around before Kay began offering lessons. The transformation was amazing. Suddenly those people became high achievers in obedience competition, capturing many advanced titles.

"Kay taught us how to win," one of them told me later. Unfortunately it didn't stick. If there had been any doubt that Kay made all the difference, it was dispelled when the Guetzloffs uprooted again in 1998 and moved to San Angelo, Texas. The collective ability of that little group has settled back to about where it was before the advent of Kay Guetzloff.

■ CHAPTER 27 ■

Tchotchkes

The rap against Dick Guetzloff was, "He wins too much." And he wasn't moved to tears upon receiving his 17,342nd ribbon and the tchotchke that accompanied it.

But in my judgment the problem had less to do with Dick Guetzloff than with the tchotchkes (virtually useless knick-knacks) given as awards at the majority of shows.

Across more than a decade of showing and sometimes winning, I have accumulated countless trophies, jars, pots, figurines, picture frames, candleholders, plaques, fake-pewter plates, coffee cups, mugs, beer steins, and God-knows-whats. Many cover every inch of flat surface in my office. The rest are on bookshelves in the family room. (We threw away several hundred books to accommodate them.) Barbara's greatest fear is that someday the tchotchkes will launch a tacky attack and take over the house.

They represent everything from high-scoring senior handler, high scoring golden retriever in such and such a class or high scoring dog in a nonregular class to our cherished high-in-trial and high-combined awards.

In our part of the country they love to give hand-painted Indian knickknacks. I have little clay-like birds, clay luminarias, clay cliff dweller building facades, and a whole set (six) of male and female Indian figurines from a day when HB and I really cleaned up.

But not all tchotchkes are worthless dust-collectors, as I learned on March 15, 1997. Honeybear and I were entered in Utility B and Open B at the obedience trial of the Kennel Club of Palm Springs.

I had entered the trial with trepidation. Southern California is a hotbed of excellent trainers and red-hot dogs. I knew we'd encounter the likes of Louise Meredith, who at the time had put OTCHs on three dogs and was closing in on a fourth. Louise was and is one of America's most formidable opponents.

The 1997 back-to-back obedience trials were held at Sunrise Park in downtown Palm Springs. That year the obedience trials were separated from the all-breed show and were a small-scale operation — particularly when compared with the current Kennel Club of Palm Springs New Year's Classic which features both conformation and obedience and draws nearly 4,000 dogs.

Our tent was only a few feet from the show secretary's tent where the trophies were displayed. As we prepared for the morning's activities, Barbara said, "Look at those God-awful things. Try not to win those."

"Oh, not to worry," I replied, "Louise (Meredith) is here."

The objects Barbara was referring to were hung high on the secretary's tent, displayed for all to see … and presumably to covet.

One was a dream catcher, a round fishnet-looking thing with eight long strands hung with feathers and beads.

The other was a medicine shield, a round dinner plate-size object made of leather and wood. The face of the "plate" was decorated with a large bear in a wilderness setting and inset with a small silver medallion and a small piece of rock with a tiny fragment of turquoise in the center.

That morning, her heeling doldrums long behind her, Honeybear was magnificent. And I must have remembered to breathe. We scored 197.5 to finish second to Louise and her border collie, Riot, in Utility B. Then we did a 198.5 in Open B to win the class.

We weren't finished. Later that afternoon a steward came rushing over. "Willard," he said, "get your dog ready. You're in a runoff for high in trial. With Louise Meredith," he added, and his face had condolences written all over it.

Oh, my God! It hadn't entered my mind. Sure, I knew Louise and Riot had beaten us in Utility B with a 198.5, the same score we had then gotten to beat them in Open B. But my thought process had stalled right there. We weren't bad, but high in trial was not part of our routine shtick. Especially in Southern California.

Somehow, by the grace of God and the flawless heeling of Honeybear, we won the runoff, high in trial, high combined, and both of those tchotchkes that had hung above the rings until they were presented to us.

Now they hang in a prominent spot in my office. Part of a display I put together so I'll never forget that magic day in the little park in Palm Springs.

The dream catcher, with its suspended strands of beads and feathers, is about five and one-half feet from top to bottom. I've hung the medicine shield so it's inside the hoop of the dream catcher, at the top and centered.

Next come the ribbons, blue for first in Open B, red for second in Utility B. Then the large rosettes and streamers. The large green-and-blue ribbon reads, "Highest Combined Scoring (sic) in Open and Utility." (We had gotten a total of 396 points out of a possible 400. Our highest-scoring day ... ever.) The blue-and-gold one says, "Highest Scoring Dog in Regular Classes."

That display is beautiful ... in its own right but mostly because of what it represents. Even Barbara, who had said, "Look at those God-awful things," now thinks they're pretty swell.

Tchotchkes? Yes. But look a bit deeper and you find meaning that transcends first impressions.

They were not made in Taiwan. They really were made by Indian craftsmen in Albuquerque, New Mexico. And each is steeped in symbolism and lore.

The dream catcher is a catcher of dreams one would like to keep, while allowing others to pass through. It allows you to hold on to your dreams and is often given to infants, children and young people as well as the elderly so that their dreams might come true.

It is decorated with turquoise, silver, white bone or mother of pearl and an arrowhead. Those symbols stand for life, wealth, purity and strength. Objects are added to the dream catcher as hopes and dreams are realized, much as a charm bracelet.

Without knowing that — because I didn't read the cards that accompanied the items until nearly five years later, researching this book — I had completed my display by adding my score-cards and ribbons. Indeed they do represent a dream come true: to beat a Louise Meredith in a runoff for high in trial, and to have my first obedience competition dog at my side when I did it.

The medicine shield holds supernatural powers.

North American Indians believe that nature possesses many powers that could come to man through a vision. Men were drawn to hilltops, lakesides or towering mountains. There they called upon the supernatural powers to give them a vision so they might fulfill their quest. Their vision became tangible as they created a medicine shield to proclaim that vision.

The supernatural power of the medicine shield was believed to be stronger than that of men. The shield was sometimes carried to war; a miniature was sometimes worn around the neck or in the hair.

Each replica of the medicine shield contains symbols and designs handed down through many generations. The true meaning of each shield is known only to the artist.

Now then, do *these* tchotchkes have real value? Oh, you bet they do!

■ ■ ■

Not too long ago I was at a trial sponsored by an obedience club in another city. It was Sunday afternoon, the second of two trial days. That club gives lots of awards for a slew of things. During the awards presentations, I was seated next to a friend who is one of the best handlers, smartest trainers and most creative thinkers in the world of dog sports.

She had won high in trial, high combined, highest scoring dog with a breed championship of record, highest scoring dog of her breed and her group. On and on. What's more, she had also cleaned our clocks the day before. And this happened the lion's share of the times she entered a show.

Pretty soon she was surrounded by tchotchkes of the Indian pottery variety. Big bowls, little bowls. Big birds, little birds. Far more than she could possibly carry to her van in one trip. And what in God's name would she do with them when she got home?

I leaned over and whispered, "What do you *do* with all this stuff?

She whispered back, "I keep it in the garage and every so often I have a yard sale."

I thought she was kidding and I began to laugh.

But she said, "I'm serious. About every two years I have enough for a yard sale. People *love* the Indian stuff." Pointing to a medium-size pot, she said, "I get $10 for that." Indicating a bird, she said, "Those go for $5."

Once in a while you get a prize that's really useful. When Honeybear finished her Utility Dog title with a first-place blue ribbon at Valley Hills Obedience Club in Woodland Hills, California, we were given a green, soft-sided, insulated box-like bag with a shoulder strap. Since then, that sturdy bag has gone to every dog show and countless training sessions. It's the most useful award we've received.

Recently I saw, but never got near, a neat high-in-trial award. An outdoor recliner with a built-in-table, cupholders and footrest. The Utah woman who won it is going to luxuriate in it at dog shows for years. They may have to wake her when it's time to go into the ring.

A few shows, precious few in our part of the country, eliminate the need for a yard sale by going directly to cash prizes.

Honeybear has shown three times in the Veterans class at Southwest Obedience Club (SWOC) of Los Angeles. She has scored 198 each time to win the class. She has also been the highest scoring dog in nonregular classes each time and won the $25 cash prize. (High in trial goes for $100; high combined fetches $50.) No big deal, but I sure can figure out what to do with 25 bucks faster than I can figure out what to do with a ceramic bird.

When you've been around the ring for a decade or so, you can empathize with Dick Guetzloff's point of view. After a while, the tchotchkes can weigh you down.

■ CHAPTER 28 ■

Our Summer Of Discontent

"Hit 'em again! Hit 'em again!
Harder! Harder!"
FOOTBALL CHEER

Shortly after the Guetzloffs moved to Prescott, it was announced they would be holding a seminar on January 29 and 30, 1994, for the benefit of PFOC — the very crowd that had hacked them up unmercifully behind their backs.

I signed up for the seminar. Naturally I wanted to soak up what they had learned in a combined 60-odd years of training and showing. I had also recently decided to get a border collie puppy, and Dick and Kay knew all there was to know about *both* golden retrievers and border collies.

At the seminar, Dick and Kay drew upon their many decades of training and showing to present a multitude of helpful hints. Information it might take you years to figure out on your own.

"When you screw up in the ring, don't give it away," Dick told us. "Let the judge think you think the exercise was perfect."

Kay recommended we keep the directed retrieve gloves rolled up or twisted. "You want them to stand up in the ring so they're easier for the dog to see and pick up," she said. "And *never* wash them; that makes them limp."

She suggested we practice our hand signals in front of a mirror so that we could see what the dog is seeing.

Dick had a great suggestion for people like me who aren't exactly ballet dancers. When pivoting, such as during the scent discrimination exercise or the directed retrieve, place a dime between your feet, then pivot in such a way that the dime is in exactly the same location relative to your feet when you finish as it was before you began the pivot. The purpose is to keep people like me from traveling all over the ring — and losing points — as we pivot.

Kay talked all too briefly about playing with your dog. That hit a nerve; Honeybear was showing signs of boredom.

Debby advocated more hands-on play. Roughhousing, tugging and the like.

Honeybear and I did some of that, but mostly at home. She loved to climb up in my lap and instigate a "game of hand." I'd make various feinting moves with my hand and she'd try to grab it. I'd move my thumb and forefinger slowly toward her nose. Slowly, slowly; closer, closer. HB would curl her lip. Then my fingers would dart in to grab her nose and she'd snap playfully. Would she get me or would I get her? The result varied. And we both loved it.

Or my fingers would walk up her hind leg or up her hip. The lips would curl. She'd wait. Could I grab her muzzle before she got me? Sometimes. Sometimes not.

That would go on for 20 minutes or half an hour if I didn't tire.

But I had trouble transferring such informal play to the training situation. Almost from Day One, Debby had been trying to get me to be less formal, less structured in my training.

If nothing else, I have become much more aware of real play versus ersatz play.

I see glaring examples of people playing *at* their dogs. I know that even at my worst I was never as bad as some of what I see.

People playing *at* their dogs run around a lot, frantic, cheer-leading. They feature a lot of upper-body flailing. Above all, they communicate with their dogs in high falsetto voices. Meanwhile, the dog is standing there, either puzzled or bored, saying, "Yeah, yeah."

The person isn't connecting with the dog and isn't giving the dog time to respond. It's more of a heckling exercise than it is play.

The point that gets lost in all this is that during play the dog, not the handler, should run around.

Once I became aware of that scenario, I saw enough of me in it that I wanted to tap more deeply into Kay's insights about playing with your dog.

■ ■ ■

I called her a week after the seminar. We agreed to meet the next morning at Granite Creek Park in downtown Prescott.

We spent the early part of the 90-minute lesson focusing on the concept of incorporating play into (rather than before and after) training. And on the natural corollary, the need for me to make my training far less formal. "You don't need to incorporate a finish into every exercise," Kay said. "Nothing can dampen a dog's enthusiasm faster than being required to front during every exercise." She advised me to practice fronts and finishes *outside* the exercises.

We finished the session with heeling, HB's insatiable urge to elevate her rear end at scorable times, and ways to clean up our fronts.

The lesson had gone well and I arranged to meet her again at the same place in two weeks. And then we scheduled a lesson for two weeks after that ... and two weeks after that.

That spring Dick and Kay began offering lessons at a Phoenix park not far from where I live. When possible, Honeybear and I took our lessons in Phoenix and I was surprised to see who else was there. As Debby put it later, "It was fascinating to see all the people who had ridiculed Dick and Kay behind their backs for many years. Here they were, right away flocking to them for lessons."

After my second lesson with Kay, feeling guilty and unfaithful, I figured I'd better fess up, so I called Debby. Feeling painful discomfort, I told her what a great job she had done to bring us this far. I told her how much I appreciated it. But I said I thought we had plateaued and it might be good to have a change of scenery and let Kay take us to the next level.

As usual, Debby was the consummate professional. She accepted my departure gracefully and expressed her good wishes for our future. That conversation brought into focus how much Debby had become a beautiful part of the tapestry of my life. I hung up in tears.

The lessons with Kay continued through spring and into summer. Often Dick was there, and he added his wealth of experience to the lesson. What a great resource! Got a problem? Dick or Kay or both had been there and knew what to do to correct it.

Trouble was, the what-to-do increasingly made me uncomfortable. In a nutshell, when the going got tough, the Guetzloffs got tougher. In their eyes, a multitude of problems could be solved by giving the dog a good whack.

Take HB's penchant for raising her butt. That had been going on since Novice A, but the frequency of the transgression as well as the height of the elevations had increased in Open. We were getting scored on it, up to three points at a pop. It was impeding our success.

I'd throw the dumbbell. Up would come Honeybear's butt in anticipation of my command, "Take it!" Or I'd leave her for the drop on recall. As I'd walk to the other end of the ring, her rear end would slowly rise in anticipation of being called.

I had received a lot of advice about the problem, from Debby and a host of others. We had done all the standard remedial things. I'd leave her, walk varying distances, then turn to face her. If she was still sitting, I'd say, "Good sit, Honeybear. Good sit." Then I'd go back, give her a treat, reposition her and do it again. Sometimes I'd walk all the way to the opposite end of the ring, turn, straighten my feet, look up as if to call her, then say, "Good sit, Honeybear. Good sit." Then I'd go back and reward her. She would be called to me maybe once out of every five repetitions.

That worked well in practice, but in pressure situations dogs revert to old behaviors. When we were in a show, Honeybear's butt would float up as if attached to a helium balloon.

In practice, when her butt came up, I'd go back and push it down, maybe giving her a rap on her hindquarters.

For a while we tried attaching a longline to her collar. Whoever was behind the dog would hold the other end of the line. When her butt started to rise, the line-holder would yell, "Sit!" while jerking the line. Her butt would go back down … only to rise again before long.

There was a second option with the line. We worked on using the opposition reflex to our advantage. The line was clipped to HB's collar and the collar rotated so that the clip was below her chin at six o'clock. The line extended straight out from HB's median line. I was on the other end. When I'd leave her, I'd immediately put pressure on the line. The dog's natural reaction was to resist, to pull back, to dig in and work hard at maintaining the sit.

Of course you can't do that in the AKC ring. As Judge Karen TenEyck had said, I needed a ten-penny nail.

So it was that one of the problems we brought to Kay was the butt-picking-up transgressions of HB.

She observed the problem and so did Dick. "You're going to have to get physical with that dog," Dick said.

"OK, here's what you need to do," Kay instructed. "Sit your dog on your left, as you would before leaving her for a recall. As you leave, give her a sharp whack in the chest with the palm of your hand."

I sat HB. "Leave her," Kay said. I gave my dog a sharp whack in the chest with my left hand and headed for a spot about 40 feet away. I wasn't even half the distance when up came HB's butt.

"Willard, you're going to have to smack her a lot harder than that," Kay yelled. (Deja vu. Maureen Black, beginners class.) Then she took over.

She sat HB on her left. The blow came from across her body via her *right* hand and exploded with a hollow sound on HB's chest. HB nearly toppled backwards. Kay walked away. Honeybear sat. I cringed.

Sometime later I traveled to Chatsworth, California for a couple of lessons with Karen Price who, with Flash, was our role model. Karen had a different approach to the ascending-butt problem.

"Willard, when you leave any dog on a sit, what's the first thing she does?" she asked.

I hadn't a clue.

"She looks around briefly to make sure she's safe. She checks the judge, the person who is closest to her. Let's give Honeybear something else to think about while you walk to the other end of the ring ... something other than picking up her butt. I'm going to be the judge this time. Give me one of your treats."

I reached into my shirt pocket and gave her one of my little Grreat Choice biscuits.

"Now as soon as you leave," Karen said, "Honeybear is going to look at me. When you get about 10 feet out, I'm going to step in and give her a biscuit."

I left. She did. HB sat.

"In order to do this, you have to recruit someone to work with you," Karen said. "It can be Barbara or someone else. You need a judge surrogate so that when you get in a show Honeybear will busy herself checking to see if the judge has a goody for her, rather than stressing out and picking up her rear end."

Karen's method worked better than anything else we tried. Was it perfect? No. Across 12 years of training, I've learned that problems that trouble you early in a dog's career tend to crop up over and over again.

■ ■ ■

Concerns had been gnawing at me about my lessons with Kay.

While Dick was often on the road with Sweep for weeks at a time, campaigning toward a new record for most OTCH points on a dog, Kay was showing locally. They figured it would make no sense for Kay to travel with Dick, compete against him and siphon off OTCH points.

We'd be in shows together. Honeybear would put on a less-than-ecstatic performance. Kay would say, "Well, she did thus-and-so wrong but her attitude is improving."

That wasn't the way I saw it. Her attitude was drifting steadily downhill.

On my way home from the chest-whacking lesson, I made my decision. It wasn't working. It wasn't my style of training.

By that time I had become convinced that my relationship with my dog was the foremost consideration in everything Honeybear and I did together.

Debby had said, "To some people, their dogs are just something to put titles on."

My relationship with Honeybear was the antithesis of that. Sure, I wanted to do well with Honeybear in competition. I hungered to win every time we walked into the ring. But not at the cost of creating an unhappy dog. I was determined that any success we had would not be built upon HB's fear of consequences.

I wanted her to want to. I was convinced that the foundation for good performance would be a warm, loving, encouraging relationship.

In mid-July I cancelled my upcoming lessons with Kay.

■ CHAPTER 29 ■

Cookie Power

When I bailed out on Kay Guetzloff after six months of lessons, she went into a sulk. In my presence, she was silent, sullen.

The Guetzloffs presented a small seminar in a dilapidated building on the Yavapai County Fairgrounds. I wasn't invited, but it was advertised, so I mailed in my registration and went. During a mid-morning break, Kay passed out copies of an article she thought attendees would find helpful. She placed the handout on every chair … except mine.

On the other hand, after three years of coping with my headstrong ways and the ups and downs of bringing up Honeybear, Debby had received my good-bye call with class. "Let me know if I can help," she had said. And she meant it.

In fact, while I was training with Kay I saw a lot of Debby. From time to time, she held practice matches at Precision Canine. HB and I were always invited and always went.

More importantly, one-on-one lessons with Kay offered no opportunity to practice the group exercises, the long sit and long down. Debby was the one holding classes, six or eight students of an evening, working at various levels. Typically, the class ended with the long sit and long down, some handlers out of sight, others staying in sight.

Debby invited me to arrive 15 minutes before the end of class. Often she'd press me into service. "Willard," she'd say, "would you go over these dogs on the stand for exam?" I'd put HB on a down and make myself useful.

Debby's unwavering decency made it at once easier and more difficult to say, "I want back."

Easier because we had maintained a cordial, almost collegial relationship during my hiatus. More difficult because the whole episode was colored with a tinge of guilt.

No one cared more than Debby. No one gave more of herself in a teaching situation. (Never mind that she holds the world record for being difficult to reach by phone.) Debby was not the kind of friend I felt comfortable dumping for any reason.

By the end of July it was time to bite the bullet, to return to Debby and Precision Canine. I called, left a message. Debby called back. It was time to return, I told her, and we needed to focus on Honeybear's attitude.

Again, amazing grace.

We scheduled a lesson for Tuesday, August 2 at 3:30 p.m. At "the building," Debby's indoor training facility. She had rented the space in 1993 in a strip mall a few blocks from her house. The main room was slightly smaller than a 40- by 50-foot obedience ring. Cramped but workable. Debby had not installed a telephone at the building — a respite for her and a blessing for her students and their dogs.

The previous tenant had been an indoor batting range. Low-grade artificial turf covered the floor, and a row of white plastic chairs sat in front of the window to the right of the door. In the far right corner, the ceiling tiles were stained and cracking, courtesy of a perpetually leaky roof and a perpetually recalcitrant landlord.

Along the wall, on the crumbling-ceiling side, Debby began hanging presentation photos of students and dogs who won titles. Across several years, it became a gallery of achievement and excellence.

The building was modest. But what went on within those leak-stained walls was intense, focused, creative, and often brilliant.

■ ■ ■

We showed up for our lesson a few minutes early. Debby had not yet arrived. I wasn't surprised. She spends her life rushing from place to place, seeming always to have 18 balls in the air. Fortunately, she has a John F. Kennedy-like ability to shift gears instantly and be 100 percent there and intensely focused the moment she arrives.

Her frenetic lifestyle was reflected in her arrival at the building for classes and lessons. She lived maybe five minutes away and she had it timed to the minute. If the appointment or class was scheduled for 3:30, Debby would arrive at 3:29, 3:30 or 3:31, depending upon the intransigence of the one traffic light enroute. On the day of our return, Debby hit it right on the nose.

In retrospect, from a training standpoint, there were two landmark days in Honeybear's competition career: January 21, 1991, the day HB and I walked into Debby's backyard for the first time, and August 2, 1994, the day we returned to Debby. The student with his tail between his legs. The dog nearly wagging her hind end out of joint.

We all went inside to begin our fresh start. Little did I know how fresh.

"First thing," Debby said, "get rid of the choke chain. Put her buckle collar on her."

I did.

Then she said, "Bring Honeybear over here, Willard." We moved to the edge of the poor man's Astroturf, in front of the white chairs, halfway between the door and the broken ceiling tiles. I could take you there today, point and say, "Right here, right on this exact spot — *this* is the spot where Honeybear was reborn!"

Next Debby asked, "Do you have treats?" She was trying to keep a straight face. It was like asking the San Francisco Giants whether Barry Bonds swings for the fences. Or New Yorkers whether Osama bin Laden acts out his aggression.

"Put HB in heel position," she continued without waiting for the wisecracking answer she knew was sure to come. "Now take a treat in your left hand like this." She showed me how to cup my hand with the treat nestled in the crotch formed by my thumb and forefinger. Grasped that way, my little Grreat Choice biscuits were visible, sniffable, but not quite grabbable, even for a chowhound like HB.

"Now cup your hand above HB's nose, not quite touching," she said. "Keep the treat up there so she can't get it until you tell her it's OK. That's it. Are you ready?"

Was I ever!

"Forward!" And off we went, Honeybear prancing, head up, eyes bright, tail wagging. We heeled half the length of the room before Debby said, "Feed her," and I opened my hand so HB could snarf down the biscuit. Then we repeated that little pattern several more times.

Honeybear was ecstatic. Her eyes said, "What's this?"

I was in shock. All those years when I had been pressed not to use food. Even vilified by The Coven for using it. The repeated warning: "Willard, if you use food in practice, then eliminate it when you get in the ring, Honeybear will think she's done something wrong. She'll think she's being punished. She'll fall apart and quit on you."

And all those days at the park — particularly days when things were going poorly and I was depressed. We'd heel with food in my hand. HB would perk up, strut and be like Flash. Then I could go home happy, saying, "She really *can* turn it on."

But never anything as blatant as this — a pure lure, right on top of her nose. That lesson, an hour that flew by in seconds, was bliss. I hadn't seen my dog that happy heeling in a long time. I sure didn't question or object. It was working and that afternoon there was no tug of war between Debby and me.

I drove home wondering, *What's gotten into Debby?*

■ ■ ■

I wasn't the only one wondering. Sandra Shults, who had worked for Debby as an instructor from the inception of Precision Canine, had become my close friend. We talked about Debby's new training methods and Sandra, too, was puzzled. "Debby has asked me to tell the students to bring their dogs to class with empty stomachs," she said. Then she went on to describe the same scenario I had encountered the day HB and I returned to Debby. Everyone in the class heeling their dogs around with hands cupped over the dogs' noses, treats snuggled between thumb and forefinger.

Sandra was one of the strongest proponents of fading the use of food early in training. When working with her border collie Ott, she left the goodies in a little bag on the sidelines. Only after an exercise was finished, or even after several exercises had been chained together, would she take Ott over to the bag for the reward.

Sandra was one of the people who had pressed me on the food issue, and she was clearly uncomfortable with the new method. "I don't understand where Debby is going with this," she told me.

Shortly thereafter, Sandra severed her relationship with Precision Canine.

Puzzled about Debby's new approach, I telephoned Chris Hill, a mutual friend, and asked her about it. "Oh yeah," she said, "that's the Patty Ruzzo stuff."

"Patty who?"

"She's a trainer from Connecticut, a big-time advocate of food training. She put an OTCH on a Terv using that method."

Of course that would catch Debby's attention, her breed being Belgian Tervurens.

Chris went on to tell me she knew about the transition in training styles because she had recently borrowed the new Patty Ruzzo tapes from Debby.

If Patty Ruzzo's techniques were valid, I had found the perfect fit. I ordered my own set of tapes.

It turned out Patty lives in Colchester, Connecticut and had indeed shown her big handsome male, Luka, to an OTCH.

The jackets of her videotapes summed up her approach: *A hands-off, correction-free, cookie-power method.* One that focused on "the proper use of food rewards that will carry over into the ring." Wow! Just what Skip, the Food King, had been looking for.

Patty wrote that she had felt increasingly guilty about some of the force-training methods she was using, and now advocated "eliminating the power struggle with your dog." (Which is exactly what it is. Whack the dog. She doesn't respond up to your expectations? Well then, whack her harder.)

She recommended "working with your dog to develop a joyous canine partner who performs with an ears-up, eyes-bright attitude." (The very response Honeybear had given me on August 2 when Debby stunned me with her new approach.)

"Great things begin to happen when you throw away your pinch collar and refuse to force your dog," Patty wrote.

I was particularly interested in the part about "the proper use of food rewards that will carry over into the ring." What had I been browbeaten with, almost from the beginning? "Willard, you need to get rid of the food. It's going to come back and haunt you when you get into the ring."

So far it hadn't, except perhaps during heeling. No doubt about it, HB heeled better when I had food in my hand. In general, she heeled well enough that most of the other handlers in the environment were envious of the attention I was getting. "I love the way she watches you," they would say.

But HB heeled *better* when she knew I had a treat in my hand, one she might get at any moment. It was a dichotomy that had become more pronounced lately as her attitude slipped.

So naturally I was intensely interested in "the Patty Ruzzo stuff."

Soon I learned it wasn't only our heeling that was to be the beneficiary of cookie power. Patty's philosophy was, "Got a problem? Put a cookie on it." She could generally figure out a way to fix a problem using treats — and lots of hands-on reinforcement (petting).

■ ■ ■

As several weeks passed and several lessons unfolded, Debby's interpretation of Patty Ruzzo's methodology became clear.

In my mind as well as in Debby's, heeling was the barometer of Honeybear's attitude. As the heeling went, so went the remainder of the performance in the ring. And Debby had a clear picture of where we were, heeling-wise and attitude-wise.

She knew where we were and I knew where we were … and we agreed. When, after a few lessons, we began to talk about the underlying philosophy of our new approach and where we were headed, she summed it up with more precision than I had been able to express in my thoughts. "Honeybear is heeling accurately but her attitude is gone," she said. "She's hanging there as opposed to driving to be there. She's less excited about heeling."

Exactly.

"Putting her on a leash won't fix it," she continued. "Giving her corrections won't fix it. All of that stuff has made her a little more apprehensive about being there (heel position). She needs to get rewarded right in the middle of heeling." *Food.*

From that point, the gospel of Patty Ruzzo according to Debby Boehm went like this:

There would be no corrections (no "Harder, Willard!"). We would work HB off leash, and teach Honeybear to *drive me.*

Prime example: Instead of saying, "Watch me," having HB look up, then popping her a treat, I would wait for her to look at me, then feed her … *instantly* and *every time.* That's what's meant by HB driving me. She controlled the rewards. We wanted HB to think, *I look at him and — voila! — a treat. I don't look … zilch.*

The idea was to build her desire to be next to me, in heel position, watching. Because *she* had decided that was a neat place to be.

In our case, Debby emphasized food as the primary reinforcer. Honeybear's food drive transcends any other drive known to man or beast.

Even more importantly, with food I could reinforce a bit of perfect performance exactly when I wanted to and in the precise position where it would be most effective.

Debby also kept drumming into my head the importance of play as a secondary reinforcer. "Food isn't enough," she said. "You want her to like *you*, not just think of you as a food-dispenser. So be tons of fun." Which I tried to be, but given a choice, my voracious golden retriever would prefer tons of food.

Above all, the new method was a game of choice, not force. The philosophy was that any sort of negative — such as a rough correction — was verboten. "Dogs are strongly place-oriented," Debby said, "You take them to the vet once and the next time they know that place and begin to shake." Roughing up the dog to induce nice heeling, then, is the antithesis of making heel position the happiest place in the world for the dog.

■ ■ ■

In my mind, the one fly in this soothing ointment was the old bugaboo about, "When you get in the ring and the treats aren't there, HB's gonna shut down on you."

One day I voiced that concern to Debby. (Surely the earth trembled. *Willard* expressing concerns about food training??!!) Her response made my day/week/career.

"The philosophy of 'the dog knows when you don't have food' is based on the unspoken assumption that deep down the dog doesn't want to do the work," Debby said. "That he gets in the ring, a gleam comes into his eye and he says to himself, 'I can get away with it here, which is what I've wanted to do for a long time.'"

That may be true if that's the kind of attitude you've fostered. But the very foundation of the philosophy we had adopted was that everything we did in training was aimed at building "want-to." I can still hear Debby telling her classes, "If first you develop want-to in your dog, the rest will follow."

Early in December Patty Ruzzo gave a two-day seminar in San Diego. It was a must for those of us who had recently begun to use her methods. I sat in the front row for two days, HB lying quietly at my feet.

For me, the high point came when Patty addressed the consequences of when the food goes away in the ring.

"Right before you go into the ring, heel your dog with lots of cookies," she said. "When the steward calls you, heel your dog to the ring entrance and pop your last cookie just before you get there.

"Then, when you finish your run, leave the ring, ignore anyone who wants to compliment you or talk to you. Grab a few cookies and do a little bit of heeling with lots of rewards. That way, your time in the ring is only a brief cookieless interlude between two highly rewarding sessions."

On the spot, I adopted that as standard practice for the remainder of HB's career.

■ ■ ■

Honeybear and I were now on a weekly schedule with Debby, Tuesday mornings at 10:30. That time was sacred. I planned all other commitments around it. Under Debby's guidance, and milking cookie power for all it was worth, HB and I were as exuberant as kids on Christmas morning.

Little by little my cupped hand elevated above HB's nose. Then my palm flattened and began to inch toward my waist. The treat was always there, nestled deep in the valley between my thumb and forefinger. Finally — and these transitions spanned many weeks — my hand was at my belt buckle, treat intact, where it would be as we heeled.

"Head up, eyes bright" — that was Patty Ruzzo's criterion for a happy, attentive dog. And now that was Honeybear.

We also enrolled in Debby's Utility class. "You've been in Open forever," she said, "it's time to move on." Of course she was right. We had finished our CDX on November 28, 1992, nearly two years earlier. But I had been obsessed with The Gaines, with competing there in Open and *placing*. We had come so close that first time in San Antonio. I *wanted* that.

I didn't want to screw up HB's Open performances by confusing her with the Utility exercises. At the time, that concern seemed ultravalid to me. The old demons of anxiety about "breaking" Honeybear were still running wild inside my head.

And now! Here it was, nearly September and we were entered in the Gaines Classic in Pasadena on November 19 and 20. *The Classic!* The best of the best.

Nevertheless, it *was* time to move on. Time to get into the Utility exercises. Time for the signals, the scent articles, the gloves, the go-outs, the directed jumping, the moving stand. Honeybear was going to love this stuff. Working more independently. Working at a distance. Lots of retrieving. Lots of jumping. And during the scent articles she'd get to sniff and it would be OK.

So we continued with one eye on Utility, the other looking toward Pasadena in mid-November.

■ ■ ■

As we embraced new training methods, moved into Utility and prepared for the Classic, I was also watching an interesting development at the park. There was big-time activity at the south end. Heavy machinery, grading. *Oh, oh!* I thought, *here comes the expressway.* But no. They were putting in two baseball diamonds.

In a sense, that was reassuring. *No way they're going to put in baseball diamonds*, I thought, *then turn right around and tear it up for a road.*

■ ■ ■

In spite of what I felt was subpar work during the first half of 1994, I had gone ahead with our entry in the Classic.

We had qualified with scores of 195 at the Palo Verde Golden Retriever Specialty at Tucson on November 19, 1993; 194.5 at Black Mountain Kennel Club of Nevada in Las Vegas on April 9, 1994, and an exhilarating third leg at Arizona White Mountain Kennel Club in Show Low, Arizona, on June 10, a 196.

With a requirement that our three qualifying scores average 195 or better, we squeaked through with an average of 195.16. Phew!

Our final AKC score, 11 days before we were to leave for the Classic, was troubling. We did a 188.5 at Phoenix Field and Obedience under Judge Harry Burke, the same judge who had awarded us a 196 at Show Low five months earlier. Hardly a confidence-building final tuneup.

Undaunted, one week before Thanksgiving Barbara and I and Honeybear loaded our stuff into the Suburban and headed west to participate in the top dog obedience competition event in America.

■ CHAPTER 30 ■

A Touch Of Class

*"Honeybear is my first obedience competition dog.
Training her to this level is simply the most
satisfying thing I have done in my lifetime."*
FROM HANDLER PROFILES

THE 1994 CYCLE UNITED STATES
DOG OBEDIENCE CLASSIC

Our judges wore tuxedos or evening gowns. The blue ring mats were placed atop a ballroom carpet. When you threw the dumbbell, it bit and stayed instead of skidding into a ring gate.

The formal name for the event was the 1994 Cycle United States Dog Obedience Classic. Better known as the Gaines Classic or just the Classic.

A Gaines tournament, under the overall aegis of the Illini Obedience Association — the founders and nurturers of Gaines events — was required to have a local sponsor. That local sponsor had to be an independent group, not an existing kennel club or obedience club. A group formed specifically to put on Gaines events. In Pasadena, the sponsoring group called itself the Pacific Obedience Association. The 1994 event was called "A Touch of Class."

In 1993, we had gone to the Gaines Western Regional in an RV ... and missed the ambience of the headquarters hotel. Not this time. I wanted to be where the action was. I wanted to mingle with the best dogs and trainers in America. I wanted to give Honeybear the opportunity to pee where the Big Dogs peed.

So we stayed at the Pasadena Hilton, a block or so from the show site, the Pasadena Center.

By acclamation and through my own experience in San Antonio, I knew Gaines events were put together and run to be models of exhibitor-friendliness.

It started as soon as we arrived at the hotel. We got off the elevator and walked down the hall toward our room. On the doors were the names of the dogs and handlers staying in each room. We came to our room. The large yellow sign featured a top hat and cane in the center. On the tophat it said "1994 Cycle Classic." At the top the words "Willard Bailey, My Partner 'Honeybear'" gave me goose bumps and brought tears ... and they still do. All those thousands of afternoons at the park — this is what they were about. Below our names, two large stars: In one, the word "Open." In the other, "from AZ." At the bottom "A Touch of Class." Indeed.

Our visit to the lobby was like touring the Hall of Fame of United States obedience dogs and handlers. There was Janice DeMello with Juice. Over there, Gary Platt and Bink. And Andrea Vaughan with Rocky.

There were 157 dogs entered in the event. As usual, the field was dominated by golden retrievers (46) and border collies (26). There were 17 Shelties among the 38 breeds represented. All were there by virtue of having won or placed at a 1994 regional. Or, like Honeybear and me, they had qualified by submitting three recent scores averaging 195 or better. The Classic attracted teams from 28 states.

The catalog showed two from Arizona: Willard Bailey with teammate Starbuc's Dream Come True, CDX (Honeybear) and Debby Boehm with Licorice Lilly, CDX (Lilly, a standard poodle owned by Kathryn Zatz). Both of us in the Open division. Imagine! HB and I competing against our mentor in the Gaines Classic.

■ ■ ■

Several levels below the lobby was the Potty Zone — the Ritz-Carlton of canine "exercise" facilities. Nothing better represented the million miserable little details the Pacific Obedience Association had deftly converted into the touches of class that made A Touch of Class a *real* touch of class.

The Potty Zone was located at one well-lighted end of the Pasadena Hilton garage's lower level, 12 floors and several long, carpeted hallways from our room — an exciting trip first thing in the morning.

The Home Depot had donated 600 square feet of sod. It was carefully laid atop several inches of straw. Pooper-scoopers and plastic bags were abundant, and used. The area was surrounded by hundreds of blown-up dog cartoons and even a graffiti board.

The sod was watered, deodorized and disinfected several times a day. On Sunday morning, because we were first in the ring at eight o'clock, we arrived at the Potty Zone at 5 a.m. There we encountered Mary Fry, co-chairperson of the event, laying fresh sod. Even the shit detail had class.

■ ■ ■

And how did the competition go? Those of us who showed in the Open division had our clocks cleaned by Terri Arnold and her golden retriever bitch Naughty — a light, fast, high-stepping dream. They lost two points out of a possible 600 during three runs. That's less than two-thirds of a point per run. About as close to perfect as you can get.

Photo: Barbara Bailey

The Gaines Classic, 1994: Skip, HB, Debby, Lilly.

Honeybear and I didn't burn up the ring, but we didn't embarrass ourselves, either. Across two intensive days in three rings with eagle-eyed judges, Honeybear heeled like ... well, like Honeybear. We lost less than two points per run on the heel free and figure eight.

Unfortunately, she also fronted like Honeybear and mouthed the dumbbell like Honeybear. All in all, our runs were sloppy, and we didn't get a perfect score on any exercise. A point here, two points there; they add up. We scored a 191 and two 190s to finish 18th out of 49 Open entries.

Debby and Lilly, on the other hand, popped off a pretty 196.5 in their second ring. They seemed to be cooking up another solid run in the third ring when Lilly, during the drop on recall, chose to sit rather than drop. There went 30 points. They finished 26th.

Closing out a not-so-hot year, we had held our own in the most demanding, exciting, satisfying dog obedience test in America.

On Monday morning we drove back across I-10. As HB rested her chin on my leg, I said, "We gotta get ready, big girl. Only nine months until the Gaines Western Regional in Salt Lake City next August."

■ CHAPTER 31 ■

Cookie Power In Action

The Gaines Classic brought down the curtain on our 1994 obedience competition season. We weren't planning to be in the ring again until the Phoenix Field and Obedience Club trial on February 25, 1995.

Once again I was teaching Honeybear new things, the part of training I enjoyed most. Watching her learn and knowing I had taught her was the most fulfilling thing I had done in my life.

Debby welcomed a time when we were free to dismantle exercise components that were malfunctioning and go hellbent about fixing them. "One of the problems with Honeybear's training," she had said from time to time, "is that you always have a show coming up in a week or two. We're always tiptoeing around the problems to avoid breaking something right before the next show."

HB was a notorious sniffing machine, right from Day One in puppy kindergarten. Now it was time to harness that. Time for HB to sniff with a purpose, sniff well and get treats for it. Learning the scent discrimination exercise came fairly easily to her, although neither Debby nor I could have predicted that she would become one of the great scent articles dogs in the sport.

Although she was far from an overnight phenom, she was having a blast learning her new exercises.

It was great fun to run out, snatch the glove and bring it back. Never mind that part of the fun was tossing it in the air and (usually) catching it on the way back.

Go-outs were fun because there was cheese on the center post or a treat on the ground at the base.

By December 16, I felt confident enough to enter HB in Utility at a Precision Canine practice match at the training building. Although Debby saw half a dozen things wrong with each exercise, HB didn't make any huge mistakes. I felt relieved to have broken the ice in Utility.

■ ■ ■

Although the focus was now on Utility, many of the same old bugaboos continued to haunt us.

My training was frenetic. Left to my own devices, I would instantly reward Honeybear as soon as an exercise was finished.

"Don't reward so quickly," Debby would say. "If it's a good finish or a good front, let her sit for a few seconds. Let her *see* the correct position, solidify it. Then reward." Which I would do for a few repetitions or even a couple of days. Then the toboggan would start down the hill again.

During heeling patterns or figure eights, I would reflexively step into my dog as we halted. During one of our first lessons in Debby's backyard in 1991, she had said, "You're stepping into Honeybear with your left foot."

That refrain was to be repeated nearly every time I heeled HB in Debby's presence. Indeed, it cost us half a point now and then throughout HB's career.

For a time, I tried lightly kicking the inside of my right ankle with my left foot as we halted. Without result. I must have a stepping-in gene that will not be denied.

Then too, despite years of Debby's admonitions, my approach to training remained too stiff, too formal, too regimented.

And of course there was the broken-record (but valid) admonition, "Willard, remember to breathe."

■ ■ ■

If Honeybear had a fan club, Barbara's parents, Gladys and Bob, were co-presidents. They'd fly in from Cincinnati twice a year and lavish attention on the dogs — buying toys, playing ball, engaging in tug-of-war.

They liked to go to the park with us, watch, even participate. They'd put out scent articles and gloves and they made dandy posts for the figure eight.

Shortly before Christmas in 1994, I invited Bob to go to class with us at the training building. He was 93 at the time and would live four more years. He sat in one of the white plastic chairs in front of the windows. Sitting there in his inevitable dark suit, white shirt and wild tie, Bob watched intently for the entire hour. When class was over, he said, "I'm glad we're going home. I'm uncomfortable in a place where the dogs are smarter than I am."

■ ■ ■

As we prepared to resume showing in late February of 1995, it became clear that Debby's relentless prodding about fundamentals had not been in vain. And our headlong plunge into the Patty Ruzzo method had been just what the doctor ordered. My over-the-top use of food had those who trained with us or competed against us rolling their eyes and shaking their heads. "He's ruining that dog," some whispered. And The Coven were seething. But it sure was working for us.

We were not yet ready to make our Utility debut, but we returned to the Open B ring smoking.

On February 25, at PFOC, we scored a 198.5.

We followed that with a 196 under Judge Marilyn Little at the Valle del Sol Golden Retriever Club Specialty Show on

March 3. Three weeks later we showed under her again at Sahuaro State Kennel Club and did a 197.

The next day, under old favorite Nancy Pollock, we got a 196 at Yuma Kennel Club. We did another 196 (HB's favorite score) under Judge Christine Wright at Cañada del Oro Kennel Club on April 9.

"Where were those scores last November at the Classic?" I asked HB.

■ ■ ■

I considered it a stroke of unusual good luck that we had showed twice under Marilyn Little that spring. We were committed to show in the Open division at the Gaines Western Regional in Salt Lake City on August 12 and 13, and I knew she would be one of our judges.

Marilyn and husband Bob — residents of Mesa, here in the Valley of the Sun — used an unusual heeling pattern. And most judges employ the same pattern whenever they judge. As one judge put it, "That's the only way I can remember the pattern."

So I saw our two spring outings under Judge Little as opportunities to get a leg and paw up on our chances at The Gaines. What's more, Barbara videotaped each ring appearance.

Therefore, not only did we showcase HB at darn near her best, I also had every command, every step of Judge Little's heeling pattern on tape, twice. Next I played the tapes over and over and counted each step of each segment of the pattern.

It started in the center of one end of the ring. Six steps to the first halt, opposite the high jump. Then forward two steps to a left turn, three steps before a right turn, three more steps before another right turn. Then a slow across the ring. And so on. The beauty of it was this wasn't someone else walking that pattern. It was Honeybear and me, with my stride length, my footwork on the halts, and so on.

From the end of March right on through the practice ring the day before Gaines competition began, there weren't many days when HB and I didn't practice Judge Little's heeling pattern, step by step, multiple times.

"Come on, HB," I'd say, "we're gonna practice Marilyn Little's heeling pattern." Honeybear would light up. After all, there were four or five treats in that exercise.

"One thing about it," I told people, "if I die of fright at The Gaines, right before Marilyn's ring, HB can go in alone and do it all by herself."

We showed in Open B through the Kennel Club of Beverly Hills on June 25, where we did a so-so 191. The rest of June, all of July and the early part of August I devoted to polishing our Open skills in preparation for my favorite event, The Gaines.

We left for Salt Lake City on August 9. Pumped. Confident. Feeling our oats.

■ CHAPTER 32 ■

Answered Prayers

"You are never given a dream without also being given the power to make it come true."
RICHARD BACH

SALT LAKE CITY, UTAH
AUGUST 13, 1995

It's a Sunday morning. I'm standing at the urinal in the Salt Palace Convention Center. Peeing and praying.

Dear God, please let us have just one more good run. You've allowed us to get this far, now let us have one more good run. Actually, the best run of our lives would be just about right.

In a few minutes Honeybear and I will enter our third and final ring of the Open division at the 1995 Gaines Western Regional Dog Obedience Championship.

The fun had begun as we drove into downtown Salt Lake City. The Wasatch Front Obedience Association, the local sponsoring group, had adorned the downtown streets with 7½-foot-tall yellow banners proclaiming the event. Each banner featured the names of one of the teams.

Suddenly, on West Temple Street, there was ours! **Willard Bailey and Honeybear**.

That was Friday. It's been wall-to-wall goose bumps ever since.

Yesterday, in Judge Marilyn Little's ring, Honeybear heeled like a dream. Those hundreds of practice run-throughs of Marilyn's heeling pattern sure hadn't hurt. HB also dropped on the spot and retrieved like a demon. But she fronted at 45 degrees and mouthed the dumbbell like it was a hambone. We lost four points, the equivalent of a 196 in AKC competition.

In Gaines tournaments, the top ten scoring teams in the Open division win ribbons, plaques and cash prizes. The first-day tabulations handed out at the cocktail party yesterday evening had shown Honeybear and me tied with another team for ninth place.

"All right, Honeybear," I had said, "I don't know what tomorrow will bring, but tonight, for this one day at least, we're in the thick of it with some of the best obedience competition teams in America. Good girl!"

Now, on Sunday morning, as we head for our final ring, we're still in the hunt.

Earlier this morning, in Judge Joe Heidinger's ring, we had popped off another minus four: sensational heeling, lousy fronts, big-time mouthing. We stand at minus eight after two Gaines rings.

Please, dear God, just one more good run.

By now a large crowd has gathered around Ring Four, aware that the Open division soon will culminate here. This ring is the domain of Judge Suzanne Mayborne, a large woman with red hair. Her presence dominates the proceedings.

We enter her ring, surrender our leash to the steward and position ourselves for the heel free exercise.

"Are you ready?" Judge Mayborne asks.

"Ready!" I respond. Honeybear's head pops up; her eyes lock on mine.

"Forward." And here we go.

Pit-pat, pit-pat, pit-pat. Blue rubber mats over concrete. I hear Honeybear's every step. She's right there through the turns, the slow, the fast. Eyes locked on mine. *Good girl.*

Finally, "Halt. Exercise finished."

Drop on recall: She comes bounding toward me, drops like she's shot, gives me a crooked front, finishes nicely.

What a trouper this dog is. Our third pressure-packed Gaines ring in less than 20 hours and she's still *charging* the dumbbell, *exploding* over the high jump, *driving* across the broad jump ... and, well, *mouthing* with gusto.

At the final "Exercise finished," I'm elated — and Honeybear is beside herself with joy. Before I can get her out of the ring, she vents her exuberance with two sharp barks.

"Half a point per bark," Judge Mayborne will tell me later. And so in our final ring, with everything on the line, we score a minus 5.5 instead of the 4.5 an excellent performance had warranted.

Lunch is subdued. We've lost 13.5 points out of a possible 600 — an average of 195.5 for three tough Gaines rings. Not bad, but possibly two barks short of a Gaines placement.

After lunch I say, "Well, let's find out. Let's count them."

Open competition has been completed. All three scores for the 41 teams in our division have been posted. Not ranked, but there they are. OK, how many have lost less than 13.5 points?

I begin to count. One, two ... eight?!

I call Barbara. "*You* count them." She does: *eight.*

YES! We are in ninth place. We have finally achieved a Gaines placement in our third Gaines tournament.

The tears come later, in the dog potty area. Only Honeybear knows.

Soon the awards ceremony begins. Bleachers packed, chairs set up in front, people standing in the wings.

August 13, 1995: At last! A Gaines placement.

Our turn. We heel to center stage. Perfect. HB is still up for whatever we do.

While the PA announcer reads our biographical information, the photographer is determined that Honeybear, seated in heel position, eyes locked on mine, is going to look at the camera. I'm unable to suppress a laugh.

A whistle. A buzzer. Clucking noises. Every trick in the photographer's book. Honeybear's eyes remain locked on mine.

"What's her name?" the photographer asks.

"Honeybear!" I respond with verve. And that clinches it. HB, now certain she's being set up, locks even tighter, hardly blinking.

Finally I say, "She isn't going to look at you. This is an obedience competition dog, she watches me." The crowd laughs and there is scattered applause.

On Monday we drive 654 miles back to Phoenix. The wheels never touch the ground.

CHAPTER 33

Sleight Of Hand

We showed once more in 1995, at Phoenix Field and Obedience Club early in November. Our Open B score of 196.5, under Judge Bob Little, set us up for a runoff for fourth place. We lost that runoff on a halt when I gave HB mixed signals. She went halfway into a sit, froze there and gave me the most confused look I had ever seen on her face.

Nevertheless, 1995 had been a banner year. We had knocked off some nice scores and above all had placed at The Gaines. That itch had been scratched once and for all. Now it was time to bear down, to focus on getting HB ready for the Utility ring.

Here she was, about to turn seven, a time when many dogs are retiring, an age when they become eligible for the Veterans ring, the nonregular class for the "old" dogs. And HB had yet to set foot in an AKC Utility ring. I felt a bit panicky about that.

Utility had finally gotten my attention, so bear down we did.

■ ■ ■

About that time the germ of an intriguing idea invaded my head. True, we were getting good scores on our heel free and figure eight. But HB's heeling *looked* better than it felt.

It was like the baseball player who hits a little Texas Leaguer that barely makes it over the infield and finds a spot in the outfield grass, just beyond diving players and outstretched gloves.

"It was just a blooper," the player will say, "but it will look like a line drive in the box score tomorrow morning."

A day or two after a show Debby would look at the video-tape and nearly always be critical of Honeybear's heeling.

"My God, we lost only a point and a half," I'd say.

Debby would counter with, "Yes, but she's pacing and hanging there, not driving."

She was right. When I was heeling HB in a show, I often had the feeling I should slow down so she would move up an inch or two. But then she'd slow down, too.

But when I had food in my left hand (the hand I placed at my belt buckle as I heeled), Honeybear drove at my side. Much prettier if not better. And prettier was important because the heel free and figure eight combined to be the first exercise. They set the tone for our entire appearance in the ring. Both in terms of my psychological state and the judge's mental set about our level of excellence.

No doubt about it, in order to get HB to *be* a line drive rather than just look like a line drive on the score sheet, I needed to have a treat in my left hand when we heeled … or have Honeybear think I did.

Hmmm. *Have Honeybear think I did.* Thus an idea was born.

Debby once commented that every shirt I owned had two breast pockets. Indeed, I sought out and bought shirts with two pockets and flaps that buttoned (the better to keep treats from spilling out when I bent over). They were my training shirts. One or both pockets always had an abundant supply of Grreat Choice small puppy biscuits.

Picture us getting ready to heel. The treats are in my left shirt pocket. I say, "Heelwork, Honeybear, heelwork." She knows exactly what that means, exactly what's coming. As I say that, I reach into my left shirt pocket, extract a treat with my left thumb and forefinger and place my hand at my belt buckle. HB has been observing my movements and responds with intense interest.

At various times as we heel, my left hand leaves its position at my belt buckle, moves down to the left side of HB's face (to force her butt in rather than allowing it to swing out as she reaches for the food) and gives her the treat.

I've used treats to reinforce many parts of a good heeling performance.

"Ready!" is my signal that here we go. As we prepare to embark on the heeling pattern, the judge asks, "Are you ready?" I want HB's head to come up and her eyes to lock on my face when she hears, "Ready!"

So we practiced that a zillion times when I was teaching HB attention, and we've revisited it periodically throughout her career. I'd say, "Ready!" She'd look up and I'd reach into my pocket and drop a treat. We did that over and over until her response was automatic.

Dogs also have a tendency to drop their heads about two steps into the heeling pattern. So we'd heel two steps, then pop a treat. Start over: two steps, pop a treat. A zillion times.

Then too, dogs also tend to relax their attention on the slow. *Aw, this is a piece of cake. I can do this with my eyes closed.* That's why I fed HB lots of treats during the slow, to encourage her to keep her head up.

Nearly always, in practice, I'd end a fast by popping Honeybear a treat. The anticipation of the reward kept her driving forward with her head up.

I also learned that a well-timed treat is good medicine for a laggy about turn. The treat is given when you are about 90 percent through the turn, just before you step out to continue straight-line heeling. Anticipation of the reward causes the dog to drive through the turn.

Honeybear, then, was conditioned to expect treats during a heeling pattern. She knew they could be expected at any point during the pattern. When she thought they were there and might be dispensed at any moment, she was driven by expectation. Ears up, eyes bright ... and driving throughout the heeling pattern.

Clearly, it was time to introduce my own brand of heeling sleight of hand.

At the time, there were abundant fun matches in our area. Two to three a month. Plenty of opportunities to practice my brainstorm.

As we moved from the ring gate to the spot where heeling was to start — whether that be across the ring or just a few feet from the gate — I'd say "Heelwork, Honeybear, heelwork." My left hand would come up, thumb and forefinger would dip into my left breast pocket, emerge and go to my belt. Of course, there was nothing in my pocket. HB had gotten the final treat as we heeled toward the ring gate.

I had refined my little prestidigitation act to the point where, as I placed my hand at my belt, my thumb and forefinger touched at the tips, as if I were clasping a treat.

It worked.

Honeybear began to heel with more spirit, driving to be at the forward limit of heel position rather than hanging at the back edge.

Several months and a slew of practice matches later it was time to swallow hard, take a deep breath and bring HB out in Utility.

CHAPTER 34

Utility ... At Last!

U tility A is a riot. It's much more demanding than Open because the dog has so much more to think about. Much of the dog's work is done independently and at a distance from the handler.

Utility is where many handlers pay the piper for a shaky foundation of sloppy fundamentals.

Lack of attention may be the biggest culprit. How is the dog going to respond correctly to your hand signals, being given at a distance of 40 feet, when he's gawking at something interesting outside the ring?

How is the dog going to get the correct glove when, instead of watching you during the pivot, he's scanning all three gloves? Deciding which one he's going to charge out and grab before you can give him a line to the glove the judge has selected.

And it's amazing how many dogs reach the Utility level without learning to heel well.

It's in Utility A that you hear handlers begin to talk about "green" dogs. In fact, Utility is so difficult that a green phase is a given. That wet-behind-the-ears stage may last for quite some time before you can begin to refer to your Utility dog as "seasoned."

Many dogs — perhaps a majority — are brought out in Utility A before they are ready to cope with the unforgiving nature of the exercises in that class. It is not uncommon for the entire class to flunk. I can still hear Harry Burke, volunteering as a steward for a Utility A class here in Phoenix, as he turned to several bystanders, shook his head and said, "It's a blood bath in there."

Therefore, I was not surprised by what happened on May 5, 1996 when I brought Honeybear out in Utility at the Greater Sierra Vista Kennel Club.

Of the 13 teams entered in Utility A that day under Judge Betty Ribble, HB and I were the only ones to qualify, with a score of 189.5. Not sensational, but it was a first place and our first UD leg in our first try.

We flunked when next we showed, June 8 at Flagstaff Kennel Club. But the next day, under Judge Alvin Lee, we did a 189 for a second place and our second leg.

Next came a cluster of three shows in Ventura, California early in July. It was called Summerfest. The shows were put on by Ventura, Channel City and Santa Maria Kennel Clubs. I had been told it was a lovely show venue — the Ventura County Fairgrounds, only a few hundred yards from the Pacific Ocean. A cool respite from the scorching heat of Phoenix in July.

Three days of obedience trials. Three chances to get that final UD leg. We entered and went.

Ventura in July lived up to the hype I had been hearing. Lovely. Cool. Just right for a dog show.

We arrived on July 3, giving us July 4 to set up and practice. Competition would begin July 5.

When they finished setting up the rings early in the afternoon on July 4, I had a mild anxiety attack. It involved Honeybear's upcoming directed jumping exercises. I had never seen so many poles at one end of an obedience ring. Honeybear was well-trained to go out to the center pole at the opposite end of the ring, or the center stanchion if ring gates were used.

That afternoon I got down on my knees at one end of the ring, at eye level of a seated Honeybear, to see what she would be looking at when I told her, "Straight."

The ring was made of white poles with white chain. With four poles across the end of the ring instead of the customary five, there was no center pole. The ring was also double-roped with rebar and blue rope (to keep spectators and hamburger-eating kids at a respectable distance). That's two rows of poles.

Immediately beyond the ring there were several light poles. A third row. Beyond the light poles a row of tents, perhaps ten more poles.

And there I was with a grass-green dog. "How will HB ever do a straight go-out?" I moaned.

We flunked all three days. But none of our mishaps had anything to do with the maze of poles. Across the three Utility classes during that early July weekend, Honeybear did six of her prettiest go-outs. She went out straight as an arrow, then turned and plopped into a sit without so much as one step. It was other Utility gremlins that got us.

On the first day, I left her on the signal stand and set out for the opposite end of the ring to give the hand signals. In front of me, the people at the opposite end of the ring were laughing. *My God*, I thought, *do I look that stressed?* Then I turned around to give the signals and saw what they were laughing at. HB had sat down to scratch behind her ear. It didn't itch, it was stress. A big zero for Day One.

On the second day she got the wrong glove. Two down.

Day Three featured her best Utility run to date. We were in the low to mid-190s when the roof fell in. We made it as far as part two of directed jumping, the final exercise in Utility. Out she went. Perfect. One for the highlights film. "Bar jump," Judge Lawrence Libeu said. Out went my right arm. "Bar!" I called. HB set sail for the bar jump, then changed her mind and her course and came straight down the middle into a rare perfect front. "Look at me," she said, "aren't I perfect?"

Oh well. Ventura is lovely in July. And so was my big girl.

■ ■ ■

Billie Rosen had raved about a show held in August at Woodland Hills, California. It was a one-night stand, the obedience trial of Valley Hills Obedience Club. It was staged inside the football stadium of Taft High School on Ventura Boulevard. Billie told me there were six rings and six judges — one for each class, so the trial clipped along smoothly.

I decided to take our next shot at a third UD leg at the Valley Hills show.

Our motel, the Vagabond Inn, was decidedly past its prime but directly across the street from the football field. If you could make it across busy Ventura Boulevard without getting run down, you were home free.

The show would be held on Saturday evening, August 17. We arrived late Friday and walked across the street to see the show site. The field was a mess. Obviously the school did not maintain the football field in the summer and the club had rented it as-is. Grass and weeds were six inches tall. How, I wondered, could they hold an obedience trial there?

The next morning I found out. Bright and early, what appeared to be the entire Valley Hills Obedience Club was out there with mowers and rakes. By show time, the field had been manicured. White posts and chains defined the rings. Green canopies covered the judges' tables.

By evening, it was a beautiful picture under the daylight brightness of the stadium lights.

Only one other dog, a dalmatian, qualified in Utility A. He was working nicely until the directed jumping exercise. At which point he ran out on both parts of the exercise and gave the pole a long, searching sniff. Finally, disappointed that the cheese wasn't there, he turned and sat. Big-time points off.

Under Judge Peggy Garic, Honeybear won Utility A that evening with a score of 189. That was her third leg. We had finished our UD in a respectable seven tries.

Indeed, HB was heeling better since I had introduced the little ploy of reaching into my empty pocket for a phantom treat before the start of the heeling pattern.

CHAPTER 35

"You've Got OTCH Points"

The Valley Hills Obedience Club trial was the last time I showed Honeybear in Utility A. The AKC had introduced a new title less than three years earlier. It was called Utility Dog Excellent (UDX) and was designed to give obedience people another rung on the competition ladder, beyond a UD but short of the ultra-demanding Obedience Trial Championship (OTCH).

The OTCH is the supreme title in AKC obedience competition and is the only title that is truly competitive. The CD, CDX, UD and UDX each requires a certain number of "legs" (ring appearances with qualifying scores). OTCH points, on the other hand, are based on the number of dogs defeated in Open B and Utility B. One hundred points are required. It's a long, tough grind, demanding skills, tenacity and financial commitment far beyond the reach of most obedience competitors.

So in the lion's share of cases, when a team finishes a UDX, the title game is over. They may continue to show in obedience competition, but given the practical aspects and ability demands of seeking an OTCH, there is nothing left to shoot for.

The UDX requires that the dog/handler team qualify in both Utility B and Open B on the same day ten times (i.e., ten legs are required).

Well, why not? HB would be seven in December, but she was in great shape, loved to work and play with me and we were getting good scores in both Open and Utility. Although she was a seasoned Open dog, she was still green in Utility. It figured we would only get better.

Recently, as we had focused on getting our UD, I had concentrated on Utility. And while I had entered HB in both Open and Utility in a few matches, she had yet to experience the pressure of doing both rings — often within minutes of one another — at an AKC trial. Of course, she had been required to compete in the Open ring twice in one morning each time we went to The Gaines. And had frisked through both rings.

■ ■ ■

We got started on our UDX as quickly as possible after Valley Hills. Shortly after we arrived home I sent in our entries for the Prescott Arizona Kennel Club shows, to be held September 14 and 15.

Those shows were held at Pioneer Park on the outskirts of Prescott. The park is a huge grassy area with a couple of baseball fields and a large multipurpose building in the center. If you survive hauling your stuff up and down the long, steep walkway that connects the lower-level field with the upper-level parking lot, it's an excellent show site.

The morning of September 14 got off to a scary start. I always make sure HB gets a decent warm-up the morning of a show. We play a little ball, then I call her over a high jump three times. The jump is set at the same height she will have to clear in the ring that morning. It may be several hours before she enters the ring, but at least she has had a chance to see and gauge the jump height in advance.

As soon as the sun came up, I took HB to the far end of the field, threw the tennis ball a few times, then led her to the high jump I had set up. I put her on a sit, walked to a position on the other side of the jump and called, "Over!"

BANG! She crashed into the jump, pulled it over and rolled over herself. She had hit it so hard she took a piece out of the top board. Fortunately, I use lightweight vinyl plastic jumps to practice. They give way and turn over easily. HB got up looking dazed, but she wasn't hurt. As as soon as I determined she was OK, I set up the jump and called her over it several more times. I never want fear to begin gestating in a dog's brain. The impression I wanted her to take from the experience was that of a successful jump … and the treat that followed.

The judges arrived a bit later. Chris Cornell and Nancy Craig are highly competent, veteran obedience judges. They took one look at the two obedience rings, constructed of heavy white ring gates, and conferred. Then they summoned the obedience chairman and asked that the rings be taken down and repositioned.

Correctly set up, outdoor obedience rings are oriented so that the long dimension (50 feet) runs north/south. Those who had set up the rings for the Prescott shows had the 50-foot dimension going east/west. The problem being that dogs would be jumping into a rising sun. Or they'd be trying to see the hand signals with that sun at the handler's back. Or both. So the start of competition had to be delayed while the rings were taken down, reoriented and set up all over again. I was happy to wait. I had already experienced one jumping near-disaster that morning. I didn't want to try for two.

That was the end of the bad news for Saturday, September 14, 1996.

Honeybear jumped enthusiastically and well in both rings. We scored 194 in Open B and 193 in Utility B (our best Utility score to date), both under Judge Cornell. We had notched our first UDX leg in our first try. But there was more.

That 193 in Utility B was good for second place. As I left the Utility awards presentation carrying our red ribbon, Dick

Guetzloff appeared at my side. "You've got OTCH points," he said. I was startled. And amused. The idea of HB and me pursuing an OTCH seemed far-fetched to the point of being ludicrous. But, in fact, second place in Utility B that morning had been good for two points.

I spent the rest of the day laughing and saying, "Well, we only need another 98 points."

■ CHAPTER 36 ■

On A Roll

With one UDX leg under our belts and feeling our oats, we flunked Open B at Scottsdale Dog Fanciers. HB was cruising along with a mid-190s score until we got to the long sit with handlers out of sight. In the adjacent Open A ring, the drop-on-recall exercise was in progress. The handler in that ring boomed out a strong, "Down!" I don't know what her dog did but in our ring two goldens dropped obediently. One of them was HB. When I returned to the ring she actually looked pleased with herself: "See, Skippy, I did as I was told even when you weren't here."

The good news is that on that same morning, under long-time favorite Nancy Pollock, we finished second in Utility B and picked up two more OTCH points. (HB did not jump on her and give her a big wet smacker this time.) Now we had four points. On the drive home from Scottsdale that afternoon I felt the first itch — the first glimmer of the impossible dream. The date was November 8, 1996.

On November 23, at Sahuaro State Kennel Club, enroute to our third UDX leg, we had a stroke of good luck. At first, our chance for a win looked slim.

Sandra Davis, from El Paso, Texas, is one of the most creative, brilliant obedience competition trainers in America. She is also one of the winningest. And she was in our Utility B and Open B classes with her splendid border collie Pepper.

In Utility B, under Judge Harry Burke, the class led off with the signal exercise — no verbal commands allowed, only hand signals. When the judge said, "Forward," Sandra said, "Heel!" She took two steps, then clasped her hand over her mouth. But the damage had been done. That little "whoops" cost her five points and first place.

HB and I won the class with a nothing-to-write-home-about 190. But it was good for four more OTCH points.

Later that day I told Barbara, "It's much too early to make any commitments, but if we have 20 OTCH points when we finish our UDX, maybe we ought to make a run for it."

I had heard the giants of our sport — most notably Dick Guetzloff — talk of the rigors of "campaigning a dog." But at the time, Barbara and I were clueless as to how much time, money, blood, sweat, and tears can be scattered along the OTCH trail.

Honeybear was working well. So was the "pocket charade." I believe HB knew there wasn't really any food in that pocket or between the clasped thumb and forefinger. But hope springs eternal in the fuzzy yellow head of a food-driven golden retriever. And the concept of *there could be* brought Honeybear new life in the competition ring.

Her fan club grew. Known wherever we went as "such a happy, happy dog," she had long since become a ringside favorite (except, of course, with The Coven). Our scores weren't bad, either. We were knocking off an amazing number of right-on-the-nose 196s in Open B. At the same time, our Utility B scores were moving steadily upward. Utility scores in the mid-190s were popping up with encouraging regularity.

The end of the year found us on a roll. By the end of 1996, we had seven of the required 10 UDX legs. We were heading into the UDX homestretch. But we had been stuck at nine OTCH points since Thanksgiving weekend.

■ ■ ■

By early 1997, Debby was saying, "HB is really steady, Willard." Honeybear was a well-seasoned Open dog. Now I considered her a seasoned Utility dog as well. She knew the exercises and she simply went into the ring and did her job — then exploded with barking, tail-wagging glee when we were done. Less proud of what she had just done than excited about the Bonz she knew she was about to get.

■ ■ ■

Our next show weekend was the PFOC spring trials, February 22 and 23. We practiced at the show site, Pierce Park, twice before that weekend.

Honeybear picked up where she had left off at the end of 1996. Prancing, wagging, frisking all weekend, she knocked off scores of 193.5 and 196.5 in Open B and 196 and 196.5 in Utility B. *And* our third high combined in our run for a UDX. *And* two more UDX legs, one short of our title. *And* six OTCH points, giving us 15.

The Coven, there in force that weekend, looked on and scowled.

■ ■ ■

In late winter here, the shows come in rapid succession. Six days later, on March 1, we were back in the ring again. This time at Superstition Kennel Club. Again, it was high excitement. Honeybear needed just one leg to finish her UDX. But she chose that morning to *again* hear the loud, "Down!" in the next ring and respond. Although this time she at least looked uneasy about it when I returned to the ring. Ah well, there's always tomorrow.

On Sunday HB and I did a 195.5 in Open B under Nancy Pollock and a 193 in Utility B under Sharon Ann Redmer. Yes, the same judge who, on our bleakest day in Novice, with good humor and light encouragement may have kept us from washing out.

I asked Judge Redmer to be the one to share our UDX photo with us.

What a pair to finish our UDX under! Nancy Pollock whose good-humored tolerance averted disaster in our first ring at our first Gaines. Sharon Ann Redmer who had been the right person in the right place at the right time.

■ ■ ■

All that year we watched a large construction project taking place on the east edge of Paradise Valley Park. It turned out to be a community swimming pool and bathhouse. OK, that clinched it. First the baseball fields three years ago. Now the swimming facilities. So much for the rumors about the expressway coming through. I wondered how such nonsense got started.

■ CHAPTER 37 ■

Guilty Until Proven Innocent

We had accumulated 15 OTCH points by the time we finished our UDX, not the 20 I had said would be required to continue. But what the hell, HB was only seven. She was in great condition. She was happy. And she was working better than at any other time in her career. Me? I was having the time of my life.

"Let's go for it!" I said.

Barbara just rolled her eyes.

■ ■ ■

We didn't stay five points short of our 20-point goal for long. Two weeks after we finished our UDX we were entered in the Kennel Club of Palm Springs obedience trials. It was one of the most spectacularly successful, memorable weekends in Honeybear's competition career. On Saturday we won Open B, finished second in Utility B, took high combined, beat Louise Meredith and Riot in a runoff for high in trial, and picked up nine OTCH points.

The following day we did a 194.5 in Open B and a 197.5 in Utility B. No OTCH points that day, but that weekend provided the psychological thrust we needed. With 24 OTCH points, we were nearly a quarter of the way there. All the way back to Phoenix I kept saying, "We're goin' for it HB! We're goin' for it!" From her position on the floor between our bucket seats, Honeybear rested her chin against my leg, looked directly into my eyes and said, "Breakfast was at four o'clock this morning, Skippy. When do we eat?"

■ ■ ■

Something else happened that weekend. Something destined to reverberate for a long time.

While HB and I stormed through Saturday's classes, a small clique of Southern California handlers watched intently.

The next day, as I heeled my red-hot dog toward the Open B ring of Judge Marilyn Little, I popped my final treat into HB's mouth. Observing that, Judge Little said, "Willard, please empty your pockets and leave the treats on the table."

I patted my upper-left shirt pocket. "Nothing there," I assured the judge.

"How about your pants pocket?"

Silence engulfed the area. The Southern California watchbirds leaned forward in their lawn chairs. It was like one of those old commercials where, over lunch, someone utters the words, "E.F. Hutton says" … and the restaurant falls silent.

I checked my pants pocket for effect. I'd never had a treat in there in my life. "Nothing," I assured the judge.

While Judge Little measured Honeybear, I explained my routine. "Before we leave our setup for ringside, I count exactly seven treats," I told her. "I slip them into my upper left pocket. As the judge tallies the score on the previous team and the stewards reset the jumps, I keep Honeybear focused by saying, 'Watch!' and occasionally popping her a treat.

"I have all this precisely timed," I said. "When the steward beckons us, I have only one treat left. Honeybear gets it before we reach the ring gate."

What I was detailing for the judge, of course, was my Patty Ruzzo cookie-power method in action. Treats all the way to the ring. Plus my own little twist, dipping into my empty left pocket right before the start of the heeling pattern.

Once that little conversation was out of the way, we proceeded with our ring run.

We didn't win either class that day. We lost a runoff for third in Open B when I accidentally ran HB into a ring pole on an about turn. Perhaps I was off balance from the weight of all those treats I allegedly had in my pockets.

Throughout the day, the Southern California watchbirds focused on us whenever we entered the ring. After all, we were carpetbaggers from Arizona and we had soundly thrashed a few of them the day before.

And perhaps Honeybear had been heard to mutter, "California dogs ... sheeit!"

Later I was told Judge Little had been asked to check me for contraband treats.

■ ■ ■

A month later we were at PFOC on Monday evening for ring run-throughs. A voice called out, "Congratulations, Willard!" It was Harry Burke, AKC judge, PFOC member and all-around good guy.

"Thanks," I answered, thinking he was referring to our big day in Palm Springs. He was, but only tangentially.

"You've arrived as a competitive handler," he said. "Now you're in the same league as Dick Guetzloff — you're a marked man."

Then he went on to explain. He had had a judging assignment in Simi Valley (northwest of Los Angeles) the previous weekend. "A group was talking about competitors who cheat," Harry said, "and your name came up. They were contending that you carry food into the ring. I told them no way. 'His dog *thinks* he has food but he doesn't. Willard doesn't need to do that, he's too good.'"

The reference to Dick Guetzloff was a compliment. At the time, Dick and Sweep were steamrollering through the obedience world, pulverizing the competition. They were averaging 25 OTCH points per weekend. That's an OTCH a month. Currently they were closing in on 7,500 points, 75 OTCHs!

Harry was right. Dick was a marked man, probably *the* most marked in the sport. Dick and Sweep had long been the subjects of outrageous rumors. His detractors liked to say, "Nobody can win that much without cheating."

The rumor of the week at that time was that Dick had some sort of homing device in his trademark black hat, or belt buckle, and a microchip in Sweep's head.

Certainly the rumors about Honeybear and me weren't *that* ridiculous. But we had cleaned a few clocks in Southern California recently and the natives were restless.

A few weeks later, PFOC President Erik Hoyer called. "Willard," he said, "one of our members was at a training session last night. The rumor there was that you've been suspended by the AKC for carrying food into the ring."

After reassuring Erik that there wasn't a grain of truth to any of it, I gave him what had by then become my standard response. "I certainly hope HB is as sure that I have food in the ring as are the watchbirds in Southern California."

That evening, before class at Precision Canine, the rumor came up again. By now it was *everywhere*. It had taken on a life of its own.

At that point I wrote an article for the PFOC Newsletter, with an eye to distributing reprints. I told the saga that I have just restated above and closed with these paragraphs:

> *I am a shameless, incorrigible, dedicated, unrepentant, in-your-face food trainer. A disciple of Patty Ruzzo. A firm believer in the statement of Ted Turner, the famous Sea World trainer: "You can't put a prong collar on a dolphin."*

My dogs may not be the best in the United States. But I doubt any, anywhere — in training or in the ring — are happier. When I see some of the poor lifeless, frightened, stressed creatures that drag around the competition rings, it reaffirms my approach to training.

Honeybear never, ever heels without treats ... except in the AKC ring. As I've said, I hope Honeybear is as convinced as are the rumormongers of Southern California that I really do have food in my pocket.

Sorry guys. Try Dick Guetzloff. Confidentially — now don't repeat this — during long sits and downs he puts his hat on a stick and holds it above the blind.

When the article came out, I sent a stack of copies to Louise Meredith — who has since become a warm, generous friend — and asked her to distribute them among her friends. Louise called. "You're going to have a lot of people in Southern California mad at you," she said.

With tongue squarely in cheek, I told her how horribly upset I'd be if that happened.

On August 16, we were entered in Valley Hills Obedience Club's evening trial in Woodland Hills, our first trip to California since the Palm Springs incident. This would be Watchbird Central. I was fascinated to see what would happen.

The watchbirds were there in force that night. Each time we entered the ring they emerged from their tents to line up at ringside. The better to get a good look.

And each time, I dipped my left thumb and forefinger into my shirt pocket before placing my hand at my belt. Then I briefly scratched my nose with the extended middle finger of my right hand.

We flunked Utility B that night but finished second in Open B with a 195.5 and picked up one OTCH point. It was our 37th.

Our next entry was at Prescott Arizona Kennel Club the

weekend of September 13 and 14. Bob Little was there, showing his Labrador retriever. Yes, the same Bob Little under whom we had had our spectacular day in Palm Springs. Bob and Marilyn live here in Mesa and are trusted, highly regarded members of the dog sports community.

Before competition began that morning, I sought out Bob and said, "Would you come over here behind our tent, I want to ask you something." I asked him if he was aware of the heartburn that was going on about my hand actions in the ring.

He said he was. (Who wasn't?)

I then demonstrated the whole charade for him and asked him if that was illegal.

"No, it's not illegal but it looks bad," he replied.

"OK," I said. "That's it. I'm going to retire that tactic." Which I did.

But my little sleight-of-hand routine had had quite a run.

■ CHAPTER 38 ■

High Noon At Rawhide

The world of dog obedience competition features an endless succession of bizarre occurrences.

We went to Costa Mesa for a dog show and stayed for the Northridge earthquake.

The 1997 Palm Springs shows were part spectacular success and part incipient firestorm.

Then came a literally rocky spot in an always rocky road. The powers that be in the Scottsdale Dog Fanciers Association, in a transcendent lapse of judgement, scheduled their March shows at Rawhide Wild West Town, a north Scottsdale tourist attraction. Gunfights, rodeos, horseback rides into the desert, cookouts, horse shows, cowboy stunt men, a steakhouse, even a fake mine — Rawhide does the whole number. If you have John Wayne fantasies, it's swell. But for a dog show?

The allure, I suppose, was the availability of several arenas, each large enough to stage one or more parts of the show.

When I heard the show would be at Rawhide, bells and whistles began going off. I was concerned about the quality of the obedience rings' surfaces. There are people who jump their dogs for years — some all the way to an OTCH — in parking lots, on cul-de-sac streets, on outdoor basketball courts. Only later to wonder why their dogs have elbow or shoulder problems …

caused or aggravated by thousands of landings on an unyield-ing surface.

An occasional hard surface for an obedience trial is not an automatic no-no. The dog has to jump only four times in Open and Utility combined. I am far more concerned about traction. Will the surface have good traction or does it have the poten-tial to cause the dog to slip on takeoff and crash the jump?

Wet grass doesn't bother me. If the dog's paws are well-groomed, if the hair between the pads is cut back, if the nails are a reasonable length, I'm not concerned. I've never had a jump-ing dog slip on wet grass, in practice or in competition.

In fact, we always welcomed rain when Honeybear was entered. We picked up a generous number of OTCH points on rainy days. Some handlers pull their dogs and run for home when raindrops start to fall. Among those who stay, usually the better, more experienced teams, you can count on one or more dogs to say, "Oh, I'm not going to _____ in that." (Fill in the blank with *sit, down, heel,* or whatever.)

Loosely packed dirt or a gravelly surface can be a problem. As can a ring with large potholes or even gopher holes. Not only are gopher holes invitations to sniff, stepping in one can cripple a dog for life.

Estrella Mountain Park, where each October Kachina Kennel Club holds its shows, features an abundance of gopher holes. Several times on show mornings, I have watched someone carry many shovels of dirt into the obedience rings to plug the holes and smooth the surface. Some of those holes weren't even there the afternoon before when the rings were set up.

I have visions of a gopher popping out of the ground right in the center of the pile while someone's dog is doing scent articles.

When I was convinced Scottsdale Dog Fanciers were seri-ous about Rawhide, I decided to check it out for myself. So one morning I got in the van and drove out Scottsdale Road, through beautiful Sonoran desert being eaten up by commercial development and look-alike homes with red tile roofs.

On weekdays Rawhide doesn't open until late in the morning, sometimes late in the afternoon. I found a side entrance and drove to the back where I discovered a large main arena and several small ones. Obedience figured to be in one of the smaller areas, conformation in the main arena.

How to describe the surface where HB would be jumping? Pea gravel would indicate a fairly uniform surface. A better description would be a dirt floor with a zillion small rocks of varying sizes. Fine for horses' hooves, maybe, but what if a dog came over the jump and landed with a paw on the sharp edge of one of those little stones?

My verdict? Risky. But how risky?

Someone told me the National Australian Shepherd specialty show had been held there and Nancy Craig had judged obedience. Nancy was local. I called her. While not bubbling with enthusiasm about the show site, she said it had worked out, "OK."

In the end I entered Honeybear in Open B and Utility B.

On the morning of the show, several people took one look at the conditions and pulled their dogs. I recall Dick Guetzloff being irate, fuming about the reckless stupidity of anyone who would schedule an obedience trial in such a place. If memory serves me right, he pulled Sweep.

Honeybear's score in Open was an uninspired 192.5, but we qualified. In Utility, on the directed retrieve, the judge gave us glove one. HB dashed out, retrieved the glove and returned on three legs. After the judge said, "Exercise finished," we examined HB's right rear paw and extracted the rock that was lodged between her pads.

Honeybear is a trouper. She got a perfect score on that exercise. We also won the class with a 195 and picked up six OTCH points. We averted disaster that morning but, in retrospect, taking HB into the ring that day was the dumbest decision I made during her long career.

The morning was capped off when, at high noon, during the Novice sits and downs, a mock gunfight was staged far too near the obedience rings. The gunfire caused several of the green dogs to panic and run to their owners.

By the way, Scottsdale Dog Fanciers never returned to Rawhide. And as far as I know there have been no dog shows there since that debacle.

■ CHAPTER 39 ■

The Coven Strikes Back

Not only does the world of obedience competition get wild and wooly with strange happenings, it harbors a goodly number of dysfunctional people.

The Judge Keith Coyne fiasco began in December of 1996. In hot pursuit of our UDX, I took Honeybear to the Los Encinos Kennel Club show at Brookside Park, next-door to the Rose Bowl in Pasadena.

The day began in Utility B under Judge James TenEyck. After we had finished our run (195), the judge said, "What a pleasure it is to judge a dog who's so happy in the ring."

Then came Open B and Keith Coyne. I had never encountered him before. He had a loud, rasping, nasal voice. But he seemed nice enough. He caught me totally off guard. Our run was finished and the steward was handing me the leash when I heard that nasal voice behind me: "Steward! Bring that man over here, I want to talk to him," the judge rasped.

Addressing me, he continued, "I almost excused you this morning for training in the ring."

My jaw dropped.

"You *ran* your dog over to the drop on recall." *I sure had. So?* When there was significant distance between the point of completion of one exercise and the starting point of the next, I ran with her. It kept her upbeat and alert.

Next the judge said, "You also made a circle before you set her up for the high jump." Right again. I made a small circle to the left as I brought HB into position. Turning left when the dog is on your left keeps her butt in and helps her find perfect heel position without a lot of jockeying around.

Finally, as everyone at ringside waited to hear what else, Coyne said, "And you slapped your dog between exercises." Oh wow! When Honeybear did an exercise well, I'd tap her on the nose with the tip of my index finger and say, "Good girl!"

I was boiling, livid. But my response was deferential. "Gee," I said, "no one has ever told me that before. Sorry."

Then I was out of there.

Despite all the heartburn, he awarded us a 194.5 in Open B and we got what we had gone to Pasadena for, a UDX leg. But the Coyne incident had been nothing short of bizarre. Particularly when contrasted with the comment Judge TenEyck had volunteered earlier that morning.

Later that week I mentioned the episode to Debby. "That's interesting," she replied. "Lisa had the same thing happen with him. He said he almost excused her because she was jazzing up her dog too much between exercises."

Debby was referring to Lisa Lit, a serious, excellent trainer of border collies. Lisa was so committed, in fact, that for several years during the mid-90s she went to England for a week or two each summer to train with Sylvia Bishop, one of England's top trainers and Crufts competitors.

Lisa's dog Jake, like Honeybear, was a perfect role model for the qualities the AKC professes to want in obedience competition dogs — fast, accurate, *joyous.*

"Keith Coyne can't stand to see anyone being happy in the ring," Debby said.

At a seminar a few weeks later, the subject of Keith Coyne came up again. Several people — none a troublemaker — offered similar anecdotes. Clearly this guy was a piece of work.

Time passed.

It was announced that Coyne and his wife Jacqueline would be the obedience judges at the Prescott Arizona Kennel Club's obedience trials September 13 and 14. By the way, I've never heard a negative comment about Mrs. Coyne.

When Kay Guetzloff heard about the selection of judges for the Prescott shows, she expressed concern. Her students had had experiences with Coyne that were quite similar to mine, she said. She wrote to Tom Frampton, an assistant to the obedience director at the AKC. She requested that an obedience representative be sent to the Prescott shows.

I also wrote to Mr. Frampton, seconding Kay's request. *Something is wrong here*, I wrote, *there are too many strikingly similar incidents involving people who never seem to have difficulty with other judges.*

Frampton's response was that all obedience reps had already been assigned to other shows that weekend.

Here we go, I thought. *This should be interesting.* And it was.

On Saturday, Jacqueline Coyne judged both Open B and Utility B. Nice lady. Good judge. HB and I should have been so competent. We managed to flunk Utility B and turned in a lackluster Open B score of 191.

Most of those present at the show were aware of the history with Judge Coyne (with the exception, apparently, of those who selected the judges). Anecdotes about his often-inappropriate comments and his penchant for loud lectures at center ring were abundant.

On Sunday he judged Utility B and Open B. At first it seemed as if someone might have cautioned the judge before his arrival in Prescott — he seemed overly solicitous. But that quickly changed.

Soon, although we were seated several ring lengths from where he was judging, we could hear his loud, nasal voice above all else. He was up to his old antics, calling exhibitors to center ring as they were about to leave and loudly lecturing them about whatever had displeased him — usually related to his bizarre definition of training in the ring.

I have had more than one judge call me aside to comment on a handler error — quietly, confidentially, in a friendly, non-threatening, nonembarrassing manner. For instance, "Do you know that you are stepping into your dog at every halt?"

Most judges seem committed to putting handlers at ease. But Coyne manages to create an atmosphere of negative stress in and around his ring. If you've been at ringside, observing and listening, you can't still an inner voice that is saying, "I wonder if he'll embarrass me in front of my friends when I get in there?"

I had come to the Prescott shows prepared with a note pad and pencil to document whatever misbehavior went on in his ring. *You never know,* I thought, *when such information might become useful.*

Here are three short anecdotes based on those notes:

- The "fun" started with the first handler to enter Coyne's Utility A ring on Saturday morning. Eve Ross, showing a standard poodle, is the corporate counsel for Flagstaff-based W.L. Gore & Co., makers of Gore-Tex and many other products.

  After the individual exercises were finished, Coyne loudly told her he had almost had to excuse her for training in the ring. Her transgression? She talked to her dog while she rubbed up the scent articles.

That hit a nerve with me. I always talked to Honeybear while I rubbed up the scent articles. "Scent articles, Honeybear, scent articles. You're really good at this." It was my way of holding HB's attention until the judge said, "Are you ready?" I have searched the Obedience Regulations to find grounds for the alleged infraction. Of course there are none. And no judge, including Coyne himself, has ever called me on it.

- Coyne must have thought it was open season on lawyers. On Sunday, Kristina Pickering and her splendid OTCH border collie Scout showed under him in Utility B. Kris is a corporate litigation expert and principal of one of the leading law firms in Nevada. She is an accomplished veteran handler with many honors — including Gaines placements — under her belt (and Scout's). After the exercises were over, she was detained in the ring and given a loud lecture about the proper presentation of the signals to the dog.

- Several times across the two days of trials, I did a double-take when I realized Judge Coyne was talking to an exhibitor *during an exercise.* One poor soul, who had traveled all the way from Albuquerque, was already flustered coming into Open B because she had rushed over from the breed ring. To make things worse, her Irish setter had run out of the ring during the heel-free exercise.

Suddenly I became aware that as she did the figure eight Coyne was keeping up a steady stream of comments. "What difference does it make?" someone seated near me said. "She's already flunked."

Irritated more by the judge's behavior than by the question, I snapped, "It makes a lot of difference. She may have NQ'd but no one has refunded her entry fee. She deserves a chance to salvage ring experience from her run without some loud-mouthed clown ruining it for her."

Throughout the weekend, Coyne's ring was the focal point for many other unsettling little confrontations that seemed out of place in a well-run ring.

■ ■ ■

Judge Coyne's foot-in-mouth coupe de grace came near the end of judging early Sunday afternoon. And guess who was the victim?

Honeybear and I found ourselves in a runoff for third place with Bonnie Lee and her dynamite papillon Rosie. Bonnie and Rosie were also working on their OTCH and were closer to it than we were.

They were from Las Vegas, and we had squared off many times in various obedience rings in the United States. We had cleaned their clocks; they had cleaned ours.

But on this day it was our turn. We won the runoff. The ribbons were presented and we all left the ring to turn our attention to Open B, also the domain of Judge Coyne.

It was not until after the group exercises in Open B that he came up with the final straw. We were leaving the ring when I heard, "Sir, I want to talk to you." And he was looking at me. *Here we go again.*

So here we were in the middle of the ring and the other Open B competitors stopped to see what it was about *this time* — the umpteenth such scolding incident of the weekend.

In his loud nasal voice the judge said to me, "Several people (and he gestured toward the stewards) told me you had food in the ring during the runoff."

I began to assure the judge that such an assertion was ludicrous but he cut me off in mid-sentence with a wave of his hand. He concluded, loudly, "I didn't see it but if I had you would have been out of here."

Wow! What a damning indictment for all to hear. From a representative of the AKC, right in the middle of the ring. Fortunately from one who had already made a spectacle of himself all weekend.

Ah, The Coven strikes back! There were the stewards: the ponderous, smart-mouthed Queen of Darkness and Dim Bulb, an attractive blond until she opened her mouth. Hard-core Covenites. The worst of the worst.

They must have salivated to the point of drooling on their red stewards' bibs when they saw an opportunity to skewer the shameless food trainer.

Never mind that the AKC guidelines for stewards specifically state:

> Stewards must keep in mind that they have
> been selected to help the judge and not to
> advise him. They should carefully refrain from
> discussing, or even seeming to discuss,
> the dog's (team's) performance with the judge.

And judges understand, or should understand, that they are not to be guided by such inappropriate comments volunteered by stewards.

But on this day fate had brought together two Coven members and a judge whose misconduct in the ring had long since shredded his credibility with many of those present.

It wasn't until several days later that I figured out exactly what had happened. As usual, Barbara had taped our runoff. Debby and I went over the "game films" together. As we watched, suddenly Debby said, "There it is!" She rewound the tape and here is what we saw:

Honeybear and I are at the point where the runoff exercise (heel free) is over. Dim Bulb is entering the ring with the leash.

Honeybear always knows when she has done well. She is euphoric, frequently darting to the steward (putting her paws on Nancy Pollock's shoulders at The Gaines and licking her in the face), occasionally barking. And I'm forever trying to prevent such point-losing behavior.

For purposes of orientation as I describe what we saw on the tape, assume I am standing in the center of the ring, facing an imaginary three o'clock. I have managed to get HB into heel position, on my left. Dim Bulb is entering the ring at 12 o'clock, approaching from our left. To prevent Honeybear from darting toward the steward, I slip my left hand down along the side of her face. At which point she turns her head and nuzzles into my hand. Well, if I hadn't been the guy on the tape, if it hadn't been *my* hand that golden retriever was nuzzling, you could have fooled me. But there was no food.

That, of course, is what Dim Bulb saw as she walked toward us with the leash. She must have busted a gut getting back to the Queen of Darkness to tell her the news. And the two of them must have come out of their skins waiting to tell the judge when he got back to the table.

So here we had a potentially damaging incident perpetrated by stewards' malicious disregard of the rules of proper conduct, and made worse by a judge's acceptance of misinformation. And by his big mouth.

The next day I sent a four-page letter to Robert Squires, director of obedience for the AKC. I described the incident in detail and summarized the history that preceded it. I sent a copy directly to Coyne at his home in Petaluma, California.

Squires and I had a couple of telephone conversations. Apparently the AKC counseled Judge Coyne about his conduct. Some time later Squires sent me a copy of a letter from Coyne to the AKC. In that letter, he admitted the need to modify his relations with exhibitors.

Our paths have not crossed since.

■ CHAPTER 40 ■

Eternity

Day after day, year after year, found us on the polo field at Paradise Valley Park. Looking back, it all melds into one seamless, matchless, life-defining experience.

Some have called it tenacity. It was nothing of the sort. It was enchantment that drew us there, sustained us there.

Outside the fence, at the south end of the field, were several large Aleppo pine trees. By late afternoon they would cast enough shade onto the field to provide relief from an often-brutal Arizona sun.

On hot afternoons we would abandon our ring for a while and move into that strip of shade. There we could practice figure eights, recalls, retrieves, and scent articles.

Just beyond the fence, those trees formed a shade canopy over a soft bed of pine needles. I came to view it as a beautiful, peaceful, soothing oasis.

I can't pinpoint exactly when it happened. Surely it built little by little for at least half a decade before it coalesced into a thought. I'd pause just inside the fence, by the gate where we parked. I'd survey the large expanse of grass, *our* field. I'd look at those Aleppo pine trees, that shade, that bed of pine needles.

One afternoon it just came out: "Wouldn't it be great, Honeybear, if we could all spend eternity here together? You and me and Barbara and Bebop and Noché and Squeakie (our other animals). Wouldn't it be great to spend eternity together here, in our very favorite place on earth?"

Obviously the City of Phoenix would not allow us to be buried there. But if all of us were cremated, our ashes could be mixed, then scattered under those pine trees.

After that day we never trained there but that I stood and looked at that shady area under those trees. Often I talked to Honeybear about it. Sometimes we walked over there, right to the spot. "All of us could be together … right here in our favorite spot," I'd tell her.

The idea was our secret for several years. I mentioned it to no one else.

■ CHAPTER 41 ■

The Wheels Come Off

Late in the fall of 1997 I began to sense that something was creeping up on us. Disquieting performances in the ring had become more and more frequent.

A month after the Prescott shows and the Keith Coyne/ Coven Strikes Back debacle, we went to Las Vegas for a two-show weekend. Although we brought home no OTCH points, we qualified in all four rings. But our Utility runs were flat with nagging little errors. We scored just 191 and 190.

Looking back, I recalled that we had done only 191 and 189.5 in Utility B at Prescott. No doubt about it, our Utility scores had slipped a few notches. I couldn't put my finger on it but Honeybear wasn't quite Honeybear during those runs. And every so often she would make goofy, unHoneybear-like mistakes — the kind that would make me roll my eyes and say to myself, *Oh, HB! You know better than that.*

At Kachina Kennel Club, near the end of October, we flunked Utility B both days — on errors that HB almost never made.

We also managed a blah 189 in Open on Saturday. That one was more humorous than worrisome.

We had barely begun the heeling pattern when I became aware that HB wasn't at my side. I looked back and she was standing stock-still, nose in the air. Less than 100 feet from our Open B ring, someone had fired up a grill and was cooking hamburgers. Our ring was directly downwind.

"Honeybear, heel!" I called. She sprinted to my side, but that whiff of meat had cost us five points on the very first exercise.

The next day, with no one cooking hamburgers, we finished second to Kay Guetzloff in Open B. Unfortunately there were only six in the class so there were no points for second.

Our slide continued two weeks later at Scottsdale Dog Fanciers. We flunked the drop on recall in Open B. HB acknowledged my drop signal by dipping her left shoulder; then she came right on in to front — albeit with a guilty look on her face.

That same day Utility B again featured nagging little errors that landed us in third place.

On Sunday, the Arizona White Mountain Kennel Club held their show in the same location, the huge polo field at WestWorld in Scottsdale.

Both of us got it right in Open B and we wound up with 195.5, second place and one OTCH point, our first in nearly three months.

However, we *won* Utility B that morning, picked up 10 more OTCH points and carried home the high combined ribbon. That put us at 48 points, nearly halfway there.

Our first place in Utility B was another of those bloop singles that looks like a line drive in the newspaper the next morning. Our score, under Judge Dorin Ladd, was only 189. Everyone else in the class of 12 flunked. At the end, HB and I were the only ones left standing. And again Harry Burke, stewarding that morning, shook his head and said, "It was a blood bath in there."

That lucky win did nothing to keep our Utility B performances from waking me at 3 a.m. If we were going to get an OTCH, we had to earn high scores in Utility B.

In addition to the 100 points needed to be awarded the OTCH title, a dog/handler team was required to accumulate one first place in Open B with at least six dogs in the class, a first in Utility B with at least three dogs in the class, and an additional first in either of the B classes, with the same entry criteria. All three blue ribbons had to be won under different judges.

At the point where I was feeling uneasy about the slippage in HB's performances, we were well beyond the AKC requirements for first-place finishes. At the time, we had three blue ribbons in each class.

As Debby put it, "All you have to do is grind out the points."

True. We had 48. We needed another 52 to reach the magic number. The objective was to accumulate points in the quickest, most efficient manner — through stellar performances in Utility B.

When the powers that be created the Obedience Trial Championship, they took into account the fact that Utility is far more difficult than Open. Both dog and handler have so much more to think about in Utility. The dog works at a distance from the handler to a much greater extent than in the earlier classes. And scent discrimination, hand signals and the concept of running *away* from the handler — and in a straight line — are introduced in Utility.

Those who developed the OTCH structured the point system accordingly. In general — and this doesn't always work out precisely — the points awarded for a Utility B first or second place are two to three times as many as for the comparable positions in Open.

For example, on a day when 12 teams showed in both Utility B and Open B, first and second places in Utility were worth 10 and three points respectively. The corresponding values in Open were just four and one.

Clearly, a dog whose Utility scores are slumping is on a treadmill to nowhere.

We plodded along for the remainder of the fall 1997 show season. Our year ended the weekend of November 15, 16 and 17 at the Pima County Fairgrounds in Tucson. Three days, six rings, a chance to pass the halfway point to our OTCH before the end of the year.

We started the weekend with Greater Sierra Vista Kennel Club on Saturday: a 191.5 in Utility B and a 195 in Open B (third place but no OTCH points).

Sunday: same site, but now under the aegis of Tucson Kennel Club. We flunked Utility B. HB blew a signal, a break in concentration that recently had crept into her repertoire. We qualified in Open B but did not place.

Honeybear's performances in Utility were increasingly puzzling. In several situations she looked confused, as though what we were doing was new to her — failing to sit on the go-outs or at front, for example.

"We've done this stuff a zillion times," I said to Barbara. "Is HB getting senile?"

Monday's show was Cañada del Oro Kennel Club. Our Utility B was a mess. Same puzzling stuff. HB traveled on the signal stand and again on the moving stand. She capped off her run by failing to sit on each go-out. Jill Jones, who had judged our 195 in Open on Saturday, gave us a 183.5. That was a shocker.

Honeybear and I had flunked our share of times during her career, but the 183.5 was our second-lowest qualifying score. Only the 180 in Novice A, nearly six years earlier, had been worse. And that had included a 10-point deduction for my sharp leash correction as we entered the ring.

We finished the day, the weekend, our year with an uninspired 190 in Open B. The low scores weren't the worst part of what was happening in the ring late in 1997. What upset me most was the look on Honeybear's face when she had one of her mental lapses.

Right at the point where she had screwed up, she'd freeze in her tracks and look at me in bewilderment. The expression on her face said so clearly: "Skippy, I know I just did something wrong but I've forgotten what I'm supposed to do. Help me." But, of course, we were in the competition ring and I couldn't help her. And that broke my heart.

Kay Guetzloff had been in every class with us and at ringside all weekend. After we finished on Monday and were packing up to slink home, Kay said, "To me, Honeybear looks intimidated in the ring." But she had no explanation and no suggestions for correcting the problem. And when Kay — who had been through it all time and time again — couldn't quickly tell you what was wrong and how to fix it, things were grim.

I was beginning to see what I thought was the big picture, a picture I desperately wanted not to see. Honeybear had been born on December 22, 1989. In scarcely more than a month she would be eight years old. I couldn't think of one dog who had started with us — in training or in matches and shows — who was not long since retired, some for two or three years.

And yet, in practice, even in matches, she was full of herself, obviously loving every minute. But when she got in the AKC ring, strange things happened.

The brutal, inescapable truth was, in an obedience competition context, Honeybear was getting old.

That afternoon during the endless drive home from Tucson, for the first time Barbara said something I would hear again from time to time across the next year and a half. "Skip," she said, "don't let her embarrass herself. She's been too fine a dog. This isn't how you want everybody to remember her."

I knew she was right. But I didn't answer. I couldn't.

CHAPTER 42

"We've Got Work To Do"

Following the Tucson shows, the cliches came easily. "Well, back to the drawing board." And, "We've got work to do."

On November 20, I wrote Debby a note. Actually, it was more of a tome.

> *Here's an analysis of Honeybear's problems.*
> *She has eye surgery scheduled for Monday,*
> *November 24 (an iris cyst, common in golden*
> *retrievers). She'll need two to three weeks*
> *to recuperate. I'd guess by mid-December*
> *we'll need to get back to work. Ready?*

Ready??!!

Good old long-suffering Debby. It was time to fix it — again. When she saw my "analysis," she probably wanted to leave town. Or at least hide under the bed. It droned on for three pages. I listed all our problems, then I broke them down by ring (Open or Utility), by exercise.

"My God," I told Barbara when I was finished, "something important is broken on nearly every exercise."

The problems, though, could all be traced to tentativeness, lack of confidence and diminished motivation. And they manifested themselves as lackluster heeling, failure to sit (on the go-outs or when coming to front), anticipation, and shutting down in the middle of an exercise with a confused facial expression.

What I saw was a bunch of broken pieces. What Debby saw was more global — a situation steeped in flawed fundamentals. Debby's response across the next few weeks was a replay of more than a few haunting refrains.

Once, early in our relationship, Debby had looked me squarely in the eye and told me, "Willard, obedience training is *not* about training dogs."

My use of additional commands was a perpetual thorn in Debby's side. "Don't give her extra commands," she'd say. "Tell her *once* and follow through."

I came to realize that I wanted so badly for HB to succeed that she "succeeded" whether she had been successful or not. I had slipped into a pattern of rewarding her for *being*. If she did the exercise, or the part we were working on — or kept breathing — she got a treat.

"Often you reward her for 50 percent effort. Look for and expect 100 percent effort, energetic and focused," Debby said.

Near the end of the year, Debby noted that my two biggest problems were:

- "Giving HB too much help instead of expecting her to do it right the first time.
- "Fear of proofing. When the dog starts to fall apart (gets confused) you back off."

It was back to the drawing board all right. And we had 10 showless weeks to work it through.

■ CHAPTER 43 ■

23 (Count 'Em, 23) OTCH Points

PHOENIX FIELD AND OBEDIENCE CLUB
FEBRUARY 21, 1998

This is where we had started, on this same weekend seven years ago. This is where we had wobbled into the ring that first time and finished second to get our first CD leg.

So we were "home" again and, I hoped, poised for a rebirth.

Our judges for the weekend would be Michael Carlucci and Fred Wohlgemuth. Carlucci was a popular judge in the midwest but I had never laid eyes on the man. Wohlgemuth, on the other hand, had judged us to a 197.5 the day HB came out in Open A and got her first CDX leg. A hopeful sign.

But as it turned out, we flunked Utility B both days — more of the same goofy mistakes. Open B scores of 194.5 under Carlucci and 192.5 under Wohlgemuth yielded no placements and no OTCH points and did little to temper my disappointment. We had been fixing *what* during the past 10 weeks?

Next up were the Superstition Kennel Club shows the following weekend, February 28/March 1.

At the time, the Superstition shows were held on the athletic fields at Mesa Community College. The whole scene was difficult and stressful. Over the years the show committee had moved the obedience rings farther and farther from the parking lot.

Remember, dog shows are staged for the conformation people; that's where the money is.

And because of restrictions imposed by the college, no one was allowed on the premises to set up until after 3 p.m. By the time we finished setting up on Friday afternoon it was after five o'clock. It was after six when we got home. I've had evenings when I was in a better mood.

I like to be at ringside shortly after 6 a.m. on show mornings, so I set the alarm for four o'clock on Saturday. I was wide awake at three. Many times during Honeybear's career I have reached major decisions at 3 a.m. on show mornings. Reality seems to come to me with unusual clarity then.

In the wee hours of February 28, 1998, I decided it was time to fish or cut bait.

We had gotten our last OTCH points — that 10-point gimme at Arizona White Mountain Kennel Club — on November 9 of the previous year. We had been stuck on 48 points for almost four months. And during that stretch we had turned in some pathetic performances.

Sure, Erik Hoyer, my neighbor and steadfast supporter (and owner/trainer of the only two OTCH bouviers in the history of the breed), had constantly reassured me: "For some reason OTCH points seem to come in clumps. You'll go for a while without getting any, then all of a sudden you'll get a whole bunch."

Swell, but the only clump I had heard lately was the sickening thud of our performances in the ring. *Enough is enough,* I told myself.

So there in the darkness that morning I promised myself, *If we don't get any OTCH points today, it's all over. I'll retire Honeybear.*

It was a promise made in secrecy, between me and myself. I said nothing to anyone else.

Photo: Barbara Bailey

"Let's Play Ball!"

■ ■ ■

As is usually the case, Utility B was our first ring that morning, under Judge Barbara Handler at 8 a.m. There were 21 entries, among them more than a few formidable dogs and handlers. Two were absent. Honeybear and I were deep in the order, 17th of the 19 who showed.

Whatever had been bugging HB recently wasn't bugging her that morning. There were the usual crooked fronts, a point or two on the signal exercise, a little traveling on the moving stand. But all in all a nice run.

Dick Guetzloff and Sweep followed us — the highest-scoring dog in the history of the sport and one of the greatest handlers. They, too, were cruising along, putting on a clinic — *this*, folks, is how Utility should be done.

Until they got to the moving stand.

"Forward," Barbara Handler said.

The greatest team in the world moved flawlessly as one. Sweep's eyes were locked on Dick.

Just before the midpoint of the ring the judge said, "Stand your dog." On Dick's command, Sweep stopped as if she had run head-on into a brick wall. She stood like a statue as Judge Handler, an imposing woman, ran both hands over her body.

Then the judge said, "Call your dog to heel."

The stand and examination had taken place about ten feet short of and eight feet to the left of the bar jump. As Dick called his dog, Sweep spied that jump to her right. She diverted, soared over the jump and returned to Dick with a perfect front, followed by a perfect finish.

One exercise later Dick and Sweep exited the ring with Dick fuming. "Goddamn Kay! Goddamn agility! I told Kay this is what would happen."

Seems his wife had decided to show Sweep in agility. Apparently Dick and Kay had had words about it, Dick fearing the double exposure would result in the sort of confusion the normally precise Sweep had exhibited in Utility B that morning. Nevertheless, Kay had prevailed.

Sweep's little caper cost the great Dick Guetzloff and his teammate five points.

Honeybear and I, with a 194, won the class and picked up 17 OTCH points.

Open B, the realm of Judge Mildred Rothrock that morning, began at 10:30. The same 19 teams competed. We were third in the ring. HB was smoking. As we left the ring, I knew we had done well so we settled back to watch the rest of the class and see if anyone could do better. No one did. Our 197 was good for first place and six more OTCH points. (A perfect example of the point disparity between Utility B and Open B. The entry was identical. We took first place in each class, but we received 17 points in Utility B versus six in Open B.)

Someone in Novice B popped off a 198 that morning so we missed high in trial. But we took home the high-combined award, two blue ribbons and 23 OTCH points.

Twenty-three OTCH points! Nearly a quarter of an OTCH in one morning.

"See," Erik Hoyer said, "I told you they come in clumps."

Meanwhile, The Coven scowled and muttered. That was the morning Marilyn Abbett asked, "Willard, how come they get so mad when you win?"

After the Open B awards, I said to Barbara, "Oh my God! Here's what you don't know. Early this morning I decided if we didn't get any points today I'd hang it up."

Not quite. That morning HB and I woke up with 48 OTCH points. That night we went to bed with 71. Good girl! Only 29 to go.

■ ■ ■

The next day we weren't so hot. Dick and Sweep had their

act back together and won Utility B. Debby with toy poodle Phooie Louie, a dog she was showing for Kathryn Zatz and Pat Korrick, took second. We cooled off a bit and finished third with a 193.

It was Open B that morning that proved interesting. Right off the bat HB's heeling was uninspired. She was hanging in heel position, not driving.

The second exercise was the drop on recall. HB came at medium speed when I called her and dropped quickly on my signal. The judge, Barbara Handler again, signaled me to call HB out of the down.

"Front!" I said crisply. HB got up, took a couple of steps, then stopped to give a small leaf a long, inquisitive sniff. Finally she came loping to me.

After the exercise was finished, the judge, speaking in a falsetto voice as if she were Honeybear, laughed and said, "Oh, I've never seen a leaf before."

The remainder of our run was equally flat. With a 191.5, we finished out of the ribbons.

Dick had watched our performance from ringside. Afterward he said, "Honeybear just plain ran out of gas in there this morning. Think about it. She's nearly $8\frac{1}{2}$, she's been in the ring for over seven years and that was her fourth ring this weekend."

I nodded. He was right. Brilliant on Saturday, HB had been pooped in Open B on Sunday.

"If I were you, I'd consider showing her only in Utility B from here on. Save her energy for the ring with the big points." Dick said.

It made sense to me. That was the last time Honeybear showed in Open B.

CHAPTER 44

The Dead Zone

Our 23-point day turned out to be nothing more than a lush, refreshing oasis on a journey across a barren, hostile desert.

Full of new hope and excitement, I entered us in Utility B at a brace of shows at WestWorld in Scottsdale. Yuma Kennel Club and Scottsdale Dog Fanciers shows were held on March 20 and 21.

We flunked the first day. HB screwed up the directed jumping exercise. At the end of that exercise, Judge Judy Myers said, "Well, you had already flunked anyhow."

"Huh?" I said, nonplussed.

"You were mouthing the words on the signal exercise," she explained. Then she proceeded to demonstrate, moving her own lips in an exaggerated, "Down, sit, come."

A hot stab of anger shot up the back of my head. What normally follows makes those who had wish they hadn't.

But my resolve not to argue with judges is unshakable. It's a no-win situation. So I mechanically began saying things like, "I had no idea." And, "No one has ever told me that before." Besides, we had legitimately flunked the directed jumping exercise, so what difference did it make?

Nevertheless, that one was bizarre. Fact: I had not mouthed the commands. What's more, if I had been able to teach HB to lip-read, that should have been worth a bunch of extra points, not an NQ.

The following morning, in the Utility B ring of Scottsdale Dog Fanciers, we slogged through a flat, error-plagued 189.

On to Las Vegas for three shows, Utility B only.

On Friday, HB was HB again under Judge Bob Little. But a 195.5 brought us no placement and no OTCH points.

At Black Mountain Kennel Club the next morning, we did another 189 under Marilyn Little. And a 189.5 under Suzanne Mayborne on Sunday.

Same hijinks from HB. Hanging in heel position. Tentativeness on the scent articles. Failure to sit on the go-outs. Or going out to a point just beyond the jumps, turning and looking at me in bewilderment. "I know I'm screwing up," she seemed to say, "but I don't know what I'm supposed to do here." That, more than any other of her strange lapses, made me want to cry. And again prompted Barbara to say, "Skip, don't let her embarrass herself."

Consummate frustration. What was I supposed to do, throw in the towel just 29 points short of our OTCH? All those thousands of afternoons at the park. All those sessions with Debby. All of Debby's deep devotion. All those miles to the far-flung outposts. All those nights in all those motels where the drains were stopped up. All those cold, dark mornings at 4 a.m. All that blood, sweat and tears. All for naught?

■ ■ ■

There are few nicer spots for a dog show than the spacious grounds of the Rancho Santa Fe Polo Club at Rancho Santa Fe, California. The weather in the San Diego area is predominantly lovely. There is a huge expanse of green grass with nary a horse pucky in sight. The sponsors have erected an extraordinary amount of shade cover. And perhaps the most exhibitor-friendly stroke of all is abundant parking within 100 feet of the obedience setup area.

Now add to that neat environment my birthday. The spring obedience trials of Cabrillo Kennel Club and Del Sur Kennel Club would be held on May 16 and 17. May 17 would be the day I turned 65.

"Here's what I want for my birthday," I said. "I want to go to San Diego and work on our OTCH."

According to plan, we entered only Utility B. By the time mid-May arrived, it had been a long dry spell. Our last OTCH points had been that 23-point extravaganza on February 28. I said, "Honeybear, you can make my birthday."

We flunked both days. I can't recall exactly what the little disasters were. But undoubtedly they involved laggy heeling followed by one or more episodes where HB would do part of an exercise, turn to me with a blank look that said, "I haven't a clue," then shut down.

On Sunday, my birthday, I came out of the ring teeth-gnashingly upset. Unusually so. All I wanted was for us — Honeybear and me — to get away from everyone, go somewhere and lick our wounds together, privately.

Several acres of deserted polo field stretched beyond our tent. "Come on, Honeybear," I said, "let's go for a walk." Some handlers — far too many to suit me — after a bad run in the ring throw their dogs into a crate (sometimes literally) and stomp around telling all who are unfortunate enough to be within earshot how badly the dog screwed up. Not me. The worse things get, the more I want Honeybear with me. We go off together, lend solace to each other and both come back feeling better.

We weren't in the polo field long before I became aware we were no longer alone. Perhaps 100 feet away, AnneMarie Silverton was walking her border collie.

In my mind, as well as in the minds of many of America's best obedience competitors, she is the greatest obedience competition teacher of our time.

AnneMarie was not entered in obedience competition that day in 1998. In fact, she has not been an exhibitor in obedience since I came into the sport more than a decade ago. Her role has been that of instructor and mentor.

In recent years she has become active in border collie conformation. Through her breed ring handler Bruce Schultz, AnneMarie has developed several wildly successful border collie breed champions. She was walking one of those dogs that morning in Rancho Santa Fe after our back-to-back Utility B disappointments.

HB and I walked over. I know AnneMarie, but not well. We exchanged pleasantries and talked a bit about her dog. Then I told her about HB's lapses across the past few months and asked her what could cause that.

"Well, Willard," she said without hesitation, "Honeybear is getting old."

One time, out of the blue, Barbara had said to me, "It's always been that way, hasn't it?"

"What's always been what way?" I asked.

"You two have spent your lives with Honeybear looking up at you," she said. And she was right.

Now, as AnneMarie laid her matter-of-fact explanation on me, Honeybear was standing next to me, looking up. And yes, that face was getting whiter and whiter.

"But she's not quite eight and a half," I protested.

"That's getting up there for a golden," AnneMarie said. "Particularly as it applies to performance in obedience competition."

Looking back, that was the day and the moment I began looking at Honeybear in a different light. AnneMarie had abruptly brought me face to face with my dog's mortality.

My 65th birthday hadn't turned out the way I had anticipated.

■ ■ ■

Nevertheless, on to Flagstaff. The shows of Flagstaff Kennel Club are among the most exhibitor-unfriendly on the circuit. At least that is true for obedience competitors.

The events are held on the athletic fields at Coconino County High School in Flagstaff. All that is difficult at those shows is made more so by the altitude. The town is perched in "the high country," of northern Arizona at 7,000 feet.

The obedience rings are located at the farthest point from the parking area, adjacent to a beautiful forest of ponderosa pines.

You drag your stuff — tent, chairs, crates, coolers, mat, equipment and, oh yes, dogs — up a long hill, then across an endless cement walk that separates several athletic fields, then through a patch of gravel deep enough to stop a runaway truck. Finally, across the outfield of the baseball diamond to the rings.

If you have as much stuff as we take to dog shows, this may involve several gasping trips up the hill through the thin air. It is not uncommon for out-of-towners to experience altitude sickness for the two or three days they are at the shows.

As a crowning insult, there have been years when the Port-O-Lets — located for the convenience of the conformation people — were at least the length of two football fields from the obedience rings.

The 1998 shows were scheduled for Saturday and Sunday, June 6 and 7. HB was entered in Utility B both days. Our run on

Saturday morning was horrible, infuriating, frustrating, disheartening beyond words.

Again HB's heeling was lifeless. Again she failed to sit at front at the end of the signal exercise. Although she got the correct scent articles, she crept back timidly.

It got worse. On the first go-out, she failed to sit, then stood at front as she returned. The second go-out terminated a foot or two beyond the jumps when she turned, confusion in her eyes, and said, "I don't know what to do." I never felt more sorry for my big girl than I did at that moment.

"Call your dog in," said the judge, Roland Speck.

I managed to croak, "Honeybear, come."

While I was putting the leash on HB, Judge Speck said, "I'm sorry." Normally I'd laugh and say, "Not half as sorry as I am."

This time I couldn't speak. Billie Rosen had said, "Willard, *you* are Honeybear's world." And Honeybear had become my world. And that world had just shattered.

Back at the tent, I put Honeybear in her crate and looked around. There were all my friends, people I had met through obedience. It was a beehive of activity. People warming up their dogs, stressing around, getting ready for the Open classes, the Novice classes. Pretending not to notice the train wreck that had just taken place in the Utility B ring.

Finally Barbara said it: "Skip, don't let her embarrass herself. She's been such a wonderful dog. You don't want them to remember her like this."

She need not have spoken. I knew. We had had enough. I said, "Let's go home."

Getting out of the Flagstaff shows is just as difficult as getting in. Only you schlep the other direction. There's no sneaking out quietly.

So there we were, late on Saturday morning, taking down our tent and packing up our stuff. On the first day of a two-day show. And there was nowhere to hide.

Everyone knew Honeybear. As a result, everyone knew me. As they saw us taking down our tent, they came over one by one and said, "Willard, are you going home?" And each time, carefully avoiding the word *senile*, I answered something like, "Yes. Honeybear just can't do it anymore; I've got to retire her."

We made several trips down that endless concrete sidewalk, then down the hill to the van. We kept running into surprised friends. Surprised acquaintances. Surprised people I couldn't remember having seen before. (The *world* belonged to Honeybear's Fan Club.)

I kept fielding the question, fighting back the tears.

The last person we ran into on the last trip was the last person I wanted to face that morning, Susy Hoelzle. Quiet, modest, unassuming Susy — by acclamation the best Arizona trainer of dogs dating back some 30 years. Susy who, with her wonderful Sheltie Ryan, had kicked our butts countless times.

She came up the walk as I pulled the cart in the wrong direction. How embarrassing. She, too, looked surprised. "Willard, are you going home?"

"Yes, Susy," I replied. "Honeybear's retired. We've run out of time. She's run out of concentration in the ring." Then we continued down the endless concrete walk.

■ CHAPTER 45 ■

A Heart-To-Heart With Kay

It's always a long ride home when you don't win. But the longest of all is when you've just thrown in the towel 29 points short of your OTCH. Honeybear had been at my side since puppy kindergarten when she was 16 weeks old. Now, at eight years, five months and six days, she had reached the end of the line.

"Well, you had quite a run," Barbara said.

True. My years with Honeybear had been like no other experience I had ever had.

As we drove down I-17, HB was in her usual spot, the well between the front seats. Peaceful, content, looking up at me — wondering how much longer until supper time.

It seemed as if there had never been a time when she wasn't there. On our way to the park to practice. To Debby's for a lesson. Snuggled in for hundreds of miles enroute to a show. That was her spot and obedience was our world.

But after all she had given me, I couldn't let my wonderful big girl continue to go into the ring and embarrass herself.

And it hurt.

■ ■ ■

Four days later I headed back up I-17 toward Prescott. I was starting a young border collie, Bebop, in obedience competition.

And I had scheduled a lesson with Kay Guetzloff for that morning.

As we drove up the expressway, the world seemed dull, and I felt flat. Of course I had gone places before with Bebop and without Honeybear. But this was the first time it was "official."

I had told Bebop, "You're the little man of the hour now. It's your turn to step up. And you have huge paw prints to fill." But on the way to Prescott that morning what really needed filling was the huge emptiness I felt.

We had finished the lesson and I was preparing to leave when Kay said, "Let's talk about Honeybear."

I was startled. "You know about that?" I asked. The Guetzloffs had not been at the Flagstaff shows the previous weekend. "I knew about it before you were halfway back to Phoenix last Saturday," she replied. That figured. Kay was definitely on the grapevine.

Honeybear's retirement was the last thing I wanted to talk about; it was too fresh and painful. Nevertheless, I sat down next to Kay under a big shade tree. Although she had not witnessed the debacle at Flagstaff, she had been at ringside for months when we competed, and she had observed the problems I was having with Honeybear.

So now for a full hour — gently, quietly and in words that conveyed hope and encouragement — Kay pressed me not to quit. She made me promise to try some new training approaches for one month. "Then see how you feel. You have nothing to lose."

I thanked her and told her I'd think about it. But I was not convinced. Barbara's words still rang in my ears: "Don't let her embarrass herself."

No, I decided on the way home, HB was retired. This was no time to begin to waffle.

CHAPTER 46

Wednesday Evenings With Ed

Even as I retired Honeybear, I realized her "retirement" would be narrowly defined. Retired from the competition ring, yes. But not from being active. I knew that if I abandoned Honeybear to being a couch potato, she would die of a broken heart.

I'd noticed that whenever HB's activities with me were curtailed for a protracted period, there was a difference in her demeanor. Her spirits sagged. She no longer initiated play with me or other dogs. The sparkle was missing from her eyes. The signs of mild depression were obvious.

Then, as soon as we'd begin to train again, she'd become more active at home, more playful, more demanding of attention.

"Of course," Barbara said, "that's been her life. Training and competing have been all she's ever known."

So, as I retired HB, the course of action was clear. Honeybear would continue to "train" with me. Same time, same places. *I'll do little things with her,* I promised myself. *She'll get to heel with treats, retrieve the dumbbell, do signals and scent articles. A few things every time we train. And we'll play lots of ball.*

And so we proceeded through June, July and August. What I didn't realize was that I had set up a pure play regimen for her. We still practiced most of the things she was used to doing in the ring, but the pressure was off. She'd explode out of the van with a "Whoop!" Overjoyed to be out there doing whatever it was we were going to do … *together*.

The AKC offers a nonregular class called Veterans, for obedience competition dogs seven years or older. It doesn't count for anything. Veteran dogs can't earn points or legs or titles in the class. Most of those entered are once-active, now-retired dogs whose owners are smart enough not to relegate them to couch potato status.

Many a tear has been shed both inside and outside the ring for those wonderful old dogs as they cavort through the exercises once more. Sometimes you can actually see the pride on those white faces as they perhaps remember the glory days.

I decided to enter HB in Veterans from time to time, just for fun. No pressure. And what a joy it would be to have her heeling along at my side again.

Veterans competition consists of the Novice exercises. Which gave me an idea.

Phoenix Field & Obedience Club conducts training classes from September through May, two nights a week.

The word on the PFOC training program is that it's a cash cow for the club but the majority of the instructors are hardly qualified to be students in the classes they "teach." But there's a wonderful diamond in this rough — ring procedures at a downtown park on Wednesday evenings.

Two rings are set up, one for Novice, one for Open and Utility. Club members volunteer to run students through the various exercises.

Although ring procedures serve largely to familiarize fledgling students and their dogs with real life in the various rings, some find it a useful way to give their dogs exposure in a simulated show situation. I'm one of those.

The magic about Wednesday evenings is that for some 20 years Ed and Bea Dunn have been ring hosts (surrogate judges for ring procedures).

The Valley of the Sun dog obedience community has been blessed for more than 40 years by the exceptionally active presence of the Dunns, both of whom are now in their 80s. They were among the earliest instructors in the Valley, turning out students who excelled in dog obedience competition, among them Susy Hoelzle.

Why not take HB into Ed Dunn's Novice ring on Wednesday evenings? I thought. *She'll enjoy it, I'll enjoy it.*

So on the evening of September 2, HB pranced into Ed Dunn's ring. She heeled like a dog possessed, forward in heel position and driving. Never before with Honeybear had I felt that much power and enthusiasm at my side!

Ed commented on what beautiful heeling he had just witnessed and suggested perhaps I could smooth my transitions (normal to fast, fast to normal) a bit.

HB finished our turn in the ring by coming to me like a shot on the recall.

"Honeybear certainly had a good time tonight," I told Barbara when we got home.

September 9, same thing. HB had always been a good heeling dog, but not like this. Driving hard. Certainly not intimidated at this point.

Same attitude on September 16. And again on September 23. "Whoop!" she would say as she burst out of her crate. Then she'd turn it on again in the ring.

Can it be? I wondered to myself as we drove home from PFOC on September 23. *Can it be that Kay is right, that this dog really isn't washed up?*

Veterans classes are few and far between. They are generally not offered as part of the obedience trial component at all-breed dog shows. But nearly all dog training and obedience clubs offer several nonregular classes, and Veterans is nearly always included.

The first (and only) Veterans opportunity of the fall show season would be at the trials of Old Pueblo Dog Training Club in Tucson on October 31 and November 1. I entered HB in Veterans both days. *If we're going to show in Veterans*, I told myself, *we might as well win*. So we continued to practice the exercises in short sessions and to go to Ed's ring procedures. And every Wednesday evening HB exploded out of her crate and worked like a demon.

Superstition Kennel Club had a sanctioned match on Saturday, October 10. Working my plan, I entered Honeybear in Novice, for exhibition only. She sparkled. Although we were ineligible for any prizes, she was, hands-down, the best obedience dog in the match, scoring 198.5.

She was excited, happy, driving. Intimidated? Give me a break. By God, we were ready to take on all comers in the Veterans ring at Tucson.

Wednesday evening, October 14: Gangbusters! Again. Now it was clear beyond a shadow of a doubt. Never had Honeybear worked with such pizzazz.

Until that point, I had not seriously waffled on my June 6 decision to retire her. As recently as September 23, I ordered an official transcript of Honeybear's career from the AKC. It was over and I wanted the final tally.

Now, though, the weekend of October 17 and 18 was one of much floor-pacing, soul-searching, reassessment. "Don't let her embarrass herself," dueled with, "This dog is reborn!"

Monday, October 19, brought a flurry of frantic activity. Entries for AKC obedience trials close the second Wednesday before the weekend of the trial. Which meant Old Pueblo would close in two days.

The show secretary was Barbara Lowe, Bonita, California.

I sent the change by Federal Express and backed it up with a phone call: "Please remove Starbuc's Dream Come True UDX from Veterans and enter her in Utility B."

I was trembling inside.

■ CHAPTER 47 ■

The Comeback Girl

We all have our favorite show venues. One of my favorites, if not the favorite, is the setting for the fall obedience trials of Old Pueblo Dog Training Club in Tucson.

The trials are held on the grounds of the Ramada Inn. The hotel is nothing to write home about. Often the electronic locks don't work. The plumbing is hit-and-miss. The heating/air-conditioning system is ancient.

But as a place for an obedience trial, it can't be beat. Request the right room and you can walk out your back door and into the ring. No tent to set up, no crates to lug a quarter of a mile. And if it happens to rain, you can duck into your room and watch the activity through the window.

On Friday, October 30, we drove the 110 miles down I-10 with anticipation and trepidation.

HB was entered only in Utility B. In less than two months she would be nine years old. I figured she had only so much giddyup left on any given day. Why not concentrate it where we could get the greatest return?

If the celebrated bank robber Willie Sutton was alive today and someone asked him why he showed only in Utility B, what would he reply? "That's where the points are."

■ ■ ■

Saturday, October 31, dawned a perfect Arizona fall day, an ideal morning for a dog show. Clear blue skies, sunny, pleasantly warm but not hot.

Old Pueblo Dog Training Club's 86th obedience trial got underway at 8 a.m. with Utility B in Ring Two under Judge Jeanne Stephens.

Eleven teams were entered. Honeybear and I, number 275, would be the 10th team in the ring.

Good! That gave me time to carefully observe all the details I like to study if I have a chance before we enter the ring.

Most importantly, I could memorize the judge's heeling pattern, go somewhere and walk it, then run my dog through it a few times. It's nice not to be victimized by an unexpected halt or an unanticipated turn.

I also like to watch where the judge places the scent articles. The better to know whether to breathe a sigh of relief or go into cardiac arrest when my dog retrieves an article.

And it can often be helpful to watch the judge's succession of gloves. If, for instance, you see the sequence 1-3-2 for a couple of cycles, in most cases you can count ahead and figure out which glove you are likely to get.

That doesn't always work, though. Some judges premark their score sheets with the glove number each team will get, sometimes randomly.

Best advice: Observe carefully, calculate, then have your weight evenly distributed on the balls of both feet as you wait for the judge to say, "The gloves are one, two and three. Take glove …"

Finally, a few minutes after nine, the time for watching was over and the time for doing had arrived. The team immediately preceding us — Pat Hansen and her border collie Otis — entered the ring.

I carried my scent articles and gloves to the judge's table. "These are for the next dog, number 275, a golden retriever," I told the steward.

"Put them right here on this chair," she said. "Good luck."

"Thanks," I replied, and restrained myself from saying, "We're gonna need it." Which Honeybear would enter the ring this morning? The poor, confused soul who had wandered through the spring shows or the happy, driving heeling machine who had been at my side on those summer evenings in Ed Dunn's ring?

Our ritual as we count down the final moments before our run never varies. Right before I get Honeybear out and head for the ring, I count the seven treats and drop them into my left shirt pocket.

Then, as we heel with perfect attention toward the ring, I dispense four. We halt about 20 feet from the ring, directly in line with the gate. There, HB sits in heel position, watching me intently, her eyes not darting away for an instant. Two more treats reward that perfect attention.

As the steward calls our number, I say, "Strut!" We move forward and HB gets the final treat as we near the gate. Once I had a judge say, "I hope she swallows it before she gets into the ring."

Now, on this comeback morning, we arrive at our holding spot, in a patch of shade, just as Pat and Otis exit the ring.

While the judge pauses at the table to do the requisite paperwork, Honeybear sits at my side, her eyes glued to mine. As the judge picks up her clipboard again, I drop HB's second-last treat. Snarf! It is gone and her eyes are locked on mine again.

Now the steward is calling, "Number 275."

"Strut," I say and we heel toward the gate. I pop the final treat and here we are. One step inside the ring I remove the leash and hand it to the steward. Honeybear slips into heel position.

"Good morning," Judge Stephens says. "This is your signal exercise. Are you ready?"

"Ready!" HB's head pops up.

"Forward," the judge says. I give a swipe of my left hand and away we go. At the first halt, I remember to breathe. And again right before the about turn.

The heeling isn't HB's all-time best, but it isn't bad. I'm aware of a wide on the about turn and, excited, she forges momentarily on the fast. Then she gives me a crooked front on the recall at the end of the hand signals.

The first scent article is the worst part of our run. HB has always held the metal article gingerly, and this morning she drops it halfway back, picks it up and gives me a lousy front.

On the second article both the front and finish are a shade crooked.

Her directed retrieve is all happy Honeybear. She dashes out to get the glove, snatches it, then plays with it merrily as she returns. Judge Stephens is kind, she deducts only half a point.

Honeybear's moving stand and examination are perfect.

She loses only half a point (a crooked finish) on the directed jumping exercise. That, all by itself, makes my day; directed jumping was where the lion's share of her springtime goofiness had manifested itself.

Done.

I heel her in a wide arc as I wait for the steward to bring us the leash, hoping to avoid the exuberant barking that at times has cost us points. As I attach the leash to her collar, Judge Stephens say, "Congratulations on a qualifying score."

"Good girl, Honeybear," I say and we begin our signature mad dash to get her Bonz.

A chocolate lab is the final dog in the class, and then it's over.

As the judge sits down to tally the scores and the placements,

I heel HB a bit to have her ready in case there is a runoff. But on this morning there is none.

Finally the steward calls, "Utility B qualifiers back to the ring." Seven of us gather in a semicircle, facing the small crowd at ringside for the presentation of awards. There have been only four casualties. No blood bath this morning.

Judge Stephens stands sideways so she can speak to us and to the spectators at the same time. At her side a steward holds the ribbons.

"This is the culmination of the Utility B class," the judge begins. "First of all, I'd like to thank my stewards. I couldn't have done it without them, and they were great." (Applause.)

"Next I'd like to ask the qualifiers to give themselves a hand. This was a very nice class. (Applause.) Eleven teams competed this morning. The seven you see here qualified." (More applause.)

She continues. "In Utility B a perfect score is 200. In order to qualify, a team must score at least 170 and receive 50 percent of the points on each exercise."

Then, "In first place this morning with a score of 193.5, dog and handler 275."

For a moment I stand stunned, in disbelief. Then it hits me. "HoneeBEAR!" I say, and we step forward to accept our blue ribbon, our green qualifying ribbon ... and 10 OTCH points!

What a way to come back. What an unbelievable, wonderful way to come back. And to think I almost had her in Veterans this morning.

Then we race back to the room for another Bonz.

CHAPTER 48

On The Disabled List

I entered Honeybear in Utility B again three weeks later at Sahuaro State Kennel Club.

On Saturday we finished second by a point to Bonnie Lee and her OTCH papillon Rosie. That was worth two points.

It rained that night and the grass was wet on Sunday morning. Rosie decided she didn't want to sit or heel or do much of anything else in that awful stuff. Our 194.5 got us first place and six OTCH points.

"And that," I told several people, "is why I welcome opportunities to train in the rain. When it's wet, HB is rarin' to go."

Those were our last OTCH points for 1998. We did show in Imperial, California, a week later. But although we qualified, we got no points.

Honeybear ended the year with 89 OTCH points. More importantly, she was gung-ho. Her summer rebirth had been no fluke. We were on a modest roll.

■ ■ ■

Our next shows were scheduled to be in Palm Springs, the weekend of January 9 and 10.

So December of 1998 was the best of times. Honeybear was back again, mentally strong and overjoyed to be working with me. And afternoons found us at our favorite place in all the world, the polo field at Paradise Valley Park.

Every afternoon I worked her lightly. Afterwards she ran with the bike and played a lot of ball.

December afternoons can be glorious for training in Phoenix. The weather has cooled. The days are mostly sunny and the joy of Christmas is pervasive.

That's also the time of year when the snowbirds (winter visitors) flock into Arizona. Which meant our friends from the North Scottsdale Polo Club had returned to practice at Paradise Valley Park. We once again were sharing the huge field with them, as we had each winter since HB and I began practicing there.

The polo ponies ignored us, and HB seldom gave them a second glance, even when they'd thunder past, sometimes no more than 35 feet away. After you reach a certain level of understanding on the dog's part, obedience competition training has a lot to do with proofing against distractions. And what better distraction than half a dozen polo ponies pounding by every few minutes?

Often when they'd take a break between chukkers (periods), the polo players would ride over to watch us train, and they'd ask a few questions. Many, in for the winter, were the scions of some of the wealthiest, most powerful families in the United States, although they never let you know that. They were interesting to talk to; they understood animal-related competitive sports and several proved quite knowledgeable about obedience competition training.

Surely the phrase, "It doesn't get any better than this," was meant to apply to those afternoons at the park — heightened, of course, by the fact that Old White Face was at my side again — big brown eyes dancing in the late fall sunshine.

But late in the afternoon of December 14, having returned home from the park, I saw Honeybear favoring her right rear leg, from time to time carrying it an inch off the ground.

Her final activity at the park that afternoon had been to chase the tennis ball a few times. I had been subliminally concerned about that game for a long time. She'd run after the ball and usually get possession of it by spinning and skidding in a cloud of dust. Putting a lot of stress on her legs. But as we left the park that afternoon, she showed no indication of lameness.

The next morning Dr. Toben diagnosed a hairline fracture in her right rear foot. Doubtlessly sustained during the ball game the previous afternoon. "There's nothing we can do about it," he said. "Just rest and let it heal."

So much for Palm Springs and the rest of the January shows.

About the same time, I was having pain, often intense, in my left ankle. A series of orthotics had accomplished nothing.

One afternoon I had set up a ring, my jumps and related equipment on the polo field and proceeded to train. By the time I was finished and had managed to get the dogs into the van, I was in severe pain. I was afraid I wouldn't be able to carry my equipment back to the van. Worse, I was the only person on the polo field that afternoon and at the time I had no cell phone.

I did manage to hobble back and forth and load the van. But clearly something had to be done. So I visited Todd Kile, M.D., an orthopedic specialist at the Mayo Clinic Scottsdale.

Dr. Kile diagnosed instability in the subtalar joint, resulting in shifting of the joint components, inflammation and pain. He prescribed a large pneumatic boot — a cast of sorts — to be worn all my waking hours for several months.

My friends in the dog training community were fascinated. They said things like, "Wow, if you wear that in the ring maybe the judges will give you sympathy points."

Honeybear was ready to practice again early in February. By that time I had become skilled at heeling a dog while wearing the boot.

I entered HB only one day of the two-show PFOC weekend, just to see how ready we were. I was wearing the boot for the first time in AKC competition. Although we failed when HB took a wrong jump, we received a perfect score on the signal exercise, composed largely of heeling. A perfect score in heeling is extraordinary. That was only the second time I remembered Honeybear accomplishing such a feat.

For the remainder of that day I was the target of numerous good-natured verbal jabs about the boot and sympathy points.

HB and I were definitely back … again.

■ CHAPTER 49 ■

What Next?!

Across the years, worriers had predicted that someday one of us was going to get whacked in the head by a polo mallet or run down by a charging horse. But disaster, when it struck, took a different form.

It was one of those perfect late winter days we have here in Arizona. The to-die-for kind right before it becomes so scorchingly hot the cacti uproot themselves, come into town and pretend to be fireplugs.

We had finished practice. I had taken the ring down, put away the jumps. Now it was time for our conditioning routine.

I would ride the bike around the perimeter of the polo field, just inside the fence. Honeybear, at nine-plus years, would chase me at her own pace. She'd run off and sniff, then gallop half the length of the field to catch up. The perfect way for an older dog to stay in competition condition ... except on this day.

I looked back and she was coming very slowly. I remember saying aloud, "Oh come on HB, you can't be tired, this is only the first lap."

Then I stopped, and as she drew closer I saw she was holding up her right rear leg, trying to catch up on three legs.

I didn't see what happened back there and HB wasn't saying. My best guess is she stepped in a gopher hole.

Off we went to Dr. Toben. "Ruptured anterior cruciate ligament," he said. And promptly referred us to veterinary orthopedic specialist Bradford Dixon.

Let's pause here for a little anatomy lesson. The anterior cruciate ligament (ACL) stabilizes the knee. That ligament prevents the tibia (the long bone of the lower leg) from sliding forward against the femur (the long bone of the upper leg) when the dog puts weight on the leg. When the ACL is ruptured, the tibia slides forward on the femur and makes the dog's leg unstable.

To better understand this and the explanation that follows, visualize a wagon sitting on a hill. The wagon is tied in place with an old, frayed rope. That rope is all that keeps the wagon from rolling down the hill. If the rope breaks, there goes the wagon. In the dog's leg, the femur is analogous to the wagon, the anterior cruciate ligament is analogous to the rope.

I knew all too well the implications of the diagnosis.

You need only read the sports pages. There you learn about Joe Megabucks of the NFL, NHL or NBA (choose your sport) who has just "blown out his knee (ruptured his ACL) and will miss the rest of the season."

About the time Honeybear sustained her injury, we learned that Moises Alou of the Houston Astros, one of major league baseball's superstars, had ruptured his ACL in spring training. "He'll be out for at least six months," the team announced.

Great! And here's my nine-year-old golden with the same injury … just 11 points shy of her OTCH.

So now we're in Dr. Dixon's office. He examines Honeybear and confirms the diagnosis. "There are two ways to repair this," he says, and he walks to the blackboard where he draws as he speaks.

First he describes the traditional ACL surgery where the ligament is repaired or replaced with suture material. Following that procedure, there may be complications such as residual lameness, continuing joint instability, reaction to the suture material or degenerative osteoarthritis — none of which is compatible with obedience competition.

Then he tells me about a procedure called a tibial plateau-leveling osteotomy (TPLO).

The method was developed by Barclay Slocum, an innovative veterinary surgeon who practices and trains other veterinarians in Eugene, Oregon.

The surgery is complex. It involves serious cutting of the bone to level the top end of the tibia, and subsequent rotation of the tibia along an imaginary vertical axis. The cutting and the rotation, together, change to zero degrees the angle of the top of the tibia. Normally, in the unmodified knee of a dog, that angle is 25 to 28 degrees — which is why the tibia slides if the restraining tension of the ACL is removed and the muscular support around the knee is not in balance. Once the cut in the bone is made and the bone is rotated, it is stabilized with a stainless steel plate while it heals in the new position.

These manipulations alter the biomechanics of the joint and the weight-bearing properties of the leg so that the dog's knee is stable when she's standing on it.

Let's now refer back to the analogy of the wagon on the hill. If the hill is leveled (as is the top of the tibia), the wagon (the femur) will not move even though the rope (the ACL) has snapped. So, following the surgery, when the femur hits the tibia it stays put.

Dr. Dixon was aware of Honeybear's life as an obedience competition dog, aware that she was on the brink of an Obedience Trial Championship.

After he finished his chalk talk, he said, "If Honeybear were a couch potato, I'd say let's do the traditional procedure. But given her lifestyle, and if money is not a factor — about $1,700 versus about $800 — I'd recommend the TPLO."

Photo: Barbara Bailey

Hydrotherapy: Suzanne Hayes with HB

The only veterinary surgeon in Arizona trained in the TPLO procedure was Jim Boulay in Tucson — a 250-mile round trip. Dr. Boulay had performed the procedure over 250 times with excellent long-term results.

So off we went to Tucson. It was March 10, 1999.

"We'll have you back in the ring in four months," Dr. Boulay said on the way to the operating room.

Maybe so ... maybe so. On the third day post-surgery, Honeybear was gingerly putting weight on the toes of the surgically repaired right hind leg. On the ninth day, she began testing her full weight on the leg. She had her staples removed on March 22 and we began hydrotherapy three days later.

■ ■ ■

Prior to Honeybear's surgery, I had investigated canine hydrotherapy and liked what I learned. Dr. Boulay approved.

Canine hydrotherapist Suzanne Hayes encouraged us to begin as soon as the stitches (actually nasty-looking staples) were removed. "The longer you have an injury, the more your body adapts to it," she counseled. "We want to prevent bad habits before they start."

Those bad habits emanate from short-circuited patterns of communication between the body and the brain of the dog. "Once a dog is injured and/or goes through the type of surgery Honeybear experienced," Suzanne told me, "the message sent back to the brain is what we call the *pain pattern*. The leg may no longer be injured, but the message the leg sends isn't telling the brain that."

The dog reacts accordingly, with all sorts of compensatory behavior. So one of the primary goals of Honeybear's hydrotherapy was to repattern the communication between her body and her brain.

There were additional goals.

Increasing Honeybear's range of motion was also important. Some of that range of motion had been lost as a result of the injury and the surgery. "The more range of motion Honeybear has, the more she'll be able to maintain her muscle mass and her strength," Suzanne explained. That made sense to me.

Hydrotherapy also provides an excellent aerobic workout. Honeybear is a dog who — thank God — had been on a serious lifelong conditioning program prior to her injury. Now her activity level had been sharply curtailed. And it became obvious before the end of her first therapy session that she loved this respite from her sudden — and puzzling to her — role as a couch potato.

Why *hydro*therapy?

First of all, the animal is virtually weightless in a swimming pool. Honeybear could work energetically in the water without having to support her body weight.

Second, Suzanne pointed out, "When you put the dog in the water, if she is compensating for the disability of a particular body part, the water level shows you where the problem is."

In Honeybear's case, the water line was uneven across her hips. It was higher on her right side ... the injured, surgically repaired side. That showed she wasn't using her right hind leg very well to keep that hip up in the water.

The pool itself is one of the players in the hydrotherapy drama. It is important that the pool in which the hydrotherapy takes place be quite warm — 90 to 92 degrees is ideal. The warm temperature induces instant relaxation, which is conducive to the best possible results.

"Those who don't understand may make a serious mistake," Suzanne cautioned. "They get as far as realizing swimming can be great therapy. So they take the dog to a cold lake or a relatively cool pool. That's going to tighten the muscles, impede the therapy, maybe even trigger further injury."

Honeybear's therapy took place in six one-hour sessions. The first three were on consecutive nights the weekend after the staples were removed. The final three took place the following weekend.

The techniques Suzanne uses are rooted in the Kern Method, developed and taught by Kathy Kern, a registered veterinary technician who is affiliated with the Animal Fitness Center in San Jose, California. (For more information, log on to *www.dogtherapy.com*.)

Suzanne introduced several swimming exercises designed to induce Honeybear to use her injured leg in a variety of non-weight-bearing ways.

- *Circles.* I would be seated at poolside. Suzanne would turn Honeybear so she was facing 180 degrees from me. Then I'd call, "Honeybear!" She would turn all the way around so she could face me. From the first session to the sixth, those circles got tighter and tighter, indicating Honeybear had increasing range of motion and leg strength and was progressing in her ability to use her hip and leg correctly.

- *Floating on her back.* From time to time, Suzanne would gently hoist Honeybear out of the water, turn her over and cradle her in her arms, steadying her as she floated on her back.

  "Floating on their backs, once they gain confidence in it, can trigger a huge relaxation release." Suzanne said. "Often the lower lumbar area will adjust itself while the dog floats on her back. Several times during these sessions, I've felt Honeybear adjust her vertebrae.

  "And of course," she added, "floating gives her a chance to catch her breath."

- *Pushbacks.* Suzanne would push the dog backward in the water, forcing the rear end to submerge. Honeybear would have to use her back legs to bring her rear end to the surface again. Suzanne introduced this exercise during the second week, after Honeybear had begun to gain strength and was able to recover more effectively from the pushbacks.

- *Massage*. Suzanne spent a great deal of time in the water working on Honeybear's shoulders and front. "When a dog's back end isn't 100 percent," she explained, "they put extra stress on the front as they compensate for the injury at the back end. So I worked quite a bit to relax the muscles of Honeybear's shoulders and thoracic area."

- Throughout the sessions, Suzanne persisted in exaggerating Honeybear's symptoms. "We have a tendency, if the dog's leg is not in the correct position, to reach down and put it where it belongs. Which accomplishes nothing," she explained.

    "To the contrary, if I saw Honeybear's leg wasn't working well as she swam, if she was kicking out rather than straight back, I'd tip her in the water to allow her to kick out even further. That would trigger the brain to send a signal to try to move the leg into the correct position. That's the repatterning which was one of our primary goals."

By the end of the third session, Honeybear had regained most of her range of motion and had noticeably more leg strength than she had during the first session. During the final three sessions, Suzanne intensified her work with the quadriceps muscles and the hamstrings of both legs.

And how did Honeybear react to her therapy sessions?

She thought she had died and gone to the nice warm pool in the sky. Arriving for her therapy, she would bark, squeal and try to jump into the pool on her own.

According to Suzanne, that was a plus. "When she's is in the pool, it's warm, she's relaxed and her body is working in a nonstressful environment. Consequently, she's producing more endorphins."

Endorphins are morphine-like chemicals secreted by the brain. Their presence causes a low level of euphoria. In humans it has been proven that if you can stimulate the production of endorphins after surgery, the patient heals more quickly.

At the time of Honeybear's rehab program, Suzanne was the only trained canine hydrotherapist in Arizona. And she may be part of the wave of the future.

"With more sophisticated surgeries on dogs," she emphasized, "it's important that we catch up with the humans and do more sophisticated rehab. We must take what we've learned on humans and apply it to the aftercare of animals."

That application, in Honeybear's case, was made difficult because Suzanne did not have her own pool. Which placed her in a position of perpetually scrounging around the Phoenix metropolitan area for a pool that met our needs in a variety of ways.

Although March is a lovely month here in the Valley, we were still many weeks short of the sizzling days when the sun can heat a pool and keep it warm 24 hours a day. And remember, the ideal water temperature for canine hydrotherapy is 90 to 92 degrees.

So we needed an indoor pool. If that narrowed the options, think what happened when the health department regulations came into play. Simply stated, it is verboten to swim dogs in a commercial pool intended for people.

But Suzanne, trying to build a business, had conducted her search with intensity — and with fragile success.

A lady in an eastern suburb had a large indoor pool devoted to teaching kids to swim. She was sympathetic to Suzanne's need and the two of them had worked out an arrangement that was steeped in intrigue.

HB and I would schlep across town, a 40-mile trip. We would arrive in the parking lot about the time the last kids' swim class was letting out. We'd lurk there until all the kids and moms and dads had left. Then Suzanne, who had arrived earlier, would give us the high sign. We'd skulk in and the therapy would begin.

Later, in June, long after Honeybear's sessions with Suzanne had ended, I used the pool of a friendly neighbor and continued many of the exercises I had learned from Suzanne. By then we also had resumed light obedience training in the evenings after the sun went down.

So several mornings a week Honeybear got to swim — and play ball in the pool! And most evenings she got to train with me.

In terms of her recovery from surgery, one might say things had gone swimmingly.

CHAPTER 50

"I Won't Jump ... Don't Ask Me"

My original plan had been to resume our quest at Ventura, California. The three-show weekend, called SummerFest, would begin July 10, exactly four months from the date of HB's surgery. But as we proceeded through our rehab, I began to think more conservatively.

Honeybear is nine and a half, I told myself. *And we're on the 11-yard line. Why not proceed cautiously, raise the jumps slowly and make sure we don't encounter another setback?*

That's what we did. The new target date for our return became the Prescott Arizona Kennel Club shows, September 18 and 19.

I should have known the remainder of our journey would be full of hair-raising episodes. Had it ever been any other way with HB?

By the time we got back to full-scale training again, it was summer here in the desert. Many people think you can't train in the summer in Phoenix unless you have an air-conditioned indoor facility. Which we don't. But necessity is the mother of invention.

For most of Honeybear's career, we trained in the late afternoon, except when it was brutally hot — say 115 degrees or more.

I'd park my van next to the fence along the polo field, leave the engine running and the air conditioning turned up full-blast.

We'd train a few minutes, then cool off a few minutes. I'd gotten quite good at reading my dog's heat tolerance. Honeybear never has gotten overheated, not once.

As Honeybear began to get older, I tried training in the morning during the summer. Up at 5 a.m. Arrive at the park between 6 o'clock and 6:15. We did that for a couple of summers. But for me, king of the hypoglycemics, it was a drag. I'm definitely not a morning person.

I decided to try evenings, with an afternoon session thrown in every so often.

Moon Valley Park is about two and a half miles from home. It has lighted tennis courts and a lighted basketball court. Together they throw off plenty of light. And the grass nearest the basketball court not only has the best illumination, it also offers the distractions of basketball games in progress on summer evenings.

We resumed HB's training late in May. It was pure euphoria. Honeybear was back! *We* were back! There she was, at my side again, her old white face shining in the artificial light. Seeming to say, "Let's go, Skippy! We have an OTCH to get!"

That first evening Honeybear's jumps were set at eight inches. I had a schedule that would bring us to 24 inches a couple of weeks before the Prescott shows. Prior to that, for an extended period, HB would jump 22 inches.

She frisked through those summer evenings of training. She hadn't forgotten a thing. She was still the same can't-miss girl on the scent articles. She'd charge out to the correct glove, snatch it up and occasionally toss it in the air and catch it on the way back. Her fake-one-way-and-go-the-other start on the directed jumping was still good for momentary cardiac arrest. But the layoffs hadn't improved her fronts one bit.

■ ■ ■

As we prepare for a trial, I like to set up whatever kind of ring we'll encounter at the show: rebar and rope, white posts with white chain, ring gates, etc. The idea is to let HB see in practice whatever she'll be looking at as I set her up for the go-outs in a show. There is a major difference between being sent 50 feet to a blue stanchion flanked by white ring gates and being sent to a piece of rusty rebar supporting a rope.

I had purchased a few sections of ring gates earlier. Now I decided to spring for the several hundred dollars worth of additional sections to complete my ring.

The day they arrived it was cloudy and not too hot. For unknown reasons, the field wasn't locked that summer. Arriving, I hauled the four heavy bags of ring gates out of the van and began setting them up. Forty-five minutes later I stood back to admire my shiny new ring, a 40- by 50-foot rectangle of white on the polo field grass. It was as pretty as the picture in the catalog.

Now to set up the jumps. Then HB and I could initiate my new ring. Except that, in my excitement about my new ring, I had left my high jump waiting silently in the garage, a 40-minute round trip.

Trapped!

I wasn't about to leave my new ring there while I scrambled home to pick up the forgotten jump. Nor was I about to take the ring down, pack the bags, hoist them into the back of the van, drive home, then come back and start over. And you can't practice directed jumping without two jumps.

By that time I had a cell phone. I called Barbara, in the middle of a busy afternoon. "OK," I began, "I've got this problem." She, of course, wasn't overjoyed, but she agreed to finish a few things, then go home, load the high jump into her car and bring it to the park. It would take about an hour, maybe a little more.

So we heeled, played some ball, heeled some more. Did a few signals, some gloves. It was July, monsoon season here in the desert, and as we waited I watched black clouds come rolling in. Would we have a thunderstorm or just a hard blow that would tear up my new ring gates on the very first day?

Finally Barbara arrived, only to tell me that the five-foot-wide high jump wouldn't fit in her car. So she had brought the other bar jump.

Half a loaf is better than none. We set up the two bar jumps. Now!

With one eye on the threatening sky, I took Honeybear into the beautiful new ring and set her up for the first go-out.

"Go-outs, Honeybear," I told her quietly. "Straight. Straight." She sat, head forward, focused on the stanchion 50 feet in front of her.

"Away!" I cried. And away she went, fast and straight toward the center stanchion.

"Honeybear!" I called, "sit!" She turned and settled into a sit about five feet in front of the stanchion. A perfect go-out.

After a momentary pause, I extended my left arm straight out from the side of my body, simultaneously calling, "Bar!"

She set sail straight for the jump on my left … and pulled up short. Afraid. Unwilling. Something. But she didn't jump.

"That's odd," I said. "I can't remember Honeybear refusing to jump." And my stomach knotted.

"Let's try the other one," I said.

Same drill. "Away!" Perfect go-out, perfect turn and sit.

Raising my right arm, I cried, "Bar!" Again she headed straight for the jump. Again she stopped short.

We tried it two more times that afternoon, with the same outcome.

"Maybe it's the jumps," I suggested. "It must look awfully funny to her, two bar jumps and no high jump."

"Maybe," Barbara said, but her voice was hollow.

When I had called Barbara to bring the jump, I realized it was going to get late before we got out of there. I asked her to bring a couple of cheeseburgers. Concerned about the gathering storm, I waited to eat until we had christened the new ring with directed jumping.

Now, as the clouds rolled in, we sat in silence and ate our sandwiches. I looked out across the polo field. All those thousands of afternoons, all those things I had taught her. That bright, fresh face at my side across almost a decade. And now this.

Although it was nearly six o'clock, I wasn't hungry.

That afternoon I realized the sand was rapidly running out of the hourglass. It had been nearly a year since AnneMarie Silverton had jolted me with a wakeup call. If I was going to put an OTCH on this dog, we would have to be superefficient about it, not diddle around show after show after show.

We were nearly finished packing and loading when the rain began. It had been a dismal afternoon.

■ ■ ■

As our rehab training progressed, I was nagged by the realization that it had been eight months since Honeybear and I had been in an AKC ring with a real judge and all the sights and sounds of an obedience trial.

The Southwest Obedience Club of Los Angeles (SWOC) was holding a trial at Alondra Park in Lawndale, California, on August 14. In addition to the regular classes, they offered a slate of nonregular classes, among them Veterans. It seemed a good opportunity to see where we were.

Veterans began right after lunch. Honeybear was excited. She had waited stoically all morning. Her performance can only be described as magnificent.

Our judge was the pleasant, experienced Shirley Indelicato. First came the heel on leash. HB was right there, head up and driving. Putting on a clinic. Next the figure eight. Same enthusiasm, same gung-ho girl.

At the end of the figure eight exercise, Judge Indelicato stood in the middle of the ring, put her hands on her hips and exclaimed, "*This* is a veteran dog?"

Honeybear won the class with a 198.

I drove back to Phoenix happy with her performance and her attitude. But the doubts about her jumping still nagged me.

■ ■ ■

My fears were valid. Some days HB would, and some days she wouldn't. It wasn't the blitzed-out confusion I had seen far too often during that depressing spring the year before. This was simply refusal to jump. It was particularly scary, as the jumps were still set at 22 inches, two inches short of her AKC jump height.

I had her checked and X-rayed. Everything was fine. The surgically repaired knee was working perfectly. The answer, everyone knew, didn't require rocket science. Honeybear was getting old. Her back end wasn't what it once was. And it wasn't going to get any better.

We were running out of time.

■ ■ ■

Friday, September 17: Up I-17 we went, full of trepidation. Honeybear was working nicely, but would she jump? "Well," I said, "when we drive back down this highway on Sunday afternoon, we'll know."

The trip home on Sunday afternoon would be special in another way, too. Sunday, September 19, would be our 40th wedding anniversary. "We'll celebrate at a dog show??!!" Barbara had said to several people, only half joking. She had no clue what was to come.

When we were much younger, and before dog sports had consumed our lives, we would go to the Bahamas or the Caribbean each year, sometimes twice. We'd lie in the sun, stroll nearly deserted beaches, scuba dive, snorkel, and sail.

After the first few years — after we discovered the *real* Caribbean, the one most tourists never see — we sought out what are referred to as "barefoot resorts." The loneliest outposts of the Caribbean. Usually small. Informal. No phones, no TV. Miles of beach where the only footprints were ours. Crystal-clear water. Teeming reefs.

Our favorite, by far, was Young Island. A tiny green gem that sits 200 yards off St. Vincent. Bali Ha'i-like with only 30 cottages scattered about the hillside, offering ocean views well down into the Grenadines.

Young Island had captured our hearts way back in the '60s. We had been back several times, but not for 20 years. What a great way to celebrate 40 years of marriage.

As I planned the trip my attitude was, *What the hell, you celebrate 40 years only once and God knows what kind of shape we'll be in when our 50th rolls around.*

As we loaded the van for the Prescott trip, I had hidden an envelope in the pocket in back of my seat. It contained two first-class airline tickets, a Young Island brochure and our reservation for cottage 17 — the highest, the one with the best view, the one where iguanas eat bananas out of your hand on the patio.

But first we had to face our two-day date with destiny. The fat was in the fire; we didn't have another year to horse around.

As we drove up I-17, HB was in her usual spot in the well between the seats. Nice and comfy with her chin against my seat, looking up at me. I had questions but I knew she wouldn't be answering.

■ CHAPTER 51 ■

You Can Cut It With A Knife

If the Ramada Inn grounds in Tucson lead my list of favorite show sites, Pioneer Park in Prescott ranks near the bottom.

The rings are situated in a bowl and the parking is on a plateau a considerable distance away. A steep concrete walkway connects the two. And that sheer schlep is how you get your stuff — tent, crates, coolers, chairs, dogs, and God knows what else — to and from ringside. On Friday, when you set up, the idea is to avoid being wiped out by your runaway cart. Then on Sunday afternoon, when you are already exhausted from two long days of stress and competition, you get to pull it all back up the hill.

Add the fact that Prescott features some of the worst motels on the circuit and you have less than wonderful conditions surrounding an otherwise nice show.

Now take all I have just said and toss it in the can. Because the Prescott Arizona Kennel Club shows are where Honeybear and I got our first two OTCH points.

So here we were three years later, back on the turf that held fond memories. Trying to come back from a retirement born of despair, followed by big-time, bone-cutting surgery.

Dorothy Holmes, a veteran trainer and competitor who shows with us frequently, had said, "If Honeybear screws up, you shouldn't get upset. After what she's been through, every time she walks into the ring it's a blessing."

So forget the tacky motels. Forget the steep climb. We were overjoyed to be going to Prescott.

■ ■ ■

When we arrived on Friday afternoon to set up, the field was soggy in spots, the result of several days of rain that week. It rained again Friday night. Saturday morning the rings were a bit mushy and the grass glistened in the sun.

Earlier in our career I would have said, "All right! This is Honeybear weather."

But this was different and I was concerned. We hadn't had much bad weather since HB's TPLO. I hadn't had a chance to test how she'd perform on slick grass. I could visualize her slipping, wrenching that knee and ending her career right there in Prescott. To say nothing of the pain and expense involved.

Besides, the big bugaboo casting a shadow over the weekend was would she jump under even the best of conditions? It was not a comfortable situation.

But luck was with us. Honeybear would be last in the ring in a Utility B class of 12, all of whom showed up. Which meant we wouldn't be in the ring until mid-morning — giving the grass a chance to dry somewhat and relieve my anxieties.

Once you pick up your armband, you are expected to go into the ring and compete. Normally I pick up mine long before the class begins.

But on this morning I told Barbara, "I'm not going to pick up for quite a while. Let's see how some of those other large dogs handle the jumps on this wet grass." Among the dogs scheduled to precede us were two Dobermans, a border collie, a bouvier, and a Rottweiler.

I got HB out and walked her several times. We played ball twice, heeled once. Meanwhile, I didn't see one dog slip. The Rottweiler was two dogs before us. By that time the sun had dried the ring considerably. I had seen enough. I picked up my armband, walked over to Honeybear's crate and said, "OK, big girl, we're gonna show!"

HB was sitting bolt upright, had been all morning — not her usual too-laid-back demeanor a couple of hours before her turn in the ring.

And then it was our turn. "Let's go, HB, let's go show," I said. Honeybear exploded out of her crate with a "Whoop!"

Our judge was Pauline Andrus, one-half of a husband/wife team. Husband Larry would be our Utility B judge on Sunday. We had shown under them a couple of times before and I knew them to be professional, exceptionally affable and fair.

■ ■ ■

Now the ring steward, Harry Burke, is calling us: "Golden retriever number 706." I give HB a hand signal to heel. Just before we get to the ring I pop my last treat into her mouth.

You can cut the tension with a knife. Thank God Honeybear and I are both seasoned. She certainly hasn't left anything in her crate this morning. Her eyes are dancing with what I call her "rascal look." I'm worried she might start her exuberant barking any second.

Her heeling is much like it was on those Wednesday evenings in Ed Dunn's ring, darn near perfect.

She gets the right scent article each time, albeit with her signature crooked fronts.

She tosses the glove joyously as she brings it to me.

Later someone tells me she traveled a step or two as I left her on the moving stand.

And now for our final exercise, directed jumping. I set HB up in heel position, facing the opposite end of the ring. "Directed jumping, Honeybear. Straight. Straight." HB's eyes lock onto the center stanchion, 50 feet away.

"This will be your directed jumping exercise," Mrs. Andrus says while I'm trying to remember to breathe.

"Are you ready?" I nod.

"Send your dog."

"Away!" Honeybear bounds out joyously between the jumps, straight as an arrow. Once, as we were leaving Judge Bud Skarbek's Utility B ring and shortly before he awarded us first place, the judge had laughed and said, "The regulations say the dog is supposed to *run* out there, not *hop* out there."

"Honeybear ... sit!" I call. She does.

"Bar jump," Mrs. Andrus says. *Dear God, please make her jump.*

Here she comes. She's up and over and back to me in a perfect front.

"Good girl! Good girl!" (*You too, God.*)

Back into heel position. *Dear God, just one more.*

Now Mrs. Andrus is saying, "Directed jumping, part two. Are you ready?"

I inhale deeply, wipe my sweaty palms on my pants and nod.

"Send your dog."

"Away!" And she's hopping merrily all the way to the other end.

"Honeybear ... sit!" *Am I going to faint? No, not if I breathe.*

"High jump," Mrs. Andrus says from somewhere out in the fog.

Up goes my right hand, "High!"

Here she comes again, over that jump like a deer. And another perfect front.

"Finish," the judge says.

I give my left-hand signal and get a perfect swing into heel position.

Then I hear, "Exercise finished." And a moment later, "Congratulations on a qualifying score." And behind me, applause.

Harry Burke brings in the leash and, in a low voice, says, "Good job."

HB strains at the leash. It's time for our mad dash back to the tent for her Bonz. All the way I fight back tears. *My wonderful big girl is back! She's back! She's back!*

I have no idea of our score or where we'll place in the class that's just concluded. But for the first time I know for dead certain that very soon, in some ring somewhere in the southwestern United States, some judge will hand me a ribbon and I'll hear applause for a newly crowned Obedience Trial Champion.

We were the final team in the ring, so the awards presentation will be coming up shortly, right after the judge and the stewards complete the endless paperwork required by the AKC.

Which means right now HB and I have work to do. Always, without fail, when the judge sits down to write I get my dog out to heel, to warm up for a possible runoff in the event of a tie.

But there are no ties this day and soon Harry Burke is calling, "Utility B qualifiers back to the ring."

Having thanked her stewards, Judge Andrus tells the spectators at ringside, "This morning there were 12 teams entered in Utility B." (That's 10 OTCH points for first, three for second.) "Three have survived."

The three surviving teams are Kathy Lena of Tucson and her border collie Megan, Adrienne Perry and her Rottweiler Melissa and us.

"In Utility a perfect score is 200," Judge Andrus continues. "We didn't have one of those this morning. But in first place with a very nice score of 194.5 we have dog and handler 706."

It takes a second for the neurons to fire. Then: "All right HoneeBEAR!" We leap forward and HB barks ecstatically as I accept the blue ribbon.

Ninety-nine OTCH points. Only one to go.

I must have driven Barbara crazy the rest of that day, saying over and over, "Oh my God, to think I almost pulled her this morning. We almost didn't go into the ring."

CHAPTER 52

It Doesn't Get Any Better

The next morning dawned clear, sunny and dry. Show days don't get any better.

Overnight the word had spread like wildfire. "Willard and Honeybear are going for their OTCH tomorrow. They need only one point."

When we arrived at Pioneer Park, the place was abuzz. People I had never seen before and haven't seen since walked up to me and said, "Good luck to you and Honeybear today."

I picked up my armband 30 minutes before the class started. Bea Dunn, who was stewarding for Larry Andrus, touched my hand and said, "Good luck, Willard."

The judging order was the same as the day before. We would be the last of 12 teams. All were present.

I pulled my chair close to the ring and settled in to watch. What's the judge's heeling pattern? Where is he putting the scent articles? What's the order of the gloves? And importantly, how long does he take between dogs? I didn't want to get HB to the ring too soon, then have her wilt while we waited for the judge. That had happened to us early in our career.

As I watched, Honeybear sat bolt upright in her crate. Yesterday I had welcomed the opportunity for the grass to dry. Today the wait was interminable.

At one point, just before our turn came, Nancy Craig, a local judge, tapped me on the shoulder. She would be judging obedience at the Kennel Club of Riverside (California) in two weeks. She knew we were entered. She also knew I would pull HB from the Riverside shows if we finished our OTCH at Prescott.

"Good luck, Willard," she said. "I have to leave now and go to the breed rings. If I don't see you at Riverside, I'll know you did it today. And I hope I don't see you."

Commenting on the performances in Utility B on Saturday, Harry Burke had said, "It was a blood bath in there." Sunday brought more of the same, only to a lesser degree. Three of 12 had qualified on Saturday. Five would pass on Sunday. Utility B is a treacherous ring. You never can predict who will go down and who will be left standing.

So we sat and waited and watched as the drama unfolded and, using Harry's metaphor, the blood flowed.

I had wondered, been slightly concerned, about how energetic Honeybear would be on Sunday. Even when HB was a young dog, a show or a match took a lot out of both of us.

Often her score would drop on the second day. And now she was nearing 10 years of age and coming off major orthopedic surgery. Make no mistake, dogs — even seasoned dogs — stress out at dog shows. You need only notice how much diarrhea is on the ground to know that.

As it turned out, I need not have worried. Again HB exploded out of her crate with a "Whoop!" that would set the tone for her Utility B performance that morning.

As our turn neared, folks began to appear, chairs in hand, to get a good seat outside Ring 2, ours.

Judging in Ring 1 had concluded and the judge and stewards were tallying up the scores. But as they saw Honeybear and me waiting outside our ring, Judge Pauline Andrus and Stewards Harry and Jo Burke temporarily put their papers aside, turned their chairs 90 degrees and sat back to watch.

■ ■ ■

Then we heeled into the ring for our moment of truth.

The heeling and signals were superb; we lost one point. We got a perfect score on the first scent article, lost half a point on the second. HB's exuberant mouthing cost us half a point on the directed retrieve exercise. She was perfect on the moving stand and examination.

We were smoking. Later I learned that as we set up for the directed jumping exercise we had lost only two points; we were working on a 198.

I heard myself thinking, *Honeybear, if you've ever jumped, jump today*.

"Send your dog," Larry Andrus said.

"Away!" I said.

Away she went … at a 45-degree angle to her right. Straight to and over the high jump. Then she stopped, turned, looked at me and said, "Oh, oh, I screwed up, didn't I?"

"Oh no!" Judge Andrus said.

And behind me, in unison, the crowd went, "Ooohhh."

So much for finishing our OTCH at Prescott.

We lined up for the second part of the exercise. This time I was aware that HB was eyeing the high jump. Sure enough, she did it again. But at that point it no longer mattered.

What Honeybear had done in Utility B that Sunday morning was not a new problem. It was one of HB's old, familiar stunts. Several times during her career something had short-circuited in her head and she had gotten into a rut where she'd fixate on one jump and take that jump on the go-outs. I knew how to fix it but it would take a few weeks.

So here we had a dog bearing down on her tenth birthday. One point shy of her OTCH. And it had come down to the last exercise in Utility B.

Under the circumstances the only thing to do is smile. So as we left Judge Andrus' Utility ring that morning, I said to the crowd, "We're having Honeybear stroganoff for dinner tonight. You're all invited."

A wonderful thing happened during the awards presentations. Erik Hoyer, who lived only a half mile away and had been a source of encouragement and support, won the class with a score of 194.5. As he stepped forward to receive the blue ribbon, he looked in the direction where I was standing outside the ring and said, "I would much rather have finished second today."

That's the spirit of dog obedience competition at its finest. It doesn't get any better than that.

■ ■ ■

Close, but no cigar. But I wasn't all that unhappy as we headed home. In fact, I wasn't unhappy at all.

First of all, HB was back. Back at my side and driving with gusto. Never before in her career — not even at The Gaines — had she worked with as much enthusiasm as she had displayed at Prescott.

Second, I had promised myself that the day she got her OTCH I would retire her from the regular classes. "You'll never have to jump again," I had told her as we practiced at Paradise Valley Park. But now as we neared our OTCH, I was haunted by the somber prospect that soon my big girl would never again be at my side in the AKC ring. Today we had been granted an extension.

As we drove toward Phoenix, Honeybear was in her usual spot in the well between the seats. I reached down, patted her on the head and said, "We've got work to do, big girl. We've got to fix those go-outs."

Then I turned to Barbara and said, "Reach into the pocket behind my seat and pull out the envelope that's in there."

■ CHAPTER 53 ■

In A Cold Sweat

Reflecting on the Prescott shows, there was bad news and good news.

The bad news was that, needing only one point and having one of the best — perhaps *the* best — Utility runs of her life, Honeybear had blown up and failed to salt it away.

The good news was she had jumped, albeit at the wrong time, going the wrong direction.

When working with a dog as experienced as Honeybear, a veteran of thousands of hours of training and hundreds of ring appearances, it's rare to encounter a training problem you haven't battled earlier in the dog's career.

Such was the case with HB's sudden meltdown in Prescott. I had first encountered the problem in Utility A.

You teach the directed jumping exercise in pieces. Jumping is the easiest piece. A dog who has made it to Utility probably loves to jump. The dog who doesn't like to jump or is physically unable will drop out of the sport shortly after Novice.

It's the go-outs that are difficult to teach. First of all, you have to convince the dog that it's wonderful to run *away* from you at top speed … after you've spent several years convincing her that the most desirable place in the world is at your side.

Not only do you want the dog to run away from you, you want her to go straight as an arrow. That means down the center, between the jumps — it does not mean leaping over one of them on the way out. The concept of straight does not come easily to a dog.

And finally, the dog must learn to run out straight and keep going until you call her name (her signal to turn) and tell her to sit. The pitfall here is that dogs get too smart too quickly. It doesn't take them long to begin to think, *Oh, I know this. I run out to about here, then I turn and sit.* Thus anticipating your command and losing points.

Go-outs are taught in various ways. Some trainers teach the go-out as a retrieve exercise. They place the retrieve object exactly where they want the dog to go: dead center at the other end of the ring. Eventually they eliminate the retrieve object and introduce the turn and sit.

Many of us use a target. There is almost always a center pole or center stanchion at the end of the ring. We put cheese or some other type of food on the stanchion. Or we put a toy on the ground at the base. The dog is eventually weaned off the food or toy.

In any case, those dogs who reach Utility B, and particularly those who are pursuing an OTCH, have long since mastered go-outs.

In general, Honeybear did beautiful go-outs, bounding out fast and straight, turning on a dime and plopping down right in the center of the far end of the ring.

Except that twice before we had faced the problem that now stymied us only one point shy of her OTCH.

Mysterious things go on in the heads of even the best-trained dogs. Suddenly, as we'd set up for the directed-jumping exercise, she'd fixate on one of the jumps. Often I wasn't even aware it was happening. Later someone who had been standing outside the ring would tell me, "She wasn't even looking straight when you set her up. Her head was straight but she was eyeing that jump." And sure enough, over she'd go.

I had learned how to fix the problem but it was not a quick fix. The cure was based upon the assumption the dog knew how to do good go-outs, which HB certainly did.

A regulation obedience competition ring is 50 feet long by 40 feet wide. Regulation Utility jumps, a bar jump and a solid high jump, are each five feet wide. They are placed at the midpoint of the long dimension of the ring — that is, 25 feet from each end. One is placed five feet in from each side of the ring. That leaves a corridor 20 feet wide down the center between the jumps. Call it the go-outs corridor.

One way to correct the problem Honeybear was having now — taking a jump on the go-out instead of running straight down the middle — is to create a situation in practice where the dog is tempted to make the mistake, then correct it and show her the right way to do it.

I gave HB the day off on Monday, September 20. We began working on the problem in earnest on Tuesday. Back on the polo field at Paradise Valley Park, I set up a ring and moved the jumps laterally toward the center until I had a go-outs corridor only six feet wide (versus the normal 20). HB's challenge was to "thread the needle," to go out between the jumps, resisting the temptation to jump.

As I recall, she took the bait only a time or two. Each time, as she angled off toward the jump, I responded with a sharp, "No!" Then I'd guide her back to the center and send her from there.

Honeybear has *such* a trainable attitude. It was almost as if she was saying, "I love this, we're working on something, *together*." In no time at all she had it figured out and the demons that had been wreaking havoc in her head had been exorcised.

Then, just to be certain, I moved the jumps a few inches farther apart each training session as we prepared for our next shows.

■ ■ ■

Saturday, September 25, was the date of the Papago Labrador Retriever Club's fun match. Fun matches are so few and far between around here that every fall when the Lab Club holds theirs we say things like, "Bless them," and we all turn out.

It happened that Debby Boehm was asked to judge the Open and Utility classes. I viewed the match as yet one more tuneup enroute to our final OTCH point.

Sticking with our plan, HB was not entered in Open that day.

In Debby's Utility ring, we began with the signal exercise. HB heeled beautifully, did the signals perfectly. One happy dog.

Next, scent articles. You had doubts?

She raced out, picked up the correct glove, tossed it around joyously, then presented it to me with her tail sweeping the grass furiously.

The moving stand was crisp. She stopped abruptly and didn't move a paw while Debby examined her. Then she gave me that crowd-pleasing flip of a finish. She was having a blast.

Finally, directed jumping. Big stress time.

Honeybear went bounding out to the far end of the ring on her first go-out. Nice tight turn, quick sit.

"Bar jump," Debby said. Out went my right arm. "Bar!" I cried. Here she came. Over she went. Straight front. Crooked finish. So far, so good.

"Directed jumping, part two," Debby said. Same arrow-straight go-out. A little traveling music may have been playing in her head as she turned, inched forward, then sat.

"High jump," Debby said.

I extended my left arm and boomed out, "High!"

Here she came. There she stopped. *Oh God.*

"Bring her back here," Debby said, indicating a spot about 10 feet out from the jump. "Now stand behind the jump and call her over."

I did. "Honeybear over!" Almost, but she pulled up short. I saw apprehension on that old white face, and in her tentative tail wag as well.

So we took her back to the 10-foot spot again. "Run with her this time," Debby said.

We took off side by side. As I ran past the jump, Honeybear cleared it.

"Let's quit on that one," Debby said. I could tell from the stricken look on her face she thought I had plenty to worry about.

I was in a cold sweat. One point to go for our OTCH. One week to go before we were scheduled to be in the ring again in Riverside, California. And now this.

■ ■ ■

Debby called the next morning. "Willard," she said, "maybe you should consider acupuncture for HB."

CHAPTER 54

They Call It "Alternative Medicine"

*A*cupuncture. The word conjured up images of wizened Chinese men performing mysterious rituals in incense-saturated chambers where fierce dragons guard the portals.

But what the hell. Debby had mentioned a veterinarian named Alice Blazer, a certified veterinary acupuncturist who had recently relocated to Phoenix from California. So I called and made an appointment for Tuesday, September 28. And I canceled our hotel reservations for the Riverside shows. First we'd tend to the acupuncture treatments, then we'd resume our OTCH quest in New Mexico in mid-October.

I knew my decision couldn't be all bad when we arrived at Dr. Blazer's office. The Village Plaza Animal Hospital was located in a strip mall next-door to the Cold Stone Creamery, a wonderful source of homemade ice cream.

Dr. Blazer was a small, pleasant middle-aged woman who did not clasp her hands at her waist and bow to greet me. So far, so good. She also turned out to be interested in obedience competition. She told me she had put a Companion Dog title on a Sheltie, and said she was interested in training another dog for competition.

Dr. Blazer was particularly interested to learn that Honeybear was mildly dysplastic in her left hip and had undergone a TPLO on her right hind leg. Her first concern was to assure that HB had no muscle soreness or other pain related to the TPLO.

"Sometimes dogs take weight off a leg that's had a problem," she explained, "and the other side bears more weight. That can screw up their backs and create imbalances that lead to other problems."

Acupuncture helps put the body back in a balanced or more normal state, she told me. So that if there are problems they can heal more quickly.

I asked her how acupuncture works and that turned out to be the $64 million question.

"I wish I knew," she replied. Then she continued, "Nobody knows exactly how acupuncture works. It does require that the nervous system be intact. If the spinal cord is interrupted, it doesn't work."

She told me it seems to deal with some kind of energy that flows in the body. A force the Chinese call *chi* (pronounced "chee").

Dr. Blazer believes it's a kind of electromagnetic field that fluctuates. When something is injured or not functioning normally, the chi doesn't flow properly. It may get congested in one area, causing pain, and it may be deficient in other areas, causing weakness. Those imbalances throw the body out of its homeostatic state.

She thinks acupuncture opens the channels through which the chi flows. If the chi is excessive (congested) in some places, acupuncture "kind of drags it along and starts it flowing again." On the other hand, if the chi is deficient in other areas, acupuncture allows the body to "suck" energy into the deprived areas. Thus improving the body's homeostasis and allowing it to heal itself.

Dr. Blazer believes acupuncture has anti-inflammatory effects as well.

"I think the brain has cells that release hormonal-type substances," she explained. "The glial (neurological) cells surround and support the neurons. I think they give off neuropeptides — endorphins and other chemical substances that have anti-inflammatory and pain-relieving properties. And I think part of what acupuncture achieves is to cause the brain to release those substances."

As Dr. Blazer prepared to give Honeybear her first acupuncture treatment, she explained the theory behind what she was about to do.

The places where the acupuncturist inserts the needles are called acupuncture points. Those points fall along lines in the body known as meridians. There are 12 major meridians that flow in a pattern along the body. The acupuncturist selects points to treat depending upon where the injury is and what meridians flow in that area.

Dr. Blazer explained that a special meridian, called the bladder meridian, runs along each side of the spine. It is important, she said, because it has points along its course that influence the other 11 meridians. Those points are called association points.

For instance, the hind leg is the site of the stomach, spleen, kidney, bladder, liver and gallbladder meridians. Those meridians run down the leg at known points. Therefore, you can treat the association point along the dog's back (i.e., along the bladder meridian) that corresponds with the appropriate hind-leg-located meridian to have a beneficial effect, according to Dr. Blazer.

And, of course, you treat the appropriate points in the area where you think the problem exists.

Here in our Western culture, acupuncture is subject to skepticism. In part, that skepticism exists because there's nothing you can see.

If you were to dissect the animal, you would not see the meridians — as you would the blood vessels. Gertrude Stein might have said, "There is no there in acupuncture."

Instead, Dr. Blazer explained, the meridians seem to be places of lowered electrical resistance. They have, however, been defined in rabbits by measuring the lowered electrical resistance of the tissue along the lines thought to be the meridians.

Dr. Blazer says, "The way I look at it is this: In our culture we are used to looking at the physical body. We treat physical things — with surgery, with manipulation, and so on. And we treat the chemical imbalances with drugs.

"Underneath all of that, I believe there's an electromagnetic field. It's an energetic reality but you can't see it. I think that's where everything starts. I think that field forms at conception and that's what tells our cells where to migrate to make an arm or a toe or whatever. I think all illness starts in that energetic field and is manifested later in physical ways. That is what we work on with acupuncture."

■ ■ ■

Based upon HB's history of a cruciate ligament tear in the right knee and mild dysplasia of the left hip, Dr. Blazer chose to treat both sides of the dog's hind end.

Each needle was removed, sterile, from its own blister package. She inserted 17 needles at appropriate acupuncture points. Those points are identified in what follows here by the name of the meridian along which they lie.

1. *Bai Hui* (pronounced "bow way"). Literally translated from the Chinese language to mean "hundreds meet," this acupuncture point is a place where many meridians intersect, producing a confluence of energy flows. Located on the midline, it is commonly used in veterinary acupuncture therapy to benefit the hindquarters and to normalize energy flow along the spine.

Bai Hui was the only acupuncture point where Dr. Blazer used but a single needle. The rest of the points were dealt with bilaterally, using pairs of needles.

2 and 3. *Bladder 11.* Two needles, one on each side of the bladder meridian, were placed at the base of the neck, just in front of the shoulder blades. Bladder 11 is believed to be an influential point for relief of bone-related problems.

4 to 7. *Bladder 13 and Bladder 21.* Dr. Blazer reasoned that Honeybear's back might be sore as a result of moving differently in the aftermath of her TPLO. She selected these two points to "try to pull energy along the dog's spine."

8 and 9. *Bladder 19.* This acupuncture point was significant because it was an *ahshi* point. That means it's an area where, upon palpation, the dog manifests soreness — the skin crawls or the animal cringes. Honeybear's skin crawled.

Dr. Blazer explained that this reaction was meaningful because Bladder 19 is an association point for the gallbladder meridian. That conduit travels down the outside of the hind leg, across the outside of the knee joint … the site of the radical bone-cutting surgery that had constituted Honeybear's TPLO.

10 to 13. *Bladder 40 and Stomach 36.* Local points located near the knee joint.

14 and 15. *Gallbladder 30.* She selected this acupuncture point for two reasons. It's an important point for the treatment of hip dysplasia. And it's on the gallbladder meridian — which we were concerned about because HB was sore at Bladder 19.

16 and 17. *Gallbladder 34.* This acupuncture point is located on the outside of the hind leg, just below the knee joint. It's also an influential point for problems with tendons and ligaments.

■ ■ ■

HB stood calmly for the 20-minute treatment, looking for all the world like a large golden retriever voodoo doll. I sat in front of her and cradled her chin in my hands. She did not respond in any way when Dr. Blazer inserted the needles; apparently she didn't even feel them.

Honeybear had three identical acupuncture treatments at one-week intervals. The final one took place on Tuesday, October 12. "Honeybear is the only dog I've treated who wags her tail throughout the entire process," Dr. Blazer said.

The day after the third treatment we left for Alamogordo, New Mexico, needing only one OTCH point to attain our ultimate goal. But the question remained: *Would she jump?*

■ CHAPTER 55 ■

The Holy Grail

*"...the OTCH, as it is known, is regarded by serious
obedience enthusiasts as the Holy Grail in obedience, the
crème de la crème of competition, the proverbial golden ring ...
the consummate display of precision teamwork.
Although it is thought of as the most prestigious title
offered by the AKC, it has also proven to be
the most elusive crown since its inception in 1977."*
THE AKC GAZETTE
SEPTEMBER 2000

Alamogordo, New Mexico is a nondescript little burg located in the foothills of the Sacramento Mountains. It is home to 27,600 hardy souls, most of them somehow involved with Holloman Air Force Base or the White Sands Missile Range.

The town's claim to fame is its proximity to an event that changed the history of the world. On July 16, 1945, in a remote section of the White Sands Missile Range, the first man-made atomic explosion sent a huge multicolored mushroom cloud surging to an altitude of 40,000 feet. And mankind was blasted into the Atomic Age.

Some 54 years later, on October 13, 1999, shortly after sunrise, we pointed the van south and east along I-10. The day's journey, a resumption of OTCH Quest '99, would take us into New Mexico, through the missile range, and 459 miles later would terminate at the Best Western Desert Aire Motel in Alamogordo.

The following day, a Thursday, we would set up our tent in Alameda Park, a narrow stretch of green that runs for several blocks. It is flanked on one side by White Sands Boulevard, the town's main drag, and on the other by railroad tracks.

On Friday Honeybear would resume her quest for that final point at Chaparral Kennel Club's all-breed dog show and obedience trial. She would compete in Utility B under Judge Joseph M. (Bud) Skarbek, the judge who had joked, "The regulations say the dog is supposed to *run* out on the go-outs, not hop out."

As we were setting up and practicing on Thursday afternoon, it became clear that even though Alamogordo might be remote, the competition was going to be tough.

Sandra Davis arrived with her OTCH border collie Pepper. Sandra is one of the most accomplished obedience trainers and handlers in America. She is also the author of books and the creator of videotapes called "Dancing With Your Dog," instructional materials about the increasingly popular sport of canine freestyle.

Late in the afternoon Dick Guetzloff pulled in with his trailer. Dick had lost his brilliant border collie OTCH Heelalong Chimney Sweep UDX on June 1. Sweep died of a cerebral hemorrhage at age 13. At the time, Dick and Sweep held the record for most career OTCH points, an astonishing 7,981. Their margin over the second-place dog was a whopping 2,360.

In Alamogordo, Dick was showing Heelalong Benjamin CDX. Ben had been bred by Kay and sold to a man in Chicago. The owner had returned Ben to the Guetzloffs when he was six, and Dick had promised to put some titles on the dog. But Dick and Ben were never able to get on the same page. For one thing, it was apparent to those of us at ringside who observed closely that Ben had rear-end structural problems that made it impossible for him to heel exactly the way Dick wanted him to.

Beyond that, Ben possessed a trait — in abundance — that makes many border collies difficult to train. He forged. That means instead of heeling with his right ear approximately even with the seam of Dick's pants leg, he insisted on getting out front, wrapping around the handler's leg and looking up into his face. There they'd go, especially on the fast, Ben running almost sideways in front of Dick, and Dick trying not to fall over him.

Ben also had a superabundance of desire to please. But the harder he tried the worse he forged. The more Ben forged the angrier Dick got. The angrier Dick got the harder Ben would try to please and the worse he would forge. And on and on it went in a defeating cycle.

Not only was it a frustrating situation for Dick, it followed immediately after the glory years with Sweep. The contrast must have been devastating.

Nevertheless, when I saw Dick's trailer pull up on that Thursday afternoon, I said, "Oh God, both Dick and Sandra." I knew based on handling skills alone, Dick Guetzloff with the world's worst dog would pose a threat.

■ ■ ■

Shortly before eight o'clock the next morning I was standing at ringside, waiting for the judge to demonstrate the heeling pattern and speculating on what effect the slightly uphill terrain would have on Honeybear's go-outs.

Dick walked up beside me, studied the ring for a moment, then said, "It's not like it used to be."

I figured he was referring to judges, show conditions, the types of things he liked to complain about. "What isn't like it used to be?" I asked.

"It just isn't the same without Sweep," he replied. He went on to say that this morning would be the first time he would be in an AKC obedience ring since Sweep had died four and one-half months ago.

Then he walked away.

■ ■ ■

Ten dogs were entered in Utility B on Friday morning. Nine showed; one was absent. First place was good for six OTCH points, second for two.

As in Prescott, we were last. We watched Sandra and Pepper do a beautiful run. And we watched Ben screw up and fail. In between, several teams did moderately well and qualified.

Our turn came shortly after nine o'clock. HB's heeling wasn't quite as good as I had recently come to expect; we lost three points on the signal exercise. Mouthing and crooked fronts cost us a point on each scent article. She was perfect on the directed retrieve as well as on the moving stand.

At that point we had lost five points which, as it turned out, gave us a four-point spread over Sandy Hill and her Belgian Tervuren. They had scored a 191 and were second as we had begun our turn.

Now for directed jumping. On the first go-out Honeybear took off like a shot, straight as an arrow. About the time she reached mid-ring, she said to herself, *Hey, I know this exercise, it's time to turn and sit*. Which she did, right beyond the jump.

Never mind how Sandra and Pepper had done or what kind of threat Dick has posed. We had just flunked.

Our plan was to show in Alamogordo on Friday, use Saturday as a travel and setup day and not show until Sunday in Las Cruces, in the El Paso Kennel Club shows.

So we took a nap at the motel that afternoon, all of us sacked out together. Which was just as well. US 70, the road that ran straight down through the White Sands Missile Range, was closed a good part of the afternoon because of a missile launch.

■ ■ ■

On Saturday morning we drove the 70 miles down US 70 to Las Cruces. Black clouds were threatening.

There are multiple theories as to how Las Cruces got its name. Most emanate from various Apache massacres in the vicinity of a fort near the Rio Grande River. Crosses were erected there and the area came to be known as El Pueblo del Jardine de Las Cruces (The City of the Garden of the Crosses).

The surrounding Mesilla Valley is a leading producer of the chiles for which New Mexico is famous.

We arrived early in the afternoon and went straight to the Best Western Mesilla Valley Inn to check in and unload what would not go to the show grounds. Then we headed for the show site at Apodaca Park. We had never shown in Las Cruces and were not prepared for what we encountered.

The park is a large oval grassy area encircled by a street. We saw a couple of tiny dirt parking areas, but for all practical purposes parking was on the one oval drive.

We had arrived at the midpoint of a two-day show, long after everyone else had staked out their spaces. On the way in, we passed Dick's van and trailer, parked at the curb quite a distance from the obedience rings. Later Dick told us he had arrived mid-Friday afternoon and that was as close as he could get.

As we drove around the oval several times, we were struck by how close to each other many of the RVs were parked. In many cases the front end of one was no more than six inches from the back end of the other. I wondered how they would get out when it was time to go home.

Finally we found a spot in a dirt lot outside the park and a long distance away. From there Barbara and I trudged back and forth, hauling our stuff. "Oh boy, this is going to be a mess tomorrow morning," I told her.

By late afternoon the wind had picked up and the clouds looked more ominous.

Friends who had been there for that morning's trial quickly filled us in on the results. Nine had shown in Utility B. Three had qualified. Sandra Davis and Pepper had totally outclassed the rest of the field, winning with a 198. My friend and training buddy Marilyn Whitmore, who had not been entered in Alamogordo, took second with her Sheltie, Mandy. She was followed by Sandy Hill and her Belgian Tervuren. Dick and Ben had not qualified.

As we returned to the motel that evening, a light rain began to fall.

■ ■ ■

On Sunday morning, I was the first up at 4 a.m. I parted the drapes and looked out the window. Rain was pouring down in sheets. I remember giving a thumbs-up there in the dark room and saying aloud, "OK, it's Honeybear weather" — mostly to bolster my own courage.

Of course HB *had* always done well on wet, muddy days. But now she was an older, post-surgical dog who was already showing a disinclination to jump. And this was severe weather.

Not only was it pouring. Not only was the wind blowing. It was also bitter cold. Only a few degrees above freezing, we learned later.

We arrived at Apodaca Park at 6 a.m. It was pitch dark and there were no lights on the drive surrounding the show area. Soon, though, we lucked into a large space on the far side of the drive. We pulled in behind an RV to wait for daylight. Shortly, Barbara said, "Turn your lights out; they're shining in the bedroom window of those people in front of us."

I did and we sat there in the blackness with the motor running and the heater turned up. Outside the rain was beating and the wind was howling.

Honeybear, terrified by the sound of the rain on the van roof, was trembling and trying to find a place to hide. Barbara covered HB's head with a towel but it did little good.

Our lucky-find space was opposite our ring and our tent. But we were at the curb on the outside of the oval street. On the inside of the oval, RVs were lined up bumper to bumper, blocking our view of the show area. Then came a row of vendors' tents, then the rings. Then, all the way across the field, our tent.

I decided to work out of the van. Honeybear had a stainless steel plate with six stainless steel screws in her right knee. I figured it would be best to keep that plate warm until ring time. I also ventured out of the van to get HB's scent articles out of the back and put them upfront, under the heater. I had visions of a cold metal scent article sticking to her tongue as she retrieved it.

For a time we were nice and comfy in the front seat of the van. Then I summoned the courage to go across the field and raise the tent, which was situated just opposite Ring Six, where Utility B would be judged. It seemed a perfect sheltered spot for Barbara to stand while she videotaped our run.

It was a long walk across the park to the tent and the rain was slanting in my face. I was wearing an undershirt, thermal underwear (top and bottom), my long-sleeved tan and white shirt that I normally wear with Honeybear in the ring, and a heavy, lined blue and gold jacket. No matter; the wind cut through all of it.

By the time I had raised the tent, my fingers were numb. But it was time to walk HB and warm her up.

As we walked, we were nearly alone. The show grounds had not yet come alive. None of the vendors had raised the awnings on their stands. Exhibitors and show personnel were still cowering in the shelter of their RVs and vans.

I put HB back in the van briefly while I got my high jump out, carried it onto the grass between the vendors' stands and the rings and set it up. It was 6:45 and the rain and wind and cold had not let up.

Suddenly Pamela Smith appeared out of nowhere. She lived in Las Cruces but we had met several times at shows in Arizona. She would be showing her Australian shepherd in Utility A later in the morning.

"Could I run my dog over that jump a few times when you are finished?" she asked.

"If you're hardy enough," I replied. "Just bring the jump back to my van when you're finished."

With that I brought HB out and threw the ball a few times. Then I sat her on one side of the jump, went to the other side, put a treat in my mouth and called, "Over!" She bounded over the jump each of the three times I called her and came to front with her tail wagging. Yes indeed, this *was* Honeybear weather.

About 7:30 the judge arrived and, with the help of the stewards, began to set up the ring. He was Floyd Harding of Arlington, Texas. We had never shown under him. He had arrived anticipating good weather and had not brought a raincoat. One of the stewards disappeared and returned with a transparent plastic slipover raincoat which Mr. Harding gratefully donned. When I went to the judge's table to pick up my armband, I told him, "You look like the dry cleaning."

By eight o'clock the rain and wind still had not slackened and it felt just as cold as it had when I walked the dogs at 4:15. I later learned it was 39 degrees at ring time.

■ ■ ■

The class began with Judge Harding wearing his "dry cleaning bag" and a hat that was already soaked. He had put his clipboard in a clear plastic Baggie, and he would reach inside to write. Water streamed down his glasses.

I hung around for the first two dogs, to see the heeling pattern and placement of the scent articles, and try to figure out the order of the gloves. A canopy stretched over the ringside table, providing a dry area meant for the two stewards and the judge. There must have been a dozen of us packed in there.

I returned to the van to walk Honeybear for a final time and do a little heeling. Any further warmup would have to be done on the way to the ring. Sandra and Pepper were second in. I saw their run and it was pretty. As I walked Honeybear, I caught a glimpse of Marilyn Whitmore coming out of the ring. The smile on her face told me they had qualified.

Thirteen were entered that morning; nine showed. There would be six points for first place, two for second. We needed only one.

Eventually Barbara left for the tent with the video camera.

About three dogs before we were due in the ring, I began to worry about what I was wearing. I always wear a long-sleeved shirt in Utility. It provides a little wider arm for the dog to see when I give the hand signals.

Going a step farther, I adapt my sleeves to the background against which those signals will be given. HB will be standing at the opposite end of the ring, her eyes about 29 inches off the ground. What picture will she see as I give those signals? What will be behind me?

I always have dark and light options available for the Utility ring. My ring shirts are white with dark bands on the sleeves. And I carry a lightweight dark blue jacket for the dark option.

Right before ring time, Barbara will stoop down at dog's-eye level near one end of the Utility ring. I stand at the other end and give the signals, first with just the shirt, then wearing the dark jacket. She tells me which would be more easily seen by my dog. If there is a background of green trees or a dark building, the white shirt is the option of choice. If we are in front of a white building, the dark jacket offers better contrast.

Then too, HB is near the ground, and I stand 6'4". That means if the sun is coming up behind me or is low in the sky or if there is an extremely bright sky, the dark jacket is a must.

On October 17, 1999, heavy dark clouds hung over the gloomy show site and there were lots of green trees. White sleeves were in order. But there was no way I could take off my heavy blue jacket in the cold rain and wind. I'd be shivering so hard I couldn't function.

Then I remembered Barbara was wearing a heavy silver jacket. I jumped out of the van, ran past the RVs and vendors' tents and began waving wildly, trying to attract her attention without yelling as she stood in our tent all the way across the field.

Finally she saw me, came running and met me halfway. "Quick," I said, "give me your jacket." And I unzipped mine and all but tore it off my body.

We exchanged jackets. I put on hers and zipped it up. The sleeves stopped halfway down my arms. White shirt sleeves continued from there.

As we parted, Barbara said over her shoulder, "The camera isn't working." *At least there'll be no permanent record of this sartorial fiasco*, I thought. But by God I had light-colored sleeves, and I wouldn't freeze to death.

As Dick took Ben into the ring, I took Honeybear's scent articles and gloves to ringside. "These are for golden retriever 704," I said as I set them down.

"Good luck," came as a chorus from the half dozen or so people clustered under the tent. Everyone knew exactly why Honeybear and I were there on this miserable morning.

I then retreated between the vendors' tents where I could still see but could dash to the van when Dick and Ben began the directed jumping exercise.

Suddenly, though, as they finished the scent articles, the steward was handing Dick the leash. Something had happened during only the second exercise. Dick had apparently asked to be excused and the judge had granted his request.

I turned and dashed for the van. I yanked the door open, grabbed HB's leash from atop the dash and my freezing hands fumbled with the clasp as I tried to attach it to the collar. After an eternity, it snapped on. "OK big girl," I said, "let's go show!" She leapt off the seat, landed on the street and began to prance.

On the way to the ring we did a fast, a couple of halts and two about turns. And they were calling us: "Dog and handler 704." It was still raining, blowing and bitter cold.

■ ■ ■

I heeled Honeybear into Ring Six and handed my leash to the steward, Pamela Smith. She was doing double duty on this rainy morning. For now, she was stewarding for our ring. At 10 o'clock she would be next-door, in Ring Five, competing in Nancy Craig's Utility A class.

Pamela ducked back under the canopy and now it was just Honeybear, me and Floyd Harding. What a sight we must have been: the judge in a dry cleaning bag with his score sheet in a Baggie, the handler in a silver jacket with sleeves that quit right below the elbows.

"Are you ready?" the judge asked.

"Ready!" I said.

"Forward," he said. And away we went.

Our run was more workmanlike (workdoglike?) than spectacular. And yet I have these wonderful flashbacks.

I left HB for the hand signals, walked briskly to the opposite end of the ring, then turned to face her. She had the expression of someone who is being pelted in the face by rain. But I don't think she even blinked, and her responses were perfect.

It's not so easy to do scent discrimination in pouring rain but, as Debby had said so often, "That dog's a scent articles machine." HB retrieved the correct article each time. Classic Honeybear, whatever the conditions.

Next she went charging out, grabbed the correct glove, whipped around, slipped on the wet grass and never missed a beat as she brought it back into a crooked front. Crooked fronts, too, are classic Honeybear.

Her moving stand may have involved a bit of traveling. But she stood stoically while the judge went over her and the rain beat her in the face. Then came her signature finish on that exercise. I said, "Place!" She came bounding to me, leaped a few inches off the ground and spun herself into a perfect finish. I've yet to see a judge who didn't crack a big smile at that point. Including the soggy Mr. Harding.

Now as we line up for directed jumping — the exercise that has been our Achilles heel so many times — the fat is in the fire.

"Go-outs, Honeybear. Straight. Straight."

"This is your directed jumping exercise. Are you ready?"

I nod.

"Send your dog."

"Away!" And there she goes, between the jumps, all the way out.

"Honeybear sit!" Beautiful.

Now my heart is in my mouth.

"Take the jump on your left."

"Bar!" Here she comes. She's off the ground. She's over. She's sitting in front of me. That wonderful old white face is looking up at me.

"Finish."

I give my hand signal and she swings into heel position.

"Exercise finished."

Oh, dear God, just one more.

"Directed jumping, part two. Are you ready?"

I nod or grunt or maybe just wet my pants.

"Send your dog."

"Away!" She's bounding. She's past the jumps, she's all the way out there.

"Honeybear! Sit!" Perfect. And she's all eyes and ears waiting for my next command. Yeah, this is Honeybear weather.

"Take the jump on your right."

"High!"

She's coming. She's launched. She's *soaring*! And now she's at front.

"Finish." We do.

"Exercise finished." A pause. "Congratulations on a qualifying score." As Judge Harding and I shake wet hands, I hear the applause from behind us.

No mad dash back to the van for a Bonz this time. We were the last team in our class. Judge Harding and the stewards sit down and immediately begin to dig their way through the mountain of paperwork.

Honeybear and I do a little heeling, just in case. Then we join the crush of people under the tent, which sags under several deep pockets of collected water.

At one point, near the end of the calculating, listing and certifying, Pamela Smith looks up, catches my eye and nods almost imperceptibly.

And that's when I know.

Several years before, enroute to something I was writing, I asked the American Kennel Club if there were any statistics that showed how many Novice A handlers (those entering AKC obedience competition for the first time) eventually make it to an OTCH. They did some number-crunching and the answer came back that it was less than one in 10,000.

Now, when Pamela Smith gave me that slight nod there under the tent, I knew we had beaten the odds. I reached down, petted Honeybear and said nothing. We'd wait until it was official.

■ ■ ■

Finally, "Utility B qualifiers back to the ring." By this time the rain has stopped. In we go. There are five of us.

After the niceties of thanking his stewards, Mr. Harding says, "In Utility B a perfect score is 200. This morning, in first place, with a score of 198, dog and handler 502."

Sandra and Pepper step forward to accept the blue ribbon.

Then the longest five-second pause in the history of time.

"In second place this morning with a score of 193, dog and handler 704."

"All right HoneeBEAR!" And we step forward to claim our red ribbon and the two OTCH points that make it 101.

The rain-shrunken crowd outside the ring is small but loud. I try not to cry.

We wait as Jane Derlin of Las Cruces and her Aussie, Rowdy, receive a yellow ribbon for third and Marilyn and Mandy accept the white fourth-place ribbon.

As we leave the ring, I kneel down, hug Honeybear and say over and over, "We did it! We did it!" Then I tell her, "Honeybear, you'll never have to jump again."

That wonderful moment also broke my heart. It was exhilarating to achieve something for which we'd worked so hard so long. But it also marked the end of the road … or so it seemed at the time.

Outside the ring Barbara threw her arms around me and gave me a big kiss. Then she stooped down and kissed HB.

After that it was all hugs and congratulations. Nancy Craig came over from the next ring, where she was judging, and gave me a big hug.

Before long, Honeybear had had enough. She swung around in front of me, looked me in the face and barked her head off. That meant, "I want my Bonz!"

So we took off for the van, on the dead run as usual. We were stopped briefly by Dick Guetzloff. Dick extended his hand and offered congratulations. He had watched the whole thing from under a tree several yards away.

Then on to the van where Honeybear got *several* Bonz.

■ ■ ■

When Honeybear finished pigging out on Bonz, we went back to the ring for our OTCH photo. It had stopped raining and Barbara and I again switched jackets.

What a beautiful place! What a beautiful day! I remember thinking as we reentered that soggy ring in that parking-clogged park on that cold, dreary morning.

Our OTCH photo now hangs on the wall in my office. It shares a frame with HB's ribbons from that day, her AKC OTCH certificate and a sheet detailing the where and when of each of her OTCH points.

That photo tells a lot about that magical day. Judge Harding is still wearing the dry cleaning bag, I have a big grass stain on my right pants leg and the coat on Honeybear's tummy is wet and stringy. And it's the most beautiful picture I've ever seen.

■ ■ ■

Nearly a decade earlier, my dream had come true. I had wanted a golden retriever puppy so badly. I had registered her with the American Kennel Club as Starbuc's Dream Come True. Now the *impossible* dream had come true. Now it was official.

OTCH Starbuc's Dream Come True UDX

Photo: Joe Rinehart

The Holy Grail: October 17, 1999

Honeybear, who had had her right knee surgically rebuilt seven months earlier, had come storming back at the age of nine years, nine months and 25 days to capture the Holy Grail of dog obedience competition.

■ CHAPTER 56 ■

Field Of Dreams And Memories

We were absent from Paradise Valley Park for the first six and a half months of 2000. HB's just-for-fun training could easily be done in the backyard.

It wasn't until sometime during the second week in July that I finally said, "OK, let's go to the park and practice." HB's eyes lit up as her tail pounded the furniture.

Into Paradise Valley Park we drove. Around the curve past the baseball fields. Toward the road that crossed the wash and wound back to the polo field. Then I hit the brakes.

Concrete slabs blocked the road before we reached the bridge. Before us, a six-foot chain-link fence stretched to our left and our right as far as I could see. What was *this*?

Just beyond the bridge, before the road angled right to meander back to the polo field, a huge chain-link gate stretched the width of the road. It was secured by a no-nonsense padlock. Someone had shut off access to our favorite place on earth. And they weren't kidding.

The next day I called Sharon Brady, the park supervisor. "What in God's name is going on?" I asked.

"They're getting ready to build the expressway interchange," she told me. "It'll be fenced off as it is now for about a year, then they'll begin grading and construction."

So there it was. Stan Bucher had been right on that afternoon long ago. The baseball diamonds and swimming pool had nothing to do with the land that had been earmarked for the expressway.

I learned that the project was an extension of State Route 51 (the Squaw Peak Expressway) north for 2.3 miles, where it would connect with and terminate at the Pima Freeway, Loop 101. The right of way would wipe out the polo field, several acres of adjacent parking lots and the meandering road that led to those areas.

In anyone's life there are wrenching transitions. Someone dies, but you've been expecting it. You get fired, but there's been a buildup of workplace tension and it was only a matter of time. You make a cross-country move away from your roots, but it was your choice.

But this! All those afternoons. A cascade of life-enriching — indeed, life-*changing* — experiences. A million fuzzy, furry memories. One day you drive up and wham! Right in the solar plexus of your soul.

■ ■ ■

Near the end of July, a group of us decided to get together on Wednesday evenings to practice sits and downs. A grassy, shady area at Paradise Valley Park, between the Northeast District administration building and the recreation center, had been left untouched by the highway construction project. It was a good spot and a reasonable drive for anyone who wanted to participate. Like me. My young border collie, Bebop, needed to practice sits and downs with a group of other dogs.

Our first group practice was at seven o'clock on the evening of Wednesday, August 3. I arrived a few minutes early and cruised slowly by the point where the road crossed the bridge and curved back toward the polo field.

Wait a minute! The big chain-link gates stood wide open. Beyond, the road — *our* road — beckoned. I turned back, joined the group exercises, then went home.

But I thought about that open gate overnight. Two weeks earlier I had bought a roomy Chevy Express van with plenty of ground clearance. I could make it over those concrete barriers with ease.

I hurried back the next morning. The gates were still wide open. I eased over the concrete blocks, up a little slope and through the gates.

How many thousands of times had I driven back here? On my right was the large dirt parking lot, but the parking blocks had been removed. Now it was just a huge dusty area, the size of several football fields placed side by side.

A solitary stone picnic table remained in the southeast corner, out in the middle of nowhere. It was a strange place for a picnic table — no shelter, just that lone table.

A guy used to sit on one of the stone benches in the afternoons and play the hell out of his bongo drums. Out there he didn't bother the neighbors.

Eventually I had decided that a guy out there playing his bongo drums everyday was no stranger than a guy out there training his golden retriever everyday. It was just that we heard the beats of different drums.

I drove slowly. On my left the golf course was still intact. Only a few brave souls were out there on this steaming August morning.

I pulled into the strip parking lot and stopped along the fence where I had parked so often. I had a precise spot, exactly where the back end of my van was closest to the gate, so I could unload and walk right in. How many snoozle marks had Honeybear put on the side window while she watched me set up?

I got out. There wasn't a soul in sight. It was silent except for the buzz of a few late summer locusts.

The fence was still in place. So was the sign that said *Please close the gate*. Now the gate stood wide open. On doomsday for the polo field, the last one out had forgotten to close the gate.

■ ■ ■

I walked through the gate. The dry field was overgrown with hardy weeds that crunched with each step. *Wow*! I thought, *light a match to this and watch it go*.

The chain-link fence was all-encompassing. The polo field, the parking areas, the road — all that constituted our favorite place on earth had been surrounded and defeated. Soon it would be gone.

I could only stand in the blazing August sun and look and remember. Out there, about halfway across, that's where Honeybear had gotten up on the long down at that flooded golden retriever specialty. How often had I stood on this very spot and said, "Right out there, you rascal, that's where you got up during the down. Remember?"

And over there, along the fence on the other side, that's where I called her off the hambone.

And right here, where I was standing, this was where I always set up our ring. The ring made of rebar and rope, that first ring, the one Barbara gave me for my birthday nine years ago. Or the shiny white ring gates that I set up one sullen afternoon when we were closing in on our OTCH ... and for the first time HB had refused to jump.

It had all happened right here. We had learned together and played together right here. Maybe I could still see the marks I used to paint so I'd know where to drive the rebar into the hard ground. Or the holes themselves. I walked around for a long time, examining the ground, weeds crunching under my feet.

Nothing. Not one mark. Not one hole. Not one scrap of anything to give a clue that we had ever been here.

Someday millions of cars will zoom over this very spot, I thought. *Not one of the drivers will have any hint of what went on here during thousands of afternoons. Not a clue that a happy golden retriever learned to be an Obedience Trial Champion here. That right here a man and a dog fell in love and grew old together. And on this field spent the most wonderful afternoons of their lives.*

I walked to the south end of the field. The Aleppo pines were still there. So far untouched. But we'd never be there. Never spend eternity there together. I had wanted that so much. But suddenly the chain-link fence. And soon the monstrous earthmovers. And...

I was overwhelmed by it all. Thank God the place was deserted; tears coursed down my cheeks. It was time to get out of there.

■ CHAPTER 57 ■

A Second Career

WestWorld, Scottsdale, Arizona
Thursday, March 21, 2002

Today is the 2002 Valle del Sol Golden Retriever Club Specialty. I have Honeybear entered in the Veterans class, for the 23rd time.

Long before our class is due to start I drop by the judge's table to pick up our armband. "Number 112, in Veterans," I tell the steward. Our judge this morning will be Richard Christ. He's a golden retriever person from way back, and when he hears me picking up my armband he pauses a moment to tell me about two wonderful senior goldens he has at home.

Yeah, I say to myself (but certainly not to him), *wait'll you see this.*

We've chosen to work out of the van, which is parked in sight but about 100 yards away. And the Veterans class is last. After sitting bolt upright, watching us for three hours, HB explodes out of the van and proceeds to put on a clinic.

When it's time for the awards, Judge Christ says, "And this old guy … I don't know how he does it with a 12-year-old dog. But I didn't see much wrong. They're in first place with 198.5."

As we step forward to accept our ribbon, I say, "Where was that score in Novice A, Honeybear?"

Photo: Marilyn Whitmore

Honeybear on the rocks: 2001

Then we're out of the ring. Honeybear is hell-bent for the van where she knows her Bonz awaits. We're on the dead run, but over my shoulder I hear Judge Christ: "Look at that, the dog's still driving!"

Honeybear has just won Veterans for the 20th time in 23 entries. With an average score of 198. Well into her 13th year, her heeling has never before been this sharp, nor her attitude this gung-ho.

■ ■ ■

I never dreamed it would turn out like this. After we finished our OTCH, I vowed not to show Honeybear in the regular classes again. I would not ask her to jump one more time. But I knew both of us would enjoy showing in Veterans. Any day that old white face is at my side looking up at me is a good day. And I knew we'd train for it; that would keep HB active on an ongoing basis.

So not long after we had finished our OTCH I entered her in Novice at a sanctioned match. She frisked through the exercises and we got some ridiculously high score.

As we were leaving the ring, a voice said, "I thought you were going to retire that dog, Willard." It was Hangdog, a core member of The Coven.

"I'm going to show her in Veterans once in a while," I said. "It'll keep her active and we'll both enjoy it."

Hangdog scowled, then responded, "Well she's still got to *work*!"

I didn't answer. I just shook my head and kept walking. That's The Coven for you. Their dogs slog through the obedience exercises and *work*. My dogs frolic through the obedience exercises and have the time of their lives.

No use explaining; it was beyond her.

So our plan was to show in Veterans from time to time, and

a good time would be had by all. I never dreamed it would evolve into a second career for Honeybear.

We entered Veterans here and there. Our early scores were 198, 198, 199.5, 199, 198.5. Occasionally we'd slump to 197 or 197.5. All the while, HB was having a blast.

Frequently we'd encounter dogs and handlers we had locked horns with across the years. Teams that had given us fits and all too often had cleaned our clocks. That's part of the charm of Veterans competition, renewing relationships that by now are as comfortable as old shoes.

In Las Vegas there were seven other dogs in the class, including two who had beaten us regularly six or seven years ago.

That day, before she presented the ribbons, Judge Pauline Andrus told those gathered at ringside, "This class is where you see the great dogs; they're retired." We won the class with a 198.5. Although Barbara, who had watched intently from ringside, said, "I'm not sure you won." She was referring to Carole Forsythe and her golden retriever Maggie Jones, from Pahrump, Nevada. They had taken our measure several times in years gone by. I, too, had watched their run and it was one of those days when I said, "Wow! Were we better than *that*?" Above all, it was great to be in that kind of competition again with Honeybear at my side.

How long can this go on? How much longer can I look down and see that old white face driving at my side?

Forever, I hope.

■ *EPILOGUE* ■

SATURDAY JUNE, 29, 2002

Yesterday afternoon Honeybear was inducted into the Arizona Animal Hall of Fame. Sponsored by the Arizona Veterinary Medical Association (AzVMA), the Hall of Fame annually "honors exceptional animals for their outstanding contributions to human life and for sharing in the wonder and joy of the human/companion animal bond."

Nominations are made by veterinarians, and final choices are the responsibility of the AzVMA Hall of Fame selection committee. Dr. Toben and the staff of Apollo Animal Hospital nominated HB in the category Unique Best Friend. The selection committee heartily endorsed the nomination.

During the ceremony, Honeybear heeled smartly to the podium, then posed for several photos, eyes locked on mine.

Last night, on her side in her bed, she ran in her sleep. Perhaps dreaming we were back on the polo field again.

Photo: Barbara Bailey

April 2002: The Hall of Fame girl

An Acknowledgment

Were it not for Billie Rosen and her infinite capacity for sharing, the journey would never have begun. Were it not for Debby Boehm, she of ineffable patience, the jouney could not have blossomed into the most fulfilling adventure of my life. My gratitude to both is greater than I can suitably express.

Sally Dye took stacks of pencil-written sheets and transformed them into beautifully typed chapters. How does a mere mortal crank out dozens upon dozens of pages with nary a typo? And it's been that great for 17 years.

Vince Martin edited my manuscript with skill and a love born of 40 years of friendship.

But for the excellence of Michele DeFilippo, the book you are holding, and its cover, would not have been so appealing to the eye.

And Barbara. How to thank my wife Barbara? For so many cold, dark mornings in far-flung outposts of the obedience circuit. For tens of thousands of boring, grinding miles to and from those outposts. And tens upon tens of thousands of dollars that could have/should have been otherwise spent. For lugging, collectively, how many tons of heavy stuff in and out of how many hundred shows and matches? For videotaping the "game films." And for enduring dog hair … everywhere.

Has Barbara complained? Oh, you bet she has! But she's always been there. And I love her for that.

Ed Dunn died on August 29, 2002 at age 84. Ed had been a pillar of the dog obedience community for 44 years. His knowledge and his gentle coaching have not and cannot be replaced.

—Willard Bailey

November 2003